D1547160

Studies in the New Testament and Gnosticism

by

George W. Mac Rae, S.J.

Selected & edited by

Daniel J. Harrington, S.J. & Stanley B. Marrow, S.J.

Wipf & Stock
PUBLISHERS
Eugene, Oregon

Wipf and Stock Publishers
199 W 8th Ave, Suite 3
Eugene, OR 97401

Studies in the New Testament and Gnosticism
By MacRae, George W., SJ
Copyright©1987 The Society of Jesus of New England
ISBN 13: 978-1-55635-595-0
ISBN 10: 1-55635-595-5
Publication date 8/30/2007
Previously published by Michael Glazier, Inc., 1987

George Winsor MacRae, S.J.

Contents

Part Three: Gnosticism

George Winsor MacRae (1928-1985)

"If greatness in biblical scholarship is defined in terms of service to the scholarly community, George MacRae was the greatest in our generation." Thus did Helmut Koester eulogize his Harvard colleague. Born on July 27, 1928, in Lynn, Massachusetts, George Winsor MacRae attended St. John's Preparatory School in Danvers and Boston College before entering the Society of Jesus in 1948. His course of studies there took him to Louvain for philosophy, to Johns Hopkins for a M.A. in Semitics, to Weston School of Theology for theology and, after his ordination in 1960, to Cambridge University for his Ph.D. in New Testament. He took up his teaching career in 1966 as Professor at Weston School of Theology, where he remained until his appointment in 1973 as the first tenured Stillman Professor of Roman Catholic Theological Studies at Harvard University. It was in the course of his ministering the Word to his fellow-ministers of the Word, that he died on September 6, 1985, "at an age neither biblical/ nor glossed by any text."

Though teaching the Word was at the center of his life, his many gifts and varied talents equipped him for a vast range of tasks in the service of the academic community: executive secretary of the Society of Biblical Literature from 1973 to 1976, associate editor of the *Catholic Biblical Quarterly, New Testament Studies,* Hermeneia, the Revised Standard Version revision committee, etc. His association with *New Testament Abstracts* began in 1957 as managing editor (1957-1960), and continued as coeditor (1967-1972), and then as associate editor (1972-1985).

He was in constant demand as a lecturer, and his topics covered the theology and exegesis of the New Testament as well as the particular field of his specialization, the Nag

7

Hammadi documents. Many of these documents he not only edited and translated but also assisted others in editing and translating. Teaching, preaching, counseling, consulting, writing, editing, and organizing meetings were tasks he did superbly well and with grace. All those that were fortunate enough to work with him found in him the same ready courtesy and an unfailing source of encouragement and good humor.

The present collection of George MacRae's articles does not represent the whole man, any more than they represent all that he did. Practically every item on his bibliography was undertaken in response to a request to deal with some topic of concern, to make a contribution to some scholarly gathering, or to honor a fellow-scholar. Since many of the articles are not easy to find, this volume tries to make available a sample of their author's range of interests and technical skills. Reading them and the other items on the bibliography will reveal his fascination with the development and adaptation of religious traditions. This life-long interest fitted him admirably for occupying the Stillman Chair at Harvard University, even as his interest in ecumenism found perfect expression in his teaching at the Harvard Divinity School. His own family's Catholic-Presbyterian background, as well as his studies both here and abroad imbued him with a humble respect for other religious traditions, a willingness to consider and reconcile opposites, and a firm loyalty to the faith he professed and lived. It was this faith that inspired his ministry to all who serve the Word, whether as scholars, as ministers of religion, or as inquirers after those things that "make for peace." "George MacRae," wrote the prominent scholar Jacob Neusner, "was a model of what scholars should be. He was learned, but imaginative. He not only knew a great deal, but he shared what he knew."

Editing George MacRae's papers has been a bittersweet experience: bitter because of the sense of loss that all who knew him felt and continue to feel at his premature passing from their midst; yet sweet because it afforded us the chance to listen anew to the accents of that most eloquent of men.

We are especially grateful to the Reverend Robert E. Manning, S.J., Provincial of the New England Province of the Society of Jesus, for the permission to prepare this collection; to the original publishers of the articles, for their permission to reprint the essays; and to Michael Glazier, for his willingness to publish the volume. It will, perchance, serve, not only as some small memorial to the many that knew him, but also as an introduction to others of a great scholar and an untiring minister of the Word.

June 1987

Daniel J. Harrington, S.J.
Stanley B. Marrow, S.J.

ABBREVIATIONS

AnBib	Analecta Biblica
BBB	Bonner Biblische Beiträge
BTB	*Biblical Theology Bulletin*
BWANT	Beiträge zur Wissenschaft vom Alten und Neuen Testament
CBQ	*Catholic Biblical Quarterly*
CG	Corpus Gnosticum
FRLANT	Forschungen zur Religion und Literatur des Alten und Neuen Testaments
HR	*History of Religions*
HTR	*Harvard Theological Review*
IDBSup	Supplement to *Interpreter's Dictionary of the Bible*
JBL	*Journal of Biblical Literature*
JNES	*Journal of Near Eastern Studies*
JTC	*Journal of Theology and the Church*
JTS	*Journal of Theological Studies*
KEK	Kritisch-exegetischer Kommentar
NHS	Nag Hammadi Studies
NT	*Novum Testamentum*
NTS	*New Testament Studies*
RB	*Revue Biblique*
RevSR	*Revue des Sciences Religieuses*
RSV	Revised Standard Version

RScPhTh	*Revue des Sciences Philosophiques et Théologiques*
SBLDS	SBL Dissertation Series
SNTSMS	Society for New Testament Studies Monograph Series
TDNT	Theological Dictionary of the New Testament
TU	Texte und Untersuchungen
TWNT	Theologisches Wörterbuch zum Neuen Testament
VC	*Vigiliae Christianae*
VD	*Verbum Domini*
VTSup	Vetus Testamentum, Supplements
ZNW	*Zeitschrift für die Neutestamentliche Wissenschaft*
ZThK	*Zeitschrift für Theologie und Kirche*

Part One

Interpretation

1

The Fourth Gospel
and Religionsgeschichte*

The publication of Raymond E. Brown's Anchor Bible commentary on the Fourth Gospel marks a significant point in the contemporary history of Johannine scholarship, for it was the first major commentary in the English language for some years and it must rank as one of the most complete and most useful.[1] In the subsequent four-year period the pace of publication on John has been markedly accelerated. But of new commentaries in English, such as the posthumous work of J.N. Sanders[2] or the Pelican commentary of John Marsh,[3] only the translation of R. Schnackenburg's first volume will rival Brown's in any respect.[4] Anyone who keeps his own supplement to E. Malatesta's excellent modern bibliography,[5] however, must be aware of the flood of new

* First published in *Catholic Biblical Quarterly* 32 (1970) 13-24.

[1]Vol. I: *The Gospel according to John (i-xii)* (Garden City, 1966); Vol. II: 1970.

[2]*A Commentary on the Gospel according to St John,* ed. B.A. Mastin (Black's New Testament Commentaries; London, 1968).

[3]*The Gospel of St John* (Harmondsworth, 1968).

[4]*The Gospel according to St John,* tr. K. Smyth (Herder's Theological Commentary on the New Testament; New York, 1968).

[5]*St. John's Gospel 1920-1965* (AnBib 32; Rome, 1967). 3120 titles are listed for that period alone.

15

monographs and articles on John. With rare exceptions such as the challenging work of Ernst Käsemann, *The Testament of Jesus*,[6] or the historical study of J.L. Martyn,[7] this most recent literature does not attempt to question the overall intention or thematic of the Fourth Gospel, but rather to center on exegesis of individual passages, special themes, word studies, elements of the elusive Johannine background, and the like.

In the pages that follow I should like to by-pass exegetical detail—not neglecting it, I hope, but presuming upon it—in order to raise some very general questions and suggest a line along which answers may lie. Most students of the Fourth Gospel are prepared to take a position within the multiple options of the classic "Johannine problem." My aim here is to test against critical reactions a general view of the intention of the Fourth Evangelist that is not one of the usual options, though a number of recent authors have approached it from several sides. In doing so, I shall be more or less consciously in dialogue, and often in disagreement, with Käsemann's book, without making the debate explicit at every turn. But first, I would like to set forth some of the problematic data that I wish to consider in unfolding a position.

The Background of John

To begin with, there is the major question of the background of the Fourth Gospel. Since the discovery of the Qumrân scrolls there has been a widespread shift toward a Palestinian-Jewish background, and this trend is an important part of what J.A.T. Robinson called the "new look" on the Fourth Gospel.[8] It is embodied in its most balanced and

---

[6]Tr. G. Krodel (Philadelphia, 1968).

[7]*History and Theology in the Fourth Gospel* (New York, 1968).

[8]In 1957 at the Oxford Congress; see his *Twelve New Testament Studies* (Studies in Biblical Theology 34; London, 1962) 94.

judicious form in Brown's commentary, and it has recently been popularized in A.M. Hunter's survey of the present position of Johannine studies.[9] But this renewed emphasis is by no means shared by all interpreters of John, some of whom argue that other factors must still be considered. For one thing, Qumrân itself has contributed greatly to the gradual break-down of neat and clear distinctions between Hellenistic and Palestinian Judaism, so that it is increasingly difficult to assign a locus to the Johannine traditions or their development. More important, many of the most striking elements of Johannine symbolism and literary technique are simply not paralleled in Qumrân literature but in other more unmistakably Hellenistic types, Jewish and pagan both.

We list here only a few examples, recent and classic, of alternative backgrounds. In a very thorough analysis of the Prologue, A. Feuillet points out to good advantage the influence of the Jewish wisdom literature, especially in its strongly Hellenistic later forms, on the Fourth Evangelist's theology.[10] C.H. Dodd had looked especially to the pagan gnosis known as Hermetism for parallels not only in language but in religious experience.[11] Bultmann's monumental commentary saw the Johannine background in a more or less unorthodox baptist sect of the East, perhaps Syria, to which the Mandaean literature furnishes our most direct access.[12] The reaction against his use of Mandaean sources has been vigorous, not least because of the anachronism

---

[9] *According to John* (London, 1968).

[10] *Le prologue du quatrième évangile: Étude de la théologie johannique* (Bruges, 1968) esp. 236-244. See also Brown, Anchor commentary, cxxii-cxxv; F.-M. Braun, *Jean le théologien*. II: *Les grandes traditions d'Israël, l'accord des Écritures d'après le quatrième évangile* (Paris, 1964).

[11] *The Interpretation of the Fourth Gospel* (Cambridge, 1953) esp. 10-53. I do not imply that Dodd interprets John solely from the Hellenistic side; see his discussion of rabbinic Judaism, 74-96.

[12] *Das Evangelium des Johannes* (Meyer Kommentar; Göttingen, 1941, 1968). See also "Die Bedeutung der neuerschlossenen mandäischen und manichäischen Quellen für das Verständnis des Johannesevangeliums," *ZNW* 24 (1925) 100-146, reprinted in *Exegetica* (Tübingen, 1967) 55-104.

involved. But here one should acknowledge a major and important change in Mandaean scholarship, sparked principally by the greatly enlarged fund of original sources made available by Lady Drower: the trend is again to date Mandaeism very early, perhaps even into pre-Christian times.[13] A careful comparative study on the one hand of the Nag Hammadi Gnostic texts, soon to become available in their entirety, and on the other of the Mandaean materials may yet have much to teach us about origins of Mandaeism. For another example of divergent Johannine background, finally, Käsemann, without appealing to Mandaeism, places the Fourth Gospel on the road the leads from the enthusiasts of Corinth to the Christian Gnostics of the second century.[14]

And so on. I have not yet read anyone who argues that John's background was Indian or Far Eastern, but I should not be greatly surprised to do so. The least one can conclude is that it is a remarkable biblical book indeed that is capable of eliciting such a variety of theories about its milieu or origin. But can one pose the question in a slightly different manner: since the age of the Fourth Gospel was the age of Roman Hellenism, characterized in many respects by a kind of religious universalism or syncretism, is it not possible that the Fourth Evangelist may have tried deliberately to incorporate a diversity of backgrounds into the one gospel message precisely to emphasize the universality of Jesus?

Sources and Redaction

By way of exploring that possibility further, we must first note two other general areas of the Johannine problematic, the question of sources and redaction. The source question became a lively issue only with Bultmann's commentary,

---

[13]See most recently K. Rudolph, "Problems of a History of the Development of the Mandaean Religion," *HR* 8 (1969) 210-235; E.M. Yamauchi, "The Present Status of Mandaean Studies," *JNES* 25 (1966) 88-96.

[14]*The Testament of Jesus*, e.g., 75.

although he himself credited A. Faure[15] with the first plausible case for a signs-source. Generally speaking, few scholars would follow Bultmann in postulating a revelation-discourse source, especially after the meticulous analysis of D.M. Smith, Jr.[16] But the existence of a signs-source has withstood the test of analysis, so much so that its nature, extent and theology are now the subject of much contemporary investigation. For example, R.T. Fortna's Union Theological Seminary dissertation, *The Gospel of Signs,* tries to go beyond Bultmann in arguing that the passion narrative is a part of this narrative source.[17] In addition, a number of scholars, such as H. Koester, are investigating the theological implications of the signs-source.[18] I am not concerned here with the source itself but with the widely accepted position that in using such a source, which probably presented Jesus as a miracle-worker, a *theios anēr,*[19] the Fourth Evangelist was critical of the miracles tradition and its *Tendenz.* In his Rome dissertation L. Erdozáin correctly notes John's ambiguous attitude to miracles but seeks a solution in different types of faith evoked by the Johannine Jesus.[20] Käsemann also deals with this problem but I think wrongly accuses John of heightening the miraculous for Christological purposes.[21] Far from heightening the miraculous, John almost consistently minimizes the actual miraculous activity of Jesus, even though he sometimes heightens

---

[15]"Die alttestamentliche Zitate im vierten Evangelium und die Quellenscheidungshypothese," *ZNW* 21 (1922) 99-121; see Bultmann, Meyer Kommentar, 78.

[16]*The Composition and Order of the Fourth Gospel* (New Haven, 1965).

[17]SNTSMS 11 (Cambridge, 1969).

[18]See, e.g., "One Jesus and Four Primitive Gospels," *HTR* 61 (1968) 203-247, esp. 230-234. See also the forthcoming work of Koester and J.M. Robinson, *Trajectories through Early Christianity* (Philadelphia, 1970), several chapters of which deal with this issue.

[19]See H.D. Betz, "Jesus as Divine Man," *Jesus and the Historian,* Colwell volume, ed. F.T. Trotter (Philadelphia, 1968) 114-133.

[20]*La función del signo en la fe según el cuarto evangelio* (Analecta Biblica 33; Rome, 1968).

[21]*The Testament of Jesus,* 21-22.

the miracle stories to give emphasis to their symbolic content. It is not enough to say that John did not approve of faith in Jesus based on signs, for then one would have to answer the question why he did not simply suppress the evidence. Why did he use the signs-source at all? Let us suspend an answer for a moment and observe simply that the Evangelist's intention in using the source must have been more subtle than mere acceptance or rejection of its implications.

Another source, not yet mentioned, underlies John, but it is both more difficult to describe and potentially more important for understanding the Gospel. That is the "source" which accounts for the gospel form of the work. I accept the widespread consensus of contemporary scholarship since P. Gardner-Smith[22] that John is not directly dependent on any of the Synoptics. But while giving full weight to the creativity of the Fourth Gospel vis-à-vis the established tradition, many scholars are now recognizing more and more clearly that John knew well the structure of the traditional gospel and even specific groupings of traditional material such as, for example, Jn 6 and the loaves cycles underlying Mk 6-8. Brown's commentary, again, is particularly rich in highlighting Synoptic or pre-synoptic traditions, structural as well as topical, in John.[23] And conversely, it is a major weakness of Käsemann's interpretation of John that he fails to come to grips with the question of why John chose to write a *gospel,* that is to adopt a literary form that is cast from the traditional gospel mold. But again, the Evangelist uses this synoptic-type "source," whatever its exact nature may have been, in a critical manner, for he both reveals and disguises his dependence on tradition. The triple prediction of the Passion, for example, structurally vital to the latter

---

[22]*Saint John and the Synoptic Gospels* (Cambridge, 1938). See also J. Blinzler's *Forschungsbericht, Johannes und die Synoptiker* (Stuttgarter Bibelstudien 5; Stuttgart, 1965) which, however, argues that John used at least Mark.

[23]Anchor commentary, Introduction xliv-xlvii and *passim* in the commentary itself.

half of Mark, is present in John in the triple *hypsothēnai* saying (3:14; 8:28; 12:32) which is one of the unifying symbols of the Johannine narrative.[24] Similarly, the Caesarea Philippi confession of Peter, the focal point of the Marcan development, appears in the option of the disciples voiced by Peter in Jn 6:68, though in this instance it has lost its structural significance.[25]

John's critical attitude toward his sources suggests again a concern on his part to incorporate as much as possible of the traditional even while creating his own gospel "style." I take this concern to be an implicit assertion of the universality of Jesus, who meets the religious aspirations of both the traditional and the innovative. But the critique of the miracles tradition invites us to take a step further, for here the Evangelist is suggesting, not merely that Jesus is the miracle-working divine man of Hellenistic Jewish and pagan tradition, but that he transcends the very category of divine man in his unique relationship to the Father. But let me return to this element of transcendence later.

The question of multiple redaction in the Fourth Gospel has seemed inevitable to commentators, again since the genial work of Bultmann, whose "ecclesiastical redactor" has survived, despite some well-grounded criticism, in the work of both Brown and Schnackenburg, though neither of them would attribute the same motives to the redactor(s) that Bultmann does.[26] The importance of the issue should not be minimized, but it is a truism that the primary exegetical task is to deal with the Gospel as we have it, as indeed it has been transmitted in the long Christian tradition since the earliest textually recoverable times. It is one thing to attempt to distinguish the viewpoint of the "Evangelist" from that of the "final redactor"; it is another to inquire into the intention of the Gospel as we have it. I should wish here to by-pass the

---

[24]See, e.g., Jn 18:32. On the relation to the predictions of the Passion, see Brown, *ibid.,* 146.

[25]Again see Brown, *ibid.,* 301-303.

[26]*Ibid.,* xxxiv-xxxix; Schnackenburg, Herder Commentary, 59-74.

redactional question without denying either its validity or its importance. But it is possible to pose in quite a different manner some of the questions which redactional analysis raises. In doing so, I am implicitly affirming that the ultimate intention of the redactor was not to alter the course of Johannine theology but to reinforce that aspect of it to which this paper seeks to call attention.

As an example, let us consider some of the eschatological statements of the Fourth Gospel, which are often adduced as the most obvious instance of redactional activity (apart from the addition of ch. 21). Here I mean simply the presence of futurist or apocalyptic eschatological statements in the midst of an otherwise uniform realized-eschatological perspective. Few, I think, could agree with Käsemann that "the distinction, gained from cosmology and anthropology, between realized and futurist eschatology in the Gospel of John can be maintained only with difficulty," even though Käsemann's attempt to interpret John's eschatology exclusively in Christological terms is admirable.[27] The ease with which subsequent Christianity accepted both types of eschatological utterance as genuine does not minimize the real conflict between these types, as modern NT theologians have long testified. Let us grant at the outset—if indeed there could be any question—that the eschatological perspective native to the Evangelist himself is that of realized or inaugurated eschatology, which, as Käsemann points out,[28] is not entirely without its futurist dimension. But there are in the Fourth Gospel other statements that are set within an almost classical apocalyptic futurist mold, e.g. 5:28-29. The most important observation to make about the statements of the latter type, which of course are the exception, is that they appear almost exclusively in contexts where they parallel statements of the realized-eschatological type: e.g., 5:25-29//5:21-24; 6:40c. 54b//6:40b. 54a; 6:44// 6:51; 11:25b//11:26.

---

[27] *The Testament of Jesus,* 16.
[28] *Ibid.,* 70-71.

Now, of course this juxtaposition could simply mean that the later redactor, in an effort to make this marginal gospel palatable to the Church, inserted such traditionally futurist statements at the most crudely appropriate points. (One may note in passing that no one seems to have felt any comparable scruple with regard to Colossians and Ephesians over against the major Pauline epistles.) But could not such a juxtaposition also be a way of saying: whatever your eschatological perspective, future-oriented or present-oriented, Jesus is the reality and fulfillment of your hopes? That is to suppose that the Evangelist—or the redactor if you will—was mainly concerned with asserting the universality of Jesus in the context of a growing divergence of eschatological viewpoints in the second- or third-generation Church. How else can one read 11:25-26, where the "I-am" saying so links the two eschatological perspectives that the intruding hand of a subsequent redactor is almost impossible to detect except on the supposition that no author would try to join both types of eschatological statement? "I am the resurrection and the life; he who believes in me, though he die, yet shall he live, and whoever lives and believes in me shall never die."[29] But even the categories of life and death are eventually recognized to be inadequate in the Fourth Gospel as a means of grasping the meaning of Jesus, for they too are more or less abandoned as the Gospel reaches its climax and conclusion.

This further hint at the element of transcendence leads us to another area of debate in Johannine studies, the question of the structure of the Gospel. But before turning to it, I wish to indicate summarily another way in which the Evangelist seeks to express the universality of Jesus, namely by heaping up Christological titles. To concentrate on just one passage, we may observe how the titles provide a theme of continuity throughout Jn 1:19-51, which derives its literary structure

---

[29]I am following the brilliant analysis of these verses by Dodd, *The Interpretation,* 364-365; for an only slightly different perspective see Bultmann, Meyer Kommentar, 307-308.

from the symmetrical arrangement of successive scenes. The section on John the Baptist (19-34) serves to deny that the titles (Messiah, Elijah, the prophet) are properly applied to him; his role is that of witness. The section on Jesus and his first disciples (35-51) introduces Jesus successively as Lamb of God, rabbi, messiah, the prophet announced by Moses, Son of God, and—outside the structural framework—Son of Man. In other parts of the Gospel this heaping up of titles is continued (Logos, Lord, Savior). The intention of this characteristic of John is again to incorporate deliberately into the understanding of Jesus whatever Christological labels are current in the Church, even though the particular Christological model of the Evangelist himself does not correspond adequately to any of them except possibly Son of God. It is precisely this deliberate intention to express the universality of Jesus, and implicitly to assert that the reality of Jesus transcends any such labeling, which explains the addition of the unconnected Son-of-Man saying in Jn 1:51. The Evangelist—not the redactor, according to Bultmann[30]— adds this isolated saying to the carefully-structured opening scenes of the Gospel to make his list of titles more complete. How appropriate the saying is at this point in the Gospel is not my point here,[31] nor is it the principal point for the Evangelist either.[32]

The Structure of John

We turn next to the structure of the Gospel in search of another argument for the author's deliberate assimilation of a variety of forms of religious understanding. The problem of ascertaining in detail the structural plan of the Gospel

---

[30] Meyer Kommentar, 68, 74.

[31] For an extended discussion of this question, see Brown, Anchor commentary, 88-91.

[32] In quite a different manner and on the basis of Jn 1:12-13 read against the wisdom background of the Prologue, Feuillet, *Le prologue,* also emphasizes the universality of Jesus and the response of faith; see, e.g., 17-18, 81-95.

fascinates many students of it. In the most recent literature I have noted in particular the work of Jan Willemse, who claims to detect an interlocking symmetrical pattern in the Gospel,[33] and of David Deeks, who sees the Gospel as structured in four main parts with chiastic order.[34] What both these studies neglect is the major break in John between ch. 12 and ch. 13, and I cannot regard any structural analysis as adequate which fails to recognize the importance of this natural division between what Dodd calls the "Book of Signs" and the "Book of Glory."[35] The existence of this natural division needs no demonstration, but several implications of it are important for understanding the Gospel as a whole.

First, it should be observed that the division within John corresponds closely in intention and significance to the main division in the Marcan Gospel either before or after the confession at Caesarea Philippi (8:27-30).[36] From that point on in Mark Jesus' activity focuses mainly on the instruction of the disciples and the implications of the Passion narrative for discipleship. The latter part of the Gospel is esoteric—within the circle of the disciples—as the earlier part is exoteric, in the framework of the Evangelist's interpretation of the life of Jesus, and it is well known how many of the characteristics of Marcan style are modified from this point onward. This matter of structure is an important way in which John takes over the concept of the traditional gospel structure without actually following Mark in any literary way. From Jn 13:1 onward, Jesus deals exclusively with his own disciples, abandoning even the language and symbolism that were the essence of his public revelation. Just as Mark

---

[33]*Het vierde evangelie. Een onderzoek naar zijn structuur* (Hilversum, 1965).

[34]"The Structure of the Fourth Gospel," *NTS* 15 (1968-69) 107-129.

[35]See Dodd, *The Interpretation,* 289; Brown, Anchor commentary, cxxxviii. The same criticism made of Willemse and Deeks would apply to the structure supposed by H. Conzelmann, *An Outline of the Theology of the New Testament,* tr. J. Bowden (New York, 1969) 347.

[36]In particular see I. de la Potterie, "De compositione evangelii Marci," *VD* 44 (1966) 135-141.

from 8:31 onward is oriented to the Passion, so Jn 13 ff. may be regarded as an interpretation of the Passion narrative.[37] But the contrast between the two sections in John is much more emphatic than that in Mark. John's independence from Mark, however, is attested by the fact that Mk 8:31— 10:45 is structured around the predictions of the Passion, whereas the Johannine equivalents of these are all in the first major division of the Gospel.

What is most outstanding about Jn 12 is the severe negative judgment it makes on the success of Jesus' ministry of sign and symbol in Galilee and Jerusalem both. It is not an exaggeration to say that the public life of Jesus ends in John on a note of failure. Jn 12:37-43 emphatically asserts the failure of the public revelation, explicitly mentioning the signs, and whether or not 12:44-50 is a redactional inter-polation, it too conveys an ominous judgment on what precedes (especially v. 48). In view of the fact that Jn 1-12 alone contains the miracles or signs and the multiplicity of basic human religious symbols—bread, wine, water, word, life, light, shepherd, etc.—one can only conclude that the Evangelist is asserting that although Jesus revealed himself in such a variety of modes, none of these adequately conveyed the basis of faith. Only the disciples "understand," but as the very important verses 2:22 and 12:16 assert unequivocally, they only understand because they have reflected backward, as is the theological movement of all the Gospels, from the Passion-death-resurrection experience.

Beginning in 13:1, the revelation to the disciples, that is to those who in fact, from the Evangelist's perspective, have understood and believed, takes on a new language and abandons the old. I do not suggest that one can detect any stylistic difference; the distinction of sources or hands (except for ch. 21) by these means has long since been discredited by E. Ruckstuhl[38] and others. But the language of

---

[37] Dodd, *The Interpretation*, 290-291.

[38] *Die literarische Einheit des Johannesevangeliums* (Freiburg, 1951). But for a critique of Ruckstuhl and a new application of the method, see Fortna, *The Gospel of Signs*, 203-218.

sign and symbol changes markedly. Instead of the great images, some of them introduced in the Prologue, which form the stuff of the Book of Signs: Logos, eternal life (but note 17:3), light, living water, bread of life, shepherd, Jewish feasts (except Passover, which was deeply embedded in the Passion tradition), the second part of the Gospel introduces the idea of love (not quite for the first time, of course; see 3:16) and dwells on it in discourse and in action. It is notable that when any of the old symbols recur, for example 19:26, 34, they do so in a context where they derive new force from their association with the Passion of Jesus. Käsemann may be correct in observing, as others have done, that the idea of love in the Fourth Gospel is scarcely adequate by the standards set by the rest of the NT,[39] but it is nonetheless the principal theme in the Book of Glory and the specific Johannine insight into the meaning of the Passion as the heart of the gospel message. And love is John's reaching out for a way to express the mode in which the event of Jesus Christ dying and rising not only fulfills the highest aspirations of man's varied religious longing, whether Jewish or Greek or even Gnostic, but transcends the symbolization of all of these to afford man a glimpse of the transcendence of God in the person of Jesus.

This is in many ways the opposite of Käsemann's interpretation of John, though he comes very close at several points to asserting my thesis. For example:

> "... the truth can never be imprisoned or objectified in any earthly object as such, not even in the earthly Jesus, whom, with the intention of objectifying, we call the historical Jesus. His dignity is to be Logos and his claim is that by means of all Logoi one can come to the Logos himself." [40]
>
> John's "doctrine provokes interpretation and kerygmatic unfolding instead of freezing and absolutizing it. John employed many means to point this out. He pictured

---

[39] *The Testament of Jesus*, 59.
[40] *Ibid.*, 43.

Jesus in Hellenistic categories as miracle-worker, as savior of the world and as pre-existent heavenly being. But in the Hellenistic world there were many miracle-workers, sons of God, and Jesus is something more than they. John also made use of the Jewish categories of prophet, teacher and Messiah, but these do not adequately disclose his cosmic significance. The symbols of water, bread, light, truth, life, shepherd and door are best suited, because every man has need of them and perishes without them." [41]

The difference in perspective between Käsemann and myself is that in my view John is not content merely with drawing on this multiplicity of basic human symbols, but he draws on a wealth of religious categories as he, a child of the Hellenistic world with at least some knowledge of Palestinian Jewish traditions, knows them. But in all cases but one he wishes to assert not only that Jesus is all in all, but that he transcends all and thus affords us, in the death and resurrection of the Son as the supreme act of love, an avenue to what divinity really is. It is my assertion that John deliberately uses whatever religious backgrounds he knows, though I remain convinced that his own is primarily in the wisdom tradition. He deliberately incorporates sources as disparate as the signs-source with a *theios anēr* Christology and the Passion-narrative gospel, but he also subsumes all except the theme of love in action under the condemnation of their failure to reveal adequately what God is.

The point is not that the Evangelist does this well, nor that he does it with the conceptual clarity the modern *Religionsgeschichtler* might aspire to. But the diversity of materials and backgrounds he uses may not only be in the eye of the beholder but in the eye of the Evangelist too. He wishes to imply that as long as one tries to grasp Jesus as a Jew or a Greek or a Gnostic or a traditional Christian would, he both succeeds and fails, for Jesus is the fulfillment of all these

---

[41] *Ibid.,* 54. See also E. Fascher, "Platon und Johannes in ihren Verhältnis zu Sokrates und Christus," *Das Altertum* 14 (1968) 83; E. Schweizer, *Ego Eimi* (FRLANT 56; Göttingen, 1939) 167.

expectations, but he is caught up in none of them. Only the great act of self-giving love which engenders love within the Christian community can reach him. It is in this sense that the predicative "I-am" sayings are to be taken as recognition-formulas in Bultmann's famous classification: [42] what you understand by the bread of life and long for in it is fulfilled in me. Yet even in the multiplicity of symbolic assertions expressed with this formula there is the further assertion that no such symbolization reaches the reality of Jesus as Son of God. This is particularly obvious when the symbols themselves conflict, as in "I am the resurrection and the life": whether your perspective is resurrection of the dead or eternal life of the believer, Jesus is both and yet more.

The Hellenistic Context

To conclude, I should like to offer an even more sweeping generalization than I have so far done, namely to suggest that the process of Johannine theology according to this interpretation of John's intentions corresponds to a process of "Hellenization" that is paralleled elsewhere in the history of ancient religion.

In the transition between Egyptian religion and Hellenistic Isis worship, for example—if I read correctly the sources upon which I depend here[43]—there is a movement from religious particularism to universalism. The gods of Egypt were local gods, and even if at a given epoch one god should resume in himself the functions of all, he remains nevertheless a universal national deity. But in the Isis literature of Hellenistic times, produced no doubt by Greeks, especially the aretalogy inscriptions such as the Kyme inscription, Isis

---

[42] Meyer Kommentar, 168.

[43] E.g., D. Müller, *Ägypten und die griechischen Isis-Aretalogien* (Abhandlungen der Sächsischen Akademie der Wissenschaften zu Leipzig, Phil.-hist. Klasse, Band 53, Heft 1; Berlin, 1961); J. Bergman, *Ich bin Isis* (Acta Universitatis Upsaliensis Historiae Religionum 3; Uppsala, 1968).

is all things to all men. She assumes not only all the good qualities of Egyptian deities, but also many of the characteristics of Zeus (e.g., author of thunder) and other non-Egyptian deities. This universalism is expressed particularly in the form of "I-am" sayings which identify Isis with all manner of universal power.

When the Isis aretalogy form is modified, for example in the Nag Hammadi document "The Thunder: Perfect Mind" of Codex VI (as yet unpublished),[44] an attempt is made to go beyond even this universalism in search of an expression of the transcendence of the divine voice. The method is simply to assert, by means of the "I-am" style again, that the deity transcends all human values and religious categories by identification with contrasting and even contradictory elements: "I am the silence ... I am the voice; I am knowledge and ignorance; I am war and peace; I am the disgraced and the honored; etc." The point is that the "I" represents more than the totality of human values, namely a reality that is of a totally other order.

Something similar to the progression from particularism to universalism takes place also, it seems to me, in the Hellenization of Judaism in the hands of Philo and, differently, of Josephus, but here the transcendent element expressed through contrasts is lacking. Perhaps we have another analogy in the Christian apologists of the second century, but I should not wish to force the parallel any further.

The aim of these analogies is to suggest that in the Fourth Gospel we have a somewhat similar Hellenization of early Christianity insofar as John attempts to assert both the universality and the transcendence of the divine Son Jesus. In the end, John's message is that Jesus can be approached in many ways, but he can only be understood on Christian

---

[44]   See M. Krause, "Der Stand der Veröffentlichung der Nag Hammadi Texte," *Le origini dello gnosticismo,* ed. U. Bianchi (Studies in the History of Religions [Supplements to *Numen*] XII; Leiden, 1967) 82-83. See also my forthcoming article "The *Ego*-Proclamation in Gnostic Sources," *The Trial of Jesus,* ed. E. Bammel (London, 1970) 122-134.

terms, not Jewish or Greek or Gnostic. That is why the Fourth Gospel was accepted as a Christian book: not, as Käsemann suggests,[45] because its gnosticizing trend was misunderstood, but because despite its gnosticizing trend it is the Christian gospel that it proclaims.

---

[45] *The Testament of Jesus*, e.g., 74-75.

2

Theology and Irony
in the Fourth Gospel*

The vitality of recent scholarship on the Fourth Gospel is virtually unparalleled in the history of exegesis—at least since Origen and the Gnostics. In the last half-century, the period since Rudolf Bultmann's first major article on John,[1] the volume of publication on the Fourth Gospel is wholly unprecedented. There has been some pattern to it, of course. The best of this scholarship has tended to concentrate on such issues as the history of Johannine sources and redaction, the problem of the historical *Sitz im Leben* of the Gospel, the meaning and origin of the Johannine symbolism, and themes of Johannine theology, especially the implications of eschatology. It is a tribute to the genius of Bultmann, the acknowledged master of modern Johannine scholarship, that a large majority of significant modern studies are devoted to exploiting, continuing, sometimes challenging the insights of his articles and his great commentary. But the

* First published in *The Word in the World: Essays in Honor of Frederick L. Moriarty, S.J.* (Cambridge, MA: Weston College Press, 1973) 83-96.

[1]"Der religionsgeschichtliche Hintergrund des Prologs zum Johannes-Evangelium," EUCHARISTION, *Festschrift Hermann Gunkel* (FRLANT, 19; Göttingen, 1923), 2, 3-26. Bultmann's commentary on John finally appeared in English near the end of the half-century period, *The Gospel of John, A Commentary,* tr. G.R. Beasley-Murray *et al.* (Philadelphia, 1971).

exploration of Johannine literary techniques, especially in relation to their significance for Johannine theology, has been somewhat neglected.[2] In particular, neither Bultmann nor many of the other recent interpreters have had more than passing things to say about the obvious and long-noted Johannine predilection for the literary device of irony.[3]

In the following pages, I propose, not to furnish a detailed study of the Johannine irony as a literary technique, but rather to raise a more general question: What does the Fourth Evangelist's use of the literary device of irony imply for our understanding of his theology?

At the outset it would be appropriate to state what is understood here by "irony," since the term itself is at once obvious and unclear. But that is in part the problem. Perhaps we can most profitably begin by employing the description of irony used by E.M. Good in his very perceptive study on irony in the OT.[4] Thus we shall understand irony in its most generic sense to be a "perception of incongruity" that is characterized by two specific qualities. First, it is normally expressed in understatement or suggestion, for example in double or multiple meanings perceptible on different levels by different hearers, or in saying the opposite of what is meant. Secondly, the ironic perception of incongruity rests upon the ironist's claim to an insight into the truth of things that is not shared by everyone.

---

[2] A few significant works were devoted, in the wake of Bultmann's source analysis, to the study of the Johannine discourses: e.g. H. Becker, *Die Reden des Johannesevangeliums und der Stil gnostischen Offenbarungsrede,* ed. R. Bultmann (FRLANT, 68; Göttingen, 1956); S. Schulz, *Komposition und Herkunft der johanneischen Reden* (BWANT, 5.1; Stuttgart, 1960). One of the more important recent works, which does relate literary analysis to theology, is H. Leroy, *Rätsel und Missverständnis* (BB, 30; Bonn, 1968).

[3] H. Clavier is an exception; he has dealt with the theme of irony in a series of articles from 1929 to 1959; see "L'ironie dans le quatrième Evangile," *Studia Evangelica* I (TU; Berlin, 1959), 261-276 (with references to earlier articles). D. W. Wead, *The Literary Devices in John's Gospel* (Theologische Dissertationen, 4; Basel, 1970), points out some of the irony in John but does not relate it to Johannine theology; J. Jónsson, *Humour and Irony in the New Testament* (Reykjavik, 1965), deals only superficially with John.

[4] *Irony in the Old Testament* (Philadelphia, 1965) 30-31.

It is not useful for our present purposes to dwell on the origin of irony as a literary device or on the well-known conflict of the *eirōn* and the *alazōn* in classical comedy. The author of the Fourth Gospel would probably not have recognized the term *eirōneia* as a designation of what he was doing, since the particular form of dramatic irony he used most has only in modern times inherited that name. The word had in John's time lost its pejorative sense, however, and the Socratic practice of dissimulation was not looked upon askance. But "irony" is a modern concept—though an ancient practice—and precisely because the modern concept has such a broad extension, there are some distinctions yet to be made.

Types of Irony

These may be briefly dealt with by way of elimination. First, the irony of the Fourth Gospel is not that which we usually associate with humor or with satire, whether humorous or biting. It is not the "militant irony" of Northrup Frye's "mythos of winter."[5] I would not want to exclude humor entirely from the Gospels, of course. It may well be that such stories as those of the Syrophoenician woman (Mk 7:24-30) or the tribute money (Mt 17:24-27) are intended to be at least wryly humorous. But the Fourth Gospel, though often heavily ironical, seems singularly humorless. To use the literary critic's terms again, John's Gospel does not, like satire, assume the guise of the world of romantic idealism in order to demolish the romantic delusion.

Secondly, the irony of the Fourth Gospel is not Socratic irony, properly speaking. The Socratic irony was a didactic method employed by the philosopher in the well-known manner and with the well-known results. Socrates as *eirōn* feigned ingenuousness to provoke the discovery of truth. G.G. Sedgewick, in his perennially readable lectures on the

---

[5]*Anatomy of Criticism, Four Essays* (Princeton, 1957) 223.

topic of irony,[6] has pointed out how our concept of Socratic irony has been purged of its offensiveness in part through the admiration of Socrates in later ages, to become an "urbane pretence." "It is a war upon Appearance waged by a man who knows Reality: now it is a process deadly to empty pretence, now a sort of kindly pruning vital to growth in truth." Socratic irony no doubt lies at the base of any concept of the ironical, but as a didactic method elaborated in dialogue it is not the main component of Johannine irony. This is not to say that it is wholly foreign to the Johannine presentation of Jesus. For example, the question of Jesus to those who "took up stones again to stone him": "I have shown you many good works from the Father; for which of these do you stone me?" (10:32). But if this stance is Socratic, the response of "the Jews" is another kind of irony, one that as we shall see gets more to the heart of the Johannine method: "We stone you for no good work but for blasphemy; because you, being a man, make yourself God."[7]

Thirdly, Johannine irony should not be identified with what is commonly called "tragic irony" (or "Sophoclean irony") either, though here again there are points of contact. The irony of the classical Greek tragedy (and of course of Shakespeare and others) functions as a dramatic technique in the service of undoing the tragic hero because of his fatal *hybris*. One of the clearest examples is the powerful dialogues of the *Bacchae* of Euripides,[8] in which the god Dionysus in disguise confronts the king Pentheus of Thebes, maddened by a spell of Bacchic frenzy. Pentheus' opposition to the god is requited by his death at the hands of the frenzied Maenads, his own mother among them, and his downfall begins with his mad desire to witness the mysteries. Of course the spectator knows the story and waits with fascination the sight of Pentheus' head in his raving mother's hands.

[6]*Of Irony, Especially in Drama* (Toronto, 1935) 13.

[7]Clavier's emphasis on the Socratic origin of Johannine irony ("L'ironie dans le quatrième Evangile") has led him to miss some of its theological significance.

[8]Also cited by Sedgewick, *Of Irony*, 24-25.

Pentheus:	True—true: we must not overcome by force The women. I will hide me midst the pines.
Dionysus:	Hide?—thou shalt hide as Fate ordains thine hiding, Who com'st with guile, a spy on Bacchanals.
Pentheus:	Methinks I see them mid the copses caught, Like birds, in toils of their sweet dalliance.
Dionysus:	To this end then art thou appointed watchman: Perchance thou shalt catch them—if they catch not thee.
Pentheus:	On through the midst of Thebes' town usher me! I am their one *man,* I alone dare this!
Dionysus:	Alone for Thebes thou travailest, thou alone; Wherefore for thee wait struggle and strain foredoomed. Follow: all safely will I usher thee, Another thence shall bring thee,—
Pentheus:	Ay, my mother!
Dionysus:	To all men manifest—
Pentheus:	For this I come.
Dionysus:	High-borne shalt thou return—
Pentheus:	Soft ease for me?
Dionysus:	On a mother's hands.
Pentheus:	Thou wouldst thrust pomp on me![9]

For comparison, several scenes in the Fourth Gospel suggest themselves, most notably the scene of the Pilate trial, which we shall deal with below. There the ironic interplay

---

[9] *Euripides,* vol. 3, tr. A.S. Way (Loeb; Cambridge, Mass., 1930) lines 953-969.

between "the Jews," symbols of the opponents of the Johannine community, and Pilate, and between both and Jesus rests on the same principle that the spectators know the story and what it means. But in John the issue is not the *hybris* of a tragic hero; not even Caiaphas, who unwittingly "prophesies" the true meaning of Jesus' death (11:49-52),[10] functions like Pentheus or Oedipus or Prometheus or Agamemnon, even though the conflict with the divine is central. For the Fourth Gospel we must distinguish dramatic from tragic irony.

Fourthly, and finally, we must distinguish the Johannine irony from the "metaphysical irony" identified by modern literary critics, though again the distinction is not a complete one. I borrow the term "metaphysical irony" from the fascinating study of modern literature by Charles I. Glicksberg.[11] What he understands by the "modern ironic vision" is the resultant of a set of contributory causes: "romantic individualism, the conflict between illusion and reality, the limitless aspirations of the self and its constraining finitude, the contradiction, always present, between freedom and necessity, spirit and matter, life and death."[12] What is specific about this form of irony is that it is "an expressive form of the metaphysical vision, the fruit of the growing suspicion that life is essentially meaningless."[13] Modern "metaphysical irony" is typified by the tragic absurdity of life, the image of Albert Camus' *Myth of Sisyphus*. The "world" of the Fourth Gospel is of course anything but absurd, yet the work borders on a dualism of God and world in which irony functions as a form of expression. This aspect of Johannine irony is reflected in the dialogue that concludes one section of the Farewell Discourse of Jesus. Here the disciples say, "Ah, now you are speaking plainly (*en parrēsia*), not in any

---

[10]Bultmann, *The Gospel of John,* 411, refers to this remark as an example of tragic irony.

[11]*The Ironic Vision in Modern Literature* (The Hague, 1969).

[12]Glicksberg, *The Ironic Vision,* 10.

[13]Glicksberg, *The Ironic Vision,* 13.

figure (*paroimian*)! ... by this we believe that you came
from God." And Jesus answers, "Do you now believe? ... I
have said this to you, that in me you may have peace. In the
world you have tribulation; but be of good cheer, I have
overcome the world" (16:29-33).

Johannine Irony

The four types of ironic expression that we have identified
are not completely distinct from one another, nor is any of
them completely distinct from the irony of the Fourth
Gospel. But it is time to turn to a more positive statement
about the latter. And here we must begin with the observation
that the Johannine irony is first of all dramatic irony in that
it presumes upon the superior knowledge of the reader to
recognize the true perspective within which the Gospel's
assertions are ironical.

Sedgewick singles out the following characteristics of
dramatic irony:[14] the conflict of forces or elements, the
ignorance of reality on the part of one of the forces, and the
spectator's recognition of both the appearance and the
reality. "Dramatic irony, in brief, is the sense of contradiction
felt by spectators of a drama who see a character acting in
ignorance of his condition." I do not wish to dispute this
definition, but I should like to call attention to a few
characteristics of Johannine dramatic irony which seem to
me the most significant.

First, like any dramatic irony, Johannine irony is born out
of a *conflict* in situation. The conflict is one that takes place
on a variety of levels simultaneously: it is the conflict
between Jesus and "the world" or "the Jews," between the
Christians contemporary with John and the Jewish communities
which have ostracized them, between the power of
truth and error, between glory and suffering, between the

----

[14] *Of Irony*, 48-49.

divine and the human. Conflict arises out of a disparity of vision. It can be historical (the debates between Christians and Jews) or theological (the conflict of immanence and transcendence) or metaphysical (the dualism of world and God). In some cases it is clearly the conflict of appearance and reality, as with the mystery of the incarnation. The Johannine statement "and the Word became flesh," as it is elaborated thematically in the Gospel, denotes not merely the fact of the incarnation, but the conflict created by the act of judgment in the human sphere on the part of the revealing word of God.[15]

Second, like the irony in tragedy, Johannine irony presumes the factor of *distance* from the events narrated. But precisely where the distance of tragedy is meant to bring about catharsis without actual terror, in the Fourth Gospel this distance has the effect of involving the spectator in the challenge of faith.[16] For the factor of distance in John is precisely the post-Easter perspective, the perspective of faith in Christ as the Logos vindicated by death and resurrection. It is this knowledge, which the Evangelist shares with the reader, which creates the ironical atmosphere that surrounds Jesus in his earthly career. "These [signs] are written that you may believe [i.e. go on believing, if the present subjunctive may bear this weight] that Jesus is the Christ, the Son of God, and that believing you may have life in his name" (20:31). It is important to note that the Evangelist does not say "these *happened* that you may believe," but "these *are*

---

[15]Cf. Bultmann, *The Gospel of John,* 61-62.

[16]S.R. Hopper, "Irony—the Pathos of the Middle," *Cross Currents* (Winter, 1962) 35, refers to the "ironic denouement of irony" in which the ironist's own ironic perception turns back upon him, involves him. The phenomenon may be somewhat analogous to the relationship between the process of faith in the situations of the Fourth Gospel—perceived ironically by both Evangelist and reader—and the process of faith in the reader himself. In a very important essay (which does not, however, deal with the theme of ironic perception in John), W.A. Meeks remarks: "The book functions for its readers in precisely the same way that the epiphany of its hero functions within its narratives and dialogues" ("The Man from Heaven in Johannine Sectarianism," *JBL* 91 [1972] 44-72, quotation from p. 69).

written that you may believe," that is to say that the *literary* perspective of the Gospel is designed to appeal to and nourish faith. In this sense, the irony in question lies in the Evangelist's perception and literary presentation of the reality of God's dealings with men.

Third, like the so-called modern metaphysical irony, Johannine irony shares the view that the world itself and the symbols it uses are *ambiguous*. These can be used as an avenue of access to the divine, but they can also lead only to themselves. Not only is the person of Jesus ambiguous, but the symbolization of his identity as the bread of life or the living water is also an essentially ambiguous process. I should like to return below to illustrate this ambiguity as a form of the Fourth Evangelist's ironic vision.

I use the term "ironic vision," for in John irony is not confined to the dramatic device but represents a whole literary (and quasi-philosophical) outlook, such as Frye identifies with the "ironic mode."[17] It is through this ironic vision that the contact with Johannine theology is made, for it is in irony that John expresses his own insight into the meaning of Christ for the world. Indeed, as we shall try to show, in the Fourth Gospel theology *is* irony. But it is time to turn to some illustrations of both the dramatic and what we shall call the "thematic" irony of John.

Dramatic Irony: The Pilate Trial

The techniques of drama which the author skillfully employs in such episodes as that of the woman at the well (4:4-42) and the story of the man born blind (9:1-41) are brought to bear with great sophistication upon the Pilate trial (18:28—19:15). In addition to the obvious device of alternating scenes outside and inside Pilate's Pretorium and the meticulous balancing of characters in these scenes, the entire passage is the clearest example of Johannine dramatic

---

[17] *Anatomy of Criticism*, 40 ff.

irony. My intention at the moment is not to offer an exegesis of the passage nor to claim any new insights into it, but merely to call attention to some elements of the irony as a Johannine reflection on the Passion narrative. The Pilate trial is a narrative, of course, and not a drama, and consequently the irony is not confined to the dialogue but also appears in the descriptive remarks. For convenience let us group our observations on the irony of the passage around the *dramatis personae*.

Bultmann points out that in this passage, as often elsewhere in John, *hoi Ioudaioi* are symbols of "the world" which is opposed to Jesus and to his revelation.[18] Other interpreters prefer to draw attention to the Jews as representative chiefly of the synagogue contemporary with the Evangelist, which has come to a clear position on the expulsion of the Christians.[19] It is not of course necessary to choose between these interpretations as long as we realize that the significance of this group is not exclusively, perhaps not even primarily, on the level of a historical narrative. Whether accurately or not it may be impossible to ascertain— and it is certainly not my purpose—but the Fourth Evangelist clearly places upon "the Jews" the major element of blame for the condemnation of Jesus, which he regards as the real criminal act that (ironically) underlies the trial. In the light of his stance, his mention of the prosecutors remaining outside the Pretorium to avoid ritual defilement (18:28) serves not only to justify the alternating scenes but to set the tone of irony. The irony develops with some curious and no doubt quite deliberate cross-references between the individual scenes. For example, in the first scene "the Jews" protest that they are not allowed to execute anyone (18:31); in the fifth scene they are made to insist, "We have a law and according to the law he must die" (19:7). A similar cross-reference is made between Pilate's taunting attempt to escape the

---

[18] *The Gospel of John,* 652 ff.

[19] Cf. e.g. the penetrating study of J.L. Martyn, *History and Theology in the Fourth Gospel* (New York, 1968).

confrontation of decision, "Take him yourselves and crucify him" (19:6) and the Evangelist's conclusion to the drama, "Then he handed him over *to them* to be crucified" (19:16). The apex of the dramatic irony with regard to "the Jews" appears as is well known, in their climactic rejection of Jesus, "We have no king but Caesar" (19:15), which also functions as a desperate rejection of the very values they are portrayed as claiming to defend.

In the figure of Pilate we are confronted again with a choice of symbolism: he may represent, as Bultmann suggests,[20] the state faced with the option of yielding to the world or confronting the issue of the source of its own authority, or he may represent the Gentile faced with the option of a decision when confronted with Jesus. In any case, Pilate plays the role of an ironical figure. Here I do not refer primarily to his famous question, "What is truth?" (18:38), which may or may not be sarcastic. Indeed if one sees in Pilate a symbol of the power of the state it might be better understood as not sarcastic at all but as reflecting the incapacity of the state to deal with issues involving the truth as Jesus reveals it from the Father. But there is irony in the brief dialogue about Pilate's authority (19:10-11): his power to release or to crucify is a power of life or death, but it is an empty boast in the presence of one who has the power from his Father to give the gift of eternal life. In some ways Pilate appears at his most ironical in his repeated protestation that he can find no guilt in Jesus (18:38; 19:4, 6); Jesus' innocence is ironically proclaimed by a person who is himself portrayed as incapable of understanding what the issue of guilt or innocence really means.

Finally, the figure of Jesus is the center of the strongest irony in the passage. Here the irony arises from the reader's faith-understanding of who Jesus really is, and the issue throughout is less that of Jesus' guilt or innocence than that of his true identity. It is the distance of the reader's—and the Evangelist's—stance, the post-Easter perspective, which

---

[20] *The Gospel of John*, 652 ff.

makes the irony possible. The most obvious example is the issue of Jesus' kingship which pervades the whole passage and is expressed both in the description and in the words of Pilate (18:33, 37, 39; 19:3, 14, 15). Jesus is the messianic King "of the Jews," but everyone in the scene—Pilate, the soldiers, and Jesus himself—is made to proclaim this kingship, except "the Jews" (who do so only indirectly in 19:12). This irony is a central theme of the Passion narrative, and it is carried over from the trial scene into the crucifixion scene when, by affixing the inscription to the cross, Pilate revenges himself on those who tried to provoke him to judgment. For the believer, for whom the Fourth Gospel is written, Jesus is God's Son, and in the trial this supreme acknowledgement of his identity comes from "the Jews" as an implicit accusation of blasphemy (19:7).

Throughout the Gospel, Jesus' mission appears as that of provoking judgment. In the trial scene it is he who is ostensibly being judged, but in fact his presence forces the Jews to bring judgment upon themselves—perhaps it so affects Pilate also, though the text does not clearly indicate this. In light of the irony accompanying the judgment theme, I am inclined to opt for the controversial rendering of 19:13: "Pilate, then, hearing these words, brought Jesus outside and sat him on the judgment-seat." The arguments for this understanding, apart from the predominance of irony in the context, are conventional and need not be rehearsed here.[21]

In light of the Johannine irony, it appears that the most ironical and theologically most profound assertion made in the Pilate trial is the *ecce homo* scene (19:5). Whether or not one wishes to relate the use of *anthrōpos* here to an anthropos myth, the assertion of Pilate, in view of its parallelism with "Behold your king" a few verses later (19:14), must call our attention, ironically, to the spectacle of the Son of God appearing as man in the lowest degradation of human suffering and humiliation. This affirmation is not

[21]See the commentaries, esp. R.E. Brown, *The Gospel according to St. John,* vol. 2 (Anchor Bible; Garden City, 1970).

intended to contradict Käsemann's insistence that Johannine Christology is not based on the humiliation-exaltation theme,[22] but it does mean that the Fourth Evangelist takes seriously the Passion narrative as a revelation of the "scandal of the cross"—the scandal of the transcendent divinity revealing itself in the paradox of humanity suffering out of the motive of love. But the Fourth Gospel is precisely not docetic, for the Evangelist does not assert that the divinity of the Son merely appears to be present in man suffering. Rather, by consistently orienting his Gospel to the supreme revelation of the passion narrative, the Evangelist asserts that man's quest for the divine must terminate in the irony of man's supreme act of self-giving in love. A thoroughly docetic Christology might indeed be expressed ironically, but it would be the irony of pretense in which man's capacity for love does not figure at all.

Thematic Irony: Johannine Symbols

Besides his use of dramatic irony, the Fourth Evangelist, as we have tried to suggest in general terms above, also expresses his ironic theological vision in some of the dominant themes throughout the whole Gospel. Given the limitations of a short essay, it is scarcely possible to do more than list some examples here, but it should easily become clear how these contribute to the ironic vision.

In the first category I would include the miracles of Jesus which the Evangelist carefully designates as signs.[23] I take it with Bultmann, Robert T. Fortna,[24] and many others that the Evangelist draws upon a signs-source and that he is critical of the Christological implications of presenting Jesus as miracle worker. But I do not place the irony merely in the

---

[22] *The Testament of Jesus,* tr. G. Krodel (Philadelphia, 1968).

[23] Clavier, "L'ironie dans le quatrième Evangile," and others also list these as examples of irony.

[24] *The Gospel of Signs: A Reconstruction of the Narrative Source underlying the Fourth Gospel* (SNTSMS 11; Cambridge, 1970).

fact that he makes use of a traditional theme with which he is not wholly in sympathy. Instead, it is the function of the signs as revelation of Jesus' glory (2:11) to those who understand them, from the post-Easter perspective, and at the same time as obstacles to true faith in Jesus as revealer ("Unless you see signs and wonders . . . " 4:48). The ambiguity of the signs becomes ironical, too, in the reactions that they provoke in people without the discovery of the revealing word: wonderment, eagerness, fear, opposition.

A second manifestation of irony is to be found in the predicative "I am" sayings and other Christological symbols which have the inherent capability of being understood on several levels. For example, the woman at the well responds to Jesus' partial revelation of himself in the symbol of living water, "Sir, give me this water so that I will not thirst nor come here to draw water"(4:15). Here the irony is heightened by a dramatic touch, the exchange of roles between Jesus, who first asks the woman for water (v. 7) and the woman, who now asks it of Jesus. Or again, the Galileans who follow Jesus not because they have seen signs, but because they have eaten the loaves and been filled (6:26), respond to his mention of life-giving bread, "Sir, give us this bread always" (6:34). The more explicit revelation through the symbol of bread, "I am the bread of life" (6:35), only elicits murmuring (6:41) and eventually rejection even on the part of some disciples (6:66). The way of self-revelation through the diverse signs and symbols of the first part of the Gospel is less than effective (cf. 12:37-43), not only because the world of human symbolization of the divine is inadequate and ambiguous,[25] but because the very presence of the divine in human experience is, in the Evangelist's view, ironical.

A more specific, yet even more fundamental, example of Johannine thematic irony occurs in the Fourth Gospel's transformation of the triple prediction of the Passion into the threefold allusion to the "lifting up" of the Son of Man

[25]Cf. G.W. MacRae, "The Fourth Gospel and *Religionsgeschichte*," *CBQ* 32 (1970) 13-24, esp. 23.

(3:14-15; 8:28; 12:32-34). Here there is consummate irony in choosing the image of an apotropaic magic rite—the bronze serpent on the pole (Num 21:8-9)—to suggest the mystery of the cross. The incongruity of the serpent, instrument of death (in the OT context to which the Evangelist refers[26]), as source of life, parallels the incongruity of the ignominious death of Jesus as source of eternal life. But again, the irony reveals a deeper perception of reality that is contrary to the appearance. For the Fourth Evangelist accepts the fundamental Christian belief in both the incarnation and the reality of the Passion. His interpretation of the death of Jesus as exaltation and return to the Father, the "lifting up of the Son," is his unique and crowning irony.

In a word, the heart of the Johannine theology is itself the irony of the Logos becoming flesh and dwelling among men, the revealing Word graciously announcing to men their own potential for eternal life in the self-giving act of love that is the return to the Father.

---

[26]Even though in the Roman Hellenistic world at large the serpent did not of itself imply death—quite the opposite, in fact, in the Asclepius cult.

3

"Whom Heaven Must Receive Until The Time": Reflections on the Christology of Acts*

One of the most important questions which the modern reader shares with the New Testament writers is "Who is Jesus?" The question is not nearly so simple and straightforward as it appears at first sight, for it is asked in the present tense. To appreciate the significance of putting the question this way, one has only to reflect on how much more natural it is to ask "Who was Augustus?" rather than "Who is Augustus?" Augustus belongs to history, and even though his influence on his own time and on subsequent history was enormous, one does not normally think of him as a present reality. Jesus belongs to history too, of course, and it was the insight of the author of the third Gospel and of Acts to think of him this way. Yet even Luke does not conceive of the christological question as properly put in the past tense. For him, Jesus is alive, risen, exalted, active. How then can we speak of a historical personage in the present tense without straining beyond limits the validity of religious language itself? This is one facet of the christological problem that is particularly appropriate for Luke.

* First published in *Interpretation* 27 (1973) 151-165.

The question "Who is Jesus?" is answered very differently by the various New Testament writers and by the specific traditions they reflect. To acknowledge the variety of responses is not only to understand better the theologies of the New Testament but also to establish an authentically Christian basis for modern Christology. For it is the task of theology in every age to discover formulations of belief which are both traditionally faithful and genuinely meaningful. The diversity of New Testament Christologies grounds that task and assures its legitimacy. It is not the purpose of this article to list or discuss the various Christologies of the New Testament authors, though some will be compared with that of Acts. But before we try to identify what is distinctive about the Christology of Acts, several preliminary observations must be made.

I

One cannot adequately describe Acts' answer to the christological question without relating it to certain positions taken on some of the critical problems of research on this controversial book. What—at least in general terms—is the historical value of the information in Acts? Are the speeches in it Luke's own composition or traditional formulas of the earlier Christian communities—or indeed of the parties themselves to whom the speeches are attributed? Does the author make use of literary sources such as an Antioch source or a Jerusalem one or the diary of a journey kept in the first person ("we" passages) by a companion of Paul?[1] When was Acts written? It is obvious that some answers to these questions would be essential for determining, for example, whether we must look for a single christological position in Acts or for several, whether Luke is responsible

[1] Another question would be that of the identity of the author; in referring to him conventionally as Luke, the present article does not assume any special position in this regard.

for the views expressed by his characters or they are, whether the appearance of primitiveness in christological development is due to early records or to an archaizing style on the part of the author. The issue is particularly acute with respect to the speeches in Acts, for many of these are the first places to go in search of the Christology of the book.

It would of course be out of place to attempt to solve all these problems, or even to take a reasoned position with respect to them, in a single article—much more so to survey the critical opinions of scholarship.[2] Two remarks, however, may be appropriate to reveal the suppositions on which many of the following reflections rest.

First, a rigid dichotomy between historicity on the one hand and free Lukan composition on the other is neither necessary nor justifiable. One example may suffice. It should be clear to anyone who takes Paul seriously that the distance between the Paul of the major epistles and the Paul of Acts outlined by Philipp Vielhauer in his famous essay "On the Paulinism of Acts"[3] is at least in its general lines solidly established. On the other hand it should be equally clear that Acts does transmit some genuine Pauline echoes and some solid information about the Apostle that does not conflict with the epistles. It is true that the discourse of Paul in Pisidian Antioch in Acts 13:16-41 cannot readily be reconciled with the kerygma of the epistles. Nevertheless there are many echoes of Pauline theology and biography in the one speech in Acts which most deserves comparison with the epistles—because it is the only one addressed to a Christian audience—namely the address to the Ephesian elders at Miletus in 20:18-35. I believe Luke composed both speeches, with some—but probably not an intimate—knowledge of his subject.

---

[2]Surveys of scholarship on Luke-Acts have multiplied in recent years. Among the more useful are the essays of W.C. van Unnik and Ulrich Wilckens in *Studies in Luke-Acts*, in L.E. Keck and J.L. Martyn, eds. (Nashville: Abingdon, 1966). The whole book is a very valuable contribution to Lukan studies.

[3]In English in *Studies in Luke-Acts*, pp. 33-50; it first appeared in *Evangelische Theologie* 10 (1950-51) pp. 1-15.

The second observation is that Luke more than once betrays his concern as a narrator to adapt what is said by Paul and others to the circumstances of the narrative. Again an example, perhaps the most obvious one: The apologia of Paul is reiterated frequently before varying audiences and with considerable variation of detail. In the account of Paul's conversion in Acts 9 the Lord instructs Ananias with a programmatic statement of Paul's fate: ". . . he is a chosen instrument of mine to carry my name before the Gentiles and kings and the sons of Israel; for I will show him how much he must suffer for the sake of my name" (9:15-16). Like Acts 1:8, which is widely recognized as a programmatic statement for the spread of the church in Acts "in Jerusalem and in all Judea and Samaria and to the end of the earth," 9:15 announces Paul's mission of suffering for the name of Jesus. Later he repeats the story of his conversion before "the sons of Israel" in 22:1-21 and before "the Gentiles and kings" in 26:2-23. In each case at least some of the detailed variations in the story can be accounted for as adaptations to the specific circumstances of audience and occasion. I take it that Luke is responsible for these and also for the structure of his book which builds into the history of early Christianity a theological—and indeed, as I hope to show, a christo-logical—motif in the career of Paul.

Both these premises suggest that it is Luke himself who is the primary architect of the christological edifice of Acts, and in agreement with a great deal of modern scholarship on Acts, I take that position here. It implies that there is a unity to the christological perspective of the book, but one which should not be exaggerated, for exegesis shows that not all the statements about Jesus in Acts are really harmonious. At least this indicates that the author himself knew something of the christological diversity in the early church. If he has made use of sources, he has done so knowledgeably and responsibly, editing them to form part of his intended picture of the growth of the Christian church.

II

It has become almost a classic method to systematize the Christology of the New Testament by examining the titles attributed to Jesus by the various authors and in their various patterns. While it is true that such a procedure does bring to light some of the christological beliefs of the early Christians, it is not necessarily the best way to discover the answer to the question "Who is Jesus?" For the Book of Acts it may be a particularly inappropriate method to follow, since the author seems at pains to introduce a very wide variety of titles of Christ,[4] perhaps in order to incorporate what he recognizes as the variety of early Christian confessions. The most frequently used title in Acts is *kyrios*, "Lord," and it is difficult to identify a specifically Lukan content for it since it is used so widely throughout the New Testament.[5] Particularly significant in any case is the fact that it is used as a title either of God or of Jesus quite indiscriminately, and once at least, in Peter's discourse before the household of Cornelius (10:36), the absolute form *pantōn kyrios*, "Lord of all," asserts the universality of Jesus' lordship over all men. Despite the frequency of "Lord," the most significant title for Acts seems to be "Christ," used in Acts more clearly and more regularly than elsewhere in the New Testament as a title and not a name. It is especially noteworthy that Acts uses the formula "Jesus is the Christ," or its equivalent, consistently for the preaching of Peter, the apostles in general, Paul, and Apollos to the Jews, who could be expected to be familiar with messianic expectations (2:36; 4:26-27; 5:42; 9:22; 17:3; 18:5, 28). Just as in the case of "Lord," however, Acts does not clearly spell out what precise content this title has. Much less frequently, Acts also presents a wide variety of titles which represent various

---

[4]For recent discussion of some of the titles, see C.F.D. Moule, "The Christology of Acts," *Studies in Luke-Acts*, pp. 159-85.

[5]For an attempt to do so see Gerhard Voss, *Die Christologie der lukanischen Schriften in Grundzügen* (Paris: Desclée de Brouwer, 1965), pp. 56-58.

backgrounds: servant (3:13),[6] holy one (3:14), just one (3:14), author of life (*archēgos,* 5:31),[7] savior (5:31), Son of God (9:20), judge (10:42), and even, in the speech of Stephen and for the only time in the New Testament apart from the sayings of Jesus in the Gospels, Son of Man (7:56). The very proliferation of titles makes it less than rewarding to pursue the christological question in Acts exclusively or even mainly along this line.

Except possibly in its use of *dikaios* as a title for Jesus (3:14; 7:52; 22:14), which may be reminiscent of the suffering just one in the Wisdom of Solomon but need not be,[8] Acts shows no influence of the wisdom tradition in its Christology. This is a remarkable deficiency when one recalls the vital role played by the assimilation of Christ to wisdom in the thought of Paul, John, Matthew, and other New Testament writers. It results in the startling omission, frequently noted by interpreters, of any notion, even a primitive one, of preexistence in the Christology of Acts or indeed of the Gospel of Luke. Not even the application of Psalm 16:8 to Jesus in the third person rather than the first in Acts 2:25, "I saw the Lord always before me," would really constitute a statement of preexistence.[9] And this is an unlikely interpretation of the passage in any case, for it is meant to be spoken by Jesus and not about him, despite the unusual introductory formula.[10]

Far from a Christology of preexistence, it is difficult to avoid seeing in Acts what later generations would call an "adoptionist" Christology, though of course the explicit grounds for the latter designation are not present in Acts itself. In the first kerygmatic proclamation on Pentecost day,

---

[6]References are usually to the first occurrences of each title. One the use of "servant" in two different senses, see Moule, "The Christology of Acts," p. 169.

[7]Possibly to be translated "the one who leads the way to life." See Ernst Haenchen, *The Acts of the Apostles* (Philadelphia: Westminster, 1971), on 3:15.

[8]For alternatives, see Haenchen, on 3:14.

[9]See Moule, "The Christology of Acts," pp. 178f.

[10]A possible and more satisfactory translation might be "with a view toward him," i.e. toward his saying the same.

Peter says: "Men of Israel, hear these words: Jesus of Nazareth, a man (*andra*) attested to you by God with mighty works and wonders and signs which God did through him in your midst, . . . Let all the house of Israel therefore know assuredly that God has made him both Lord and Christ, this Jesus whom you crucified" (2:22, 36). In Paul's kerygmatic speech at Antioch the formulation is even more striking, for here Psalm 2:7, so often quoted by the early Christians for christological purposes, is explicitly applied to the "today" of Easter; it is the resurrection that makes Jesus God's Son: "And we bring you the good news that what God promised to the fathers, this he has fulfilled to us their children by raising Jesus; as also it is written in the second psalm, 'Thou art my Son, today I have begotten thee'" (13:32-33). Though Acts is perfectly consistent in its "adoptionist" stance toward Jesus, it is not uniform in the way this is presented. For example, while in Acts 13:33 it is the resurrection which is decisive for Jesus' status of divine sonship, in 2:32-36, although the resurrection is the key event in the kerygma, it is the exaltation of Jesus—in Lukan thought distinct from the resurrection[11]—which is decisive: "Being therefore exalted at the right hand of God, and having received from the Father the promise of the Holy Spirit, he has poured out this which you see and hear" (2:33). The point is made more clearly, also by Peter, in 5:30-31: "The God of our fathers raised Jesus whom you killed by hanging him on a tree. God exalted him at his right hand as Leader and Savior, to give repentance to Israel and forgiveness of sins." There is another example of lack of uniformity in the contrast between Acts 2:36, "God has made him both Lord and Christ," and the language of the Petrine sermon in Acts 3, that ". . . God foretold by the mouth of all the prophets, that his Christ should suffer, ... Repent therefore, and turn again, that your sins may be blotted out, . . . and that he may send the Christ appointed for you, Jesus" (3:18-20). The

---

[11]See Helmut Flender, *St. Luke, Theologian of Redemptive History* (Philadelphia: Fortress Press, 1967), pp. 18ff.

characteristic distinction between resurrection and exaltation in Acts, which is most clearly mirrored in the separation of the ascension from the resurrection, is in marked contrast to the theology of other New Testament writers, for example the Fourth Evangelist, for whom the resurrection itself is seen as the elevation of Jesus to the right hand of the Father. The real force of the Lukan distinction lies in his notion that Jesus in his glorified state belongs essentially to another world, even though he remains a living force in the world of men.

III

We have not yet in fact identified what is most specific and most distinctive of the Christology of Acts, and to this we must turn. A good insight into it can be had by contrasting briefly the endings of the Gospels of Matthew and Luke. Both end with an emphasis on the missionary enterprise of the apostolic community, but the relationship of Jesus to that enterprise produces two fundamentally different images. In Matthew the concluding words are of the risen Jesus: "Go therefore and make disciples of all nations, . . . and lo, I am with you always, to the close of the age" (28:19-20). In Luke, Jesus also mentions the mission, but the final promise is a different one, and the concluding words are Luke's own:

> (he) said to them, "Thus it is written, that the Christ should suffer and on the third day rise from the dead, and that repentance and forgiveness of sins should be preached in his name to all nations, beginning from Jerusalem. You are witnesses of these things. And behold, I send the promise of my Father upon you; but stay in the city, until you are clothed with power from on high."
>
> Then he led them out as far as Bethany, and lifting up his hands he blessed them. While he blessed them, he parted from them. And they returned to Jerusalem with great joy, and were continually in the temple blessing God (24:46-53).

The difference is a sharp one: In the first case the focus is on Jesus' presence with his disciples until the end; in the second case, Jesus' *absence* from them is graphically portrayed by the brief mention of the ascension.

Of course, unlike Matthew, Luke was to supplement his Gospel with a second volume in which the beginnings of the mission would be described. There too the initial focus is on the departure of Jesus ("a cloud took him out of their sight," 1:9), on the mission of the apostles ("you shall be my witnesses," 1:8), and on the promise of the Father which is to confer power, the Holy Spirit ("you shall receive power when the Holy Spirit has come upon you," 1:8). The remainder of the book is characterized by a depiction of the witnessing of the apostles and of Paul *in the absence of Jesus.* Especially in the opening chapter, Acts lays heavy stress on this motif: "This Jesus, who was taken up from you into heaven, will come in the same way as you saw him go into heaven" (1:11). The "day when he was taken up" (1:2, 22) marks the boundary between the period of Jesus and the period of the church, in the well-known division of salvation history proposed by Hans Conzelmann.[12] The kerygmatic speeches, which, as we have observed, are an important vehicle of Acts' Christology, also stress this theme of the absence of Jesus—implicitly in the emphasis on his exaltation in heaven (e.g. 2:33-36) or explicitly in the mention of his second coming: "that he may send the Christ appointed for you, Jesus, whom heaven must receive until the time for establishing all that God spoke by the mouth of his holy prophets from of old" (3:20-21). Even the story of the martyrdom of Stephen makes it clear that the presence of Jesus is perceived only by a vision of heaven itself, for Jesus is absent from among men: "But he, full of the Holy Spirit, gazed into heaven and saw the glory of God, and Jesus standing at the right hand of God; and he said, 'Behold, I see the heavens opened, and the Son of man standing at the

[12]In *The Theology of St. Luke,* trans. by Geoffrey Buswell (New York: Harper & Row, 1960).

right hand of God'" (7:55-56).

This motif is so strikingly present in Acts that C.F.D. Moule has spoken of the "absentee Christology" of the book.[13] The full force of it is brought out best, not only by contrast with Matthew's Gospel, where the mode of Christ's ongoing presence is not clearly spelled out despite its prominence,[14] but also by contrast with the Christology of the Pauline epistles, with their repeated themes of "in Christ" and "with Christ" and above all with their image of the body of Christ as the mode of his ongoing presence in the world. So central is this theme of the presence of Christ that it is carried on in various ways by those later epistles of the New Testament which reflect the Pauline tradition, the Pastorals and Ephesians-Colossians. Its virtually complete absence in Acts tends to reinforce the argument of Vielhauer and others that the author of Acts did not really know or at least understand the theology of Paul.

Admittedly the author of Acts was addressing a radically different situation. For him the issue was to account for a Christian existence that had already settled down, as it were, in ongoing history. Enough has been said and written about the role of the delay of the parousia in the eschatological perspective of Luke to make it unnecessary to survey the question again here. Whatever qualifications one might wish to place on the redactional study of Conzelmann which derives the entire Lukan perspective from this one factor,[15] it is undeniable that Luke's Christology is influenced by his salvation-history viewpoint. Not only does man himself belong to a history that has its past, its present, and its future orientation, but even Jesus belongs to such a history. He is a figure from the past who, thanks to his resurrection from the dead, has his own future in his coming again—which for Luke was no less real because it recedes from the horizon of

---

[13]"The Christology of Acts," p. 180.

[14]Note the correspondence between the Emmanuel title (Matt. 1:23) and the concluding promise of Christ to "be with" his disciples (28:20).

[15]*The Theology of St. Luke,* especially pp. 95-136.

immediacy that is characteristic of other New Testament books. And he has his own present, not in the world of ongoing history, but in heaven, where reality is not conditioned by time and movement. Here, then, is a first major nuance of Luke's answer to the present-tense question "Who is Jesus?" Jesus is the man who having died a martyr's death has been raised from the dead and exalted to become Lord and Savior of all men in heaven where he awaits the moment of his return.[16]

But is the concept of "absentee Christology" adequate to account for all the christological implications of Acts? Are there not exceptions, for example in the conversion experience of Paul? To begin with, it must be acknowledged that the texts of the biblical books are never as neatly consistent as the modern interpreter's schematization of them. Luke was less concerned with expounding a rigorous Christology than we are with discovering one. There are a few passages which on the surface seem inconsistent with the picture of Jesus as absent in the heavenly world during the period of the apostolic church's activity. The most obvious is indeed the story of Paul's conversion in which Jesus not only speaks to Paul and then to Ananias (to the latter "in a vision") but even seems to invoke a corporate concept of his presence in the world by the statement—which remains constant amid the fluctuating details of the three accounts—"I am Jesus, whom you are persecuting" (9:5; 22:8 "Jesus of Nazareth"; 26:15). But in the first instance this is unmistakably a visionary experience, sometimes explicitly described as such (9:10; 26:19). It is a communication from the heavenly world itself, not so much a presence of the voice of Christ in the world of Paul. The same observation would have to be made about the dialogue between Jesus and Paul in 22:17-21, which takes place in "a trance" (*ekstasis*), and the command of Jesus to Paul in 23:11, given in a night vision.

Secondly, it is somewhat less easy to show beyond doubt

---

[16]Flender, *St. Luke,* attaches considerable importance to Luke's application of the Hellenistic pattern of the heavenly and earthly worlds to the modes of Christ's existence.

that there is no trace of a collective concept analogous to the Pauline body of Christ in the formulation "I am Jesus, whom you are persecuting." Yet because the claim refers to the "historical" Jesus (especially clear in 22:8), the more apt parallel is the Jesus saying found in a variety of forms in the Marcan, Q, and Johannine traditions: for example, Luke 10:16a, "He who hears you hears me, and he who rejects you rejects me." The latter does not imply a corporate-Christ idea but merely one of association between the Christian and Jesus in whose fate he shares, for example by imitation. With this notion, as we shall mention below, Luke is quite familiar.

IV

One question remains to be put to Acts to discover the heart of its christological orientation, and that is the most important question of all. For our emphasis on the "absentee" character of the Christology of Acts is only half the story. How does the growing Christian community relate to the Christ who is exalted in heaven? Or to put the question differently, Is there any sense in which the "absent" Christ is nevertheless present to his church? Conzelmann points to two ways in which Christ may be said to be present,[17] but in fact there seem to be four modes of "presence" at least. Let us review them briefly.

To begin with, though Christ himself reigns as Lord in heaven, his work of guiding his followers is carried on by the Holy Spirit poured out on the apostolic community and indeed on all whom the apostles convert in their ministry. The role of the Spirit in Acts is so dominant that it hardly needs to be emphasized here; moreover, a full exposition of it constitutes a study in itself. It will be enough here to point out how the giving of the Spirit and its action constitute a

---

[17] *The Theology of St. Luke,* pp. 185-87, refers to the presence of the Holy Spirit and the presence of Jesus' words and deeds as part of history.

mode of the presence of Christ to his followers. The key is to recall the distribution of the Holy Spirit in the total work of Luke—a pattern which strongly reinforces in broad lines the periodization of salvation history outlined by Conzelmann. In the infancy narrative of Luke 1—2 (which Conzelmann is often criticized for leaving out of account in his analysis of Lukan theology[18]) the Holy Spirit functions as in the Old Testament or the period of Israel, and in fact Luke seems to regard the time of Jesus as beginning only after the infancy narrative. In Luke 1—2 the Spirit is primarily the Spirit of prophecy and it fills nearly all the characters of the narrative except the infant Jesus: John the Baptist, Mary, Elizabeth, Zechariah, Simeon. But in the remainder of the Gospel, starting with the baptism of Jesus, the temptation, and the programmatic scene in the synagogue of Nazareth (4:16-30), the Holy Spirit functions exclusively in Jesus. To the disciples the Spirit is a promise of the future to teach them and empower them to perform the mission of witnessing to Jesus (12:12; 24:49; see also 11:13). Though it is not explicitly stated, the promise of the Spirit in Acts 1 (compare Acts 1:2 with 1:5 and Lk 3:16, also with Acts 1:8) and the conferral of the Spirit in Acts 2 are a handing on to the apostles of the motivating force of Jesus' own mission. They are not only to witness to him, but in a sense to be animated by his own source of power.

More explicitly, the Holy Spirit who guides the mission of Paul is identified in Acts 16:7 with the continuing force of the Jesus who first commanded Paul to undertake his mission. The Holy Spirit who forbade Paul and Timothy to speak the word in Asia (16:6) is set in strict parallelism with the "Spirit of Jesus" who restrained them from entering Bithynia (16:7). Thus Paul is guided not only by visions of the exalted Jesus in heaven but by his Spirit as well.

The second mode of Christ's presence to his church is in the theme of the name, which pervades Acts in a great many

---

[18]E.g. by P.S. Minear, "Luke's Use of the Birth Stories," *Studies in Luke-Acts,* pp. 120-25.

passages. The application of Joel 2:32 to Jesus in the Pentecost discourse of Peter sets the tone for the whole book: "And it shall be that whoever calls on the name of the Lord shall be saved" (Acts 2:21). Calling upon the name is the mark of being a follower of Jesus (9:14, 21; 22:16), more primitive, Luke implies, than being called *by* Christ's name, that is, "Christian" (11:26). And it is this act of invoking the name which relates the believer to salvation itself: "And there is salvation in no one else, for there is no other name under heaven given among men by which we must be saved" (4:12). In Peter's speech to Cornelius the forgiveness of sins is mediated by the name (10:43). Baptism in Acts, which functions to introduce men into the community of salvation and either to confirm the gift of the Holy Spirit or to induce it, is baptism in the name of Jesus Christ or of the Lord Jesus (2:38; 8:16; 10:48; 19:5). Among other uses of the theme, the apostles and Paul preach in the name (4:17-18; 9:27-29); Philip preaches about it (8:12); they work cures and exorcisms in the name (3:6; 16:18); Paul, who had once opposed the name (26:9), is called upon to suffer for it (9:16) as the apostles do (5:41).

Against an Old Testament background the sense of the reality and power of the name as a presence, especially in worship, is very strong. As is well known, the presence of Yahweh in his temple, though he himself dwells in heaven, is expressed by the notion of the name. The temple is the place where his name dwells, as is the city of Jerusalem. The prayer of Solomon at the consecration of the temple makes explicit the contrast between God whom "heaven and the highest heaven cannot contain" and his name which dwells in the house to hear the prayer of his servant (1 Kgs 8:27-30). Acts nowhere appeals expressly to this Deuteronomic theme of the divine name as a divine presence in the world; nevertheless, something analogous to it seems to underlie Luke's many uses of the expression with respect to Jesus.

The third mode of Jesus' presence in Acts is one to which we must reason from the structure and theological intention of the Lukan writings. Put very simply, it is that Jesus is present and real precisely because he belongs to history and history is present to men who reflect upon it, recall it, proclaim it. A redaction-critical comparison of the Synoptic Gospels draws our attention immediately to the fact that unlike Mark or Matthew, Luke is concerned to present the story of Jesus as a part of history—not to relegate it to the domain of the dead past which is forever behind us, but to proclaim it as always present in the preaching and lives of Christians. Luke's use of the conventional historian's prologue (Lk 1:1-4 and Acts 1:1) and his elaborate "dating" of the Gospel narrative (Lk 3:1-2) have as at least part of their purpose to reflect his historical perspective. Of course this perspective must be carefully distinguished from that of the modern historian. It is still best referred to as "salvation history," not only because it is the history of God's saving act in Jesus Christ, but because as history it exercises a saving function by making Jesus present to the church in the proclamation of its leaders.

In Acts this mode of Christ's presence may best be seen in the kerygmatic sermons of Peter and Paul which, unlike the kerygma of Paul in 1 Cor 15:3-5, for example, tell the story of the "historical Jesus" as well as the saving message of his death and resurrection.[19] Peter's Cornelius speech (10:34-43) is a lucid example, Paul's Antioch sermon (13:16-41) an even clearer one, for it not only summarizes the life of Jesus but it places it in the perspective of Old Testament salvation history from the Exodus to David. This recital is explicitly called the *logos tēs sōtērias tautēs*, "the message of this salvation" (13:26). In the light of Luke's attitude toward the history of Jesus as saving recital, the interpreter must be slow to emphasize his apparent concern for history on the model of the secular historians of his day. What he borrows from them—which on balance is really not very much—he uses not merely to declare that Jesus is a part of the world's

---

[19]The homogeneity of the kerygma in Luke and Paul discovered by C.H. Dodd in his famous study, *The Apostolic Preaching and Its Developments* (London: Hodder & Stoughton, 1936), does not seem justified by this comparison. On the formal analysis of the speeches see Eduard Schweizer, "Concerning the Speeches in Acts," *Studies in Luke-Acts,* pp. 208-16.

history, but to declare that God works in history through Jesus. And by virtue of the witnessing function of the apostolic church to this saving history—a function which Paul to whom Luke denies the title of apostle shares with the Twelve (compare Acts 1:8 with 22:15 and 26:16)[20]—the reality of Christ in history is made constantly present in the preaching of the Gospel.

Finally, the fourth mode of Christ's presence to his church, likewise to be perceived in the overall structure of Luke-Acts, is closely related to Jesus' "historical presence." We might call this Jesus' presence as a model of discipleship, incorporated in the lives of his followers. It is this understanding of the relationship of Jesus to his witnesses in Acts that no doubt stands behind the unusual christological title *archēgos*, "leader." We have already commented upon the way in which the role of Jesus is in some sense reenacted in his followers by virtue of the outpouring of the Holy Spirit. It is equally well known that in Acts the apostles and Paul exercise a miracle-working power that is closely analogous to the miraculous activity of Jesus in the Gospel. In these respects there is an element of the Hellenistic "divine man" Christology to which Luke, unlike Mark or especially John and Paul, saw no major objection.[21] The true followers of the divine man are those who recreate the evidence of his supernatural status in their own lives as his preachers.

The emphasis on Christ as a model that I wish to place here, however, is one that is less often commented upon. It is the extent to which the career of Jesus as the one who suffers is reproduced in the life of Paul. On the surface, Paul plays in Acts the role of missionary par excellence through whose almost boundless industry the Christian message spread through the lands of the Gentiles and ultimately to the center of the world, to Rome itself—even though there is already a

[20]See the interesting study of Christoph Burchard, *Der dreizehnte Zeuge* (Göttingen: Vandenhoeck und Ruprecht, 1970).

[21]Cf. H.D. Betz, "Jesus as Divine Man," *Jesus and the Historian,* in F. Thomas Trotter, ed. (Philadelphia: Westminster Press, 1968), pp. 114-33.

Christian community there when Paul arrives. There is no doubt that part of Luke's literary intention was to dramatize the spread of Christianity according to the programmatic formula in Acts 1:8 which we have already mentioned. But in addition, like Jesus whose mission was one of suffering as well as of preaching, Paul is called to suffer and his journey is toward suffering as his Master's was in the Gospel.

In the story of Paul's calling on the road to Damascus the theme of suffering is on a par with that of mission. Jesus tells Ananias that Paul is "a chosen instrument of mine to carry my name before the Gentiles and kings and the sons of Israel;"—a reference to the captivity of Paul as well as to his preaching—"for I will show him how much he must suffer for the sake of my name" (9:15-16). The ensuing history of Paul is reminiscent of the outset of Jesus' mission in the Nazareth synagogue (Lk 4:28-30), for Paul's preaching results in a plot on the part of the Jews to kill him and he is forced to escape by being lowered over the wall in a basket (Acts 9:23-25). When summarizing his own career in the Miletus speech, Paul emphasizes both the suffering that he has already undergone as an authentication of his mission (compare 2 Cor 6:1-10 and 10:7—12:10) and the suffering to which his journey to Jerusalem, and ultimately to Rome, summons him (Acts 20:19-23).

It is precisely the journey motif as a structural principle of both Luke's Gospel and Acts that reveals how deep-rooted in Luke's Christology was the concept of Christ's presence to his church in the sufferings of his witnesses. Everyone is familiar with the journey narrative of the Gospel (9:51—19:27), which is the most obvious sign of Luke's redactional activity in the presence of his Marcan source. Jesus' journey to Jerusalem is his movement toward his martyr's death, but it is also, as the opening verses make abundantly clear (Lk 9:51-62 especially) a lesson in the realities of discipleship. The journey of Paul in Acts first to Jerusalem and then to Rome analogously occupies a major part of the book (effectively 19:21—28:31) and represents the working out in the life of the model disciple the same journey toward suffering and death that was Jesus'. The difference is of course that Jesus has already made the journey. Paul can face the prospect of his fate with the confidence that was won for him by Jesus whose journey to death was crowned with resurrection and exaltation. Paul is guided on his way through one danger after another by the Holy Spirit (20:22-23) and by the vision of the Lord Jesus (23:11). And perhaps it is the confidence of this divine assurance that enables the author of Acts to end his work not with the actual martyrdom of Paul but with the serenity of the Christian mission being fulfilled in Paul's ministry in Rome. The fact that this function of Jesus as the model for Paul is really a presence of Jesus to the whole church emerges from the manner in which Paul himself, in his following of Jesus in suffering, serves as a model for the elders of Ephesus in their exercise of the Christian ministry (20:31-35).

The Christology of Acts, of which we have seen some of the main features, is complex and comprehensive. It involves a claim for the universality of Jesus reflected in his many titles. It involves a movement of the divine action from the sphere of humanity, through resurrection and exaltation, to universal lordship in heaven. Especially it involves an answer to the problem of history expressed both in the notion of Jesus' absence from the world and in the sense of his presence in the world acting through the Holy Spirit, through the name, through the present reality of history, and through the lives of his witnesses. Of the various Christologies in the New Testament, no case is made here for preferring Luke's to the exclusion of others. But by the same token no Christian answer to the question "Who is Jesus for us today?" should leave the Lukan answer out of account.

4

Romans 8:26-27*

Paul's insistence on constant prayer (Rom 12:12; Phil 4:6; 1 Thess 5:17) and his own example of prayer in all the circumstances of his life (Phil 1:3-5 and *passim*) make it quite clear how important prayer is for the Christian life in his understanding. It is probably not too much to claim that for Paul prayer in its many forms is constitutive of being a Christian. In this light it is startling, therefore, to find him saying in Romans 8:26 that we really do not know what to pray for as we should. Yet there is a sense in which this is quite true, for in the universality of prayer there can be a danger of distorting the very dependence on God that prayer is meant to express. To pray for all our human needs, for ourselves and others, for our material as well as spiritual well-being, is to run the risk of dictating to God a program for Christian living that is largely of our own making. Such a risk is inherent in prayer, of course, and it should not become a pretext for failing to pray for all these things. But it should remind the Christian that even in constant prayer one sometimes does not know what to pray for properly. In its own context this surprising statement of Paul may have a more specific meaning also, and to discover it we must probe a bit deeper.

* First published in *Interpretation* 34 (1980) 288-292.

Romans 8:26-27 is a more difficult passage to understand than appears at first sight. For one thing, it is almost completely unparalleled in the Pauline letters and indeed in the New Testament as a whole. It contains some unusual vocabulary and some expression that are not entirely clear. Short of undertaking a detailed criticism of the major current Bible translations, it may be helpful to begin with a fairly literal rendering of the Greek with which one might compare the standard versions. Even a "literal" translation contains some elements of interpretation.

> And in a similar manner the Spirit comes to the aid of our weakness: for we do not know what to pray for as is proper, but the Spirit himself intercedes with unutterable groans. And he who searches hearts knows what is the mind of the Spirit because he intercedes for the saints according to (the mind of) God.

Singular as these verses are, they are not isolated but have several points of contact with their context and are in fact explicable only in the light of it. Chapter 8 of Romans brings to completion, and indeed to a climax, the central section of the letter (chaps. 5—8) in which Paul sets forth in a variety of ways his fundamental understanding of what God has accomplished for humanity in the death and resurrection of his Son: freedom from sin, death, and the Law. In this eloquent chapter that accomplishment is expressed in terms of the ultimate gift of God's own Spirit, the Spirit of Christ (8:9), which blends, as it were, with the human spirit, actually dwells within the Christian (8:9-11) to raise ordinary human life to God's level by making the Christian a child of God, one who by grace has the right to call God Abba, Father (8:15-17). The intercessory prayer of the Spirit in our passage is already prepared for to some extent by what one might call the "simultaneous" or the "cooperative" prayer of the Spirit who "bears witness together with our own spirit" when we utter the simple yet profound prayer "Abba."

The intercessory prayer one prays not so much together with another as for the other, even at times in place of the other. And in Romans 8 the Spirit of God is not the only

intercessor. Christ, "who is at the right hand of God," also
intercedes for us (8:34). The image here is that of one who
addresses the heavenly court on behalf of the suitor, as
contrasted with one who brings a charge against him. The
intercessory roles of Christ and the Spirit are of course
similar, but they are distinguished by Paul in the choice of
images used. It is difficult for Christians steeped in the
classical Trinitarian doctrine of the church not to read Paul
here and elsewhere in the light of the developed doctrine. But
it is worth the effort to avoid the anachronism as much as
possible in order to recapture some of the freshness of Paul's
bold imagery. The Spirit, who is that intimate dimension of
God's own selfhood and Christ's as well—that is analogous
to the human spirit, pleads with God on behalf of the
Christian from within, precisely when human weakness
renders the human spirit mute in prayer.

There is another important link with the context in
chapter 8 which modern translations often obscure by their
choice of words. It hinges on the repetition of the word
"groan," noun and verb, in verses 18-27, and it revolves
about the very important issue of hope in this section of the
chapter. Despite his emphasis on the transforming power of
the Spirit of God dwelling within the Christian, Paul's well-
known eschatological reserve prevents him from portraying
the redeemed life as a full realization of all that it is destined
to be. The experiential dimension of life is still one in which
"the sufferings of the present time" (8:18) are prominent, but
thanks to the presence of the Spirit which empowers
Christians to know they are God's children and heirs (8:16-
17), suffering is relativized by the hope of glory. Paul
contrasts the experience of suffering with the confidence of
hope by using the image of groaning, figuratively expressing
in sound the longing for the full realization of what is hoped
for.

In a particularly bold metaphor, he portrays the creation
itself as groaning with the pangs of one giving birth (8:22) for
its ultimate freedom from bondage and decay. Not only does
the creation groan for its freedom, "but also we ourselves,
who possess the Spirit as first fruits, groan within ourselves

as we wait for adoption as sons, the redemption of our body" (8:23). And thirdly—Paul says "likewise" or "and in a similar manner" (8:26)—the Spirit pleads on our behalf with "unutterable groans" for the consummation of our hope of glory, especially when we do not know how to express our own prayer for what we hope for but do not see. The inadequacy of our human "groaning" is made up for in the Spirit's intercession. Creation, the believers, and the Spirit of God share a common prayer for the eschatological fulfillment of God's promise.

With these remarks on the context in mind, we may return to what our passage actually says and ask a series of questions about its meaning. First, what is the "weakness" in which we need the help of the Spirit? Here is is important not to generalize too much or too quickly. On the one hand the weakness is defined by the statement that "we do not know what to pray for as is proper." On the other hand, the context illuminates the meaning of both our weakness and our ignorance of what to pray for. Christians are weak because, still subject to "the sufferings of this present time," they hope for what they do not see (8:25) and thus do not clearly understand the eschatological realization of divine sonship, the redemption of the body, the inheritance of glory, assimilation to the image of the Son, ultimate justi-fication, and the true freedom of the children of God. These are all symbols of the reality of the transformation of human sinfulness into an existence that is so pleasing to God as to share in his own life. We have the Spirit of God within us as its first fruits—"down payment," *arrabōn,* is the image Paul uses elsewhere (2 Cor 1:22; 5:5)—yet we lack not only the fulfillment but the full knowledge of what its fulfillment will be like. In such weakness we need the Spirit's intercession.

How does the Spirit intercede? There is no suggestion in the text, at least no overt one, that the Spirit prays together with the Christian, as is explicitly stated, for example, in the case of the Abba prayer in Romans 8:15-16. Rather, the implication is that when we are too weak to pray as we ought, the Spirit prays in our place, intercedes in a strict sense. This may be Paul's way of saying that not only does

God freely grant his righteousness to whoever believes in the efficacy of Christ's saving death and resurrection, but his divine Spirit reminds him of the ultimate gift of glory which is implied in that righteousness. The language is metaphorical, to be sure, but unlike some theological metaphors, it is intensely personal. The "groans" of the Spirit are of course likewise metaphorical; they do not imply any kind of human prayer. Human "groaning" was mentioned in verse 23 and does not need to be repeated here. The particular metaphor, of course, is dictated by the parallelism with creation and "we ourselves" in the preceding verses. The word *alalētois* which describes the groans of the Spirit is unique here in the New Testament and rare in any case. It has long been disputed whether it means something like "without words, unuttered" or "incapable of being expressed in words, unutterable." In reality the difference is significant only as long as one envisions some kind of human prayer. The Spirit's prayer needs no sound, articulate or otherwise, for it is "according to the mind of God."

Verse 27 is the least clear part of the passage, and in a brief exposition one can do no more than present two alternative interpretations. The first supposes that Paul is recalling his previous discussion in 8:5-8 in which he contrasts the "mind," that is, the intention, what one "sets his mind on" (the same word *phronēma* is used in both contexts), of the spirit, both human and divine, with that of the flesh. In this instance he might be saying that the Spirit of God can effectively or appropriately intercede for the Christian in that he knows what the spiritual Christian really wants even when the latter is unable to formulate it in prayer. And the Spirit has this power because it is *kata theon,* "according to the mind of God," that he offers his intercessory prayer. One must bear in mind that the word "spirit" poses a difficult problem for the translator at many points in the New Testament and nowhere more acutely than in this chapter of Romans. The problem is to know when to capitalize the word to refer to God's Spirit; in Romans 8 both God's Spirit and the human spirit are mentioned. One might paraphrase verse 27 in this sense as follows: "And the Spirit who searches human hearts (see 1 Cor 2:10-13) knows what the human spirit has its mind set on because it is according to the mind of God himself that he intercedes for the saints."

It may be safer, however, and it is certainly closer to the tradition of interpretation, to understand the word *pneuma* here as still a reference to the Spirit of God. In this sense the argument is that God who knows the human heart also knows the mind of his own Spirit when he intercedes. A paraphrase might then be: "And God who searches human hearts knows what the Spirit has set his mind on because it is according to God's own mind that the Spirit intercedes for the saints."

Some interpreters—and in recent years some weighty ones at that—have preferred to see in this passage a reference to that type of prayer which Paul calls "speaking in tongues," *glossolalia.* For them the "wordless groans" of the Spirit's intercession are actually human sounds, an example of that inarticulate speech about which Paul is ambivalent in the long discussion of 1 Corinthians 14. The New English Bible rendering "through our inarticulate groans" could lend support to such a view, though it need not necessarily be taken this way. For some, the point of the passage would then be that whenever Christians pray in tongues in the context of worship, they are witnessing to the fact that the Spirit of God is publicly making up for their inability to pray "properly," through the gift of tongues, which is one of the manifestations or gifts of the Spirit mentioned in 1 Cor 12:10. Verse 27 would follow quite naturally by implying that God needs no interpretation of such inarticulate prayer because the Spirit prays "according to the mind of God."

Such an interpretation of the passage is certainly possible, and it would have obvious relevance for contemporary situations of charismatic renewal, whether or not one sees in the passage an implicit critique of speaking in tongues as prayer. But there are many reasons, in addition to the positive, contextual interpretation given above, for thinking it unlikely. For one thing, there is no indication in this passage or indeed in the whole chapter that Paul has in mind the situation of community worship that is envisioned in 1

Corinthians 14, even though in general Paul does not think of Christians in purely individualistic terms. Moreover, he does not project onto the Roman church, which he does not know first hand, the excesses of pneumatic enthusiasm with which he is all too familiar at Corinth. Speaking in tongues, for example, is not included in the list of gifts in Romans 12:6-8. Where such a gift is mentioned, as in 1 Corinthians 12—14, it is given to some Christians only, while others have different gifts; Romans 8:26-27 refers to all Christians in whom the Spirit is operative. Most significantly, verse 26 does not attribute the "unutterable groans" to the Christians themselves, but only to the intercession of the Spirit. In the light of all this, it is best not to involve this passage in a discussion of ancient or modern forms of charismatic prayer.

The wealth of this difficult passage for homiletic purposes, once one has wrestled with its problems, is abundant. Its main lesson may be that when Christians pray, however inadequately, they do not pray alone: The Spirit of God himself prays with them, in them, and even for them. The indwelling of the Spirit gives to prayer as to all other aspects of Christian life a profound dimension that surpasses human understanding. Likewise the context of the passage is a reminder that Christian prayer is an expression of eschatological hope in the fulfillment of God's promises. Only a true spirit of prayer can enable the Christian, with Paul, to "consider that the sufferings of this present time are not worth comparing with the glory that is to be revealed to us."

5

A Note on 1 Corinthians 1:4-9*

Modern translations uniformly—and wisely—adopt the principle that the same Hebrew, Aramaic, or Greek word need not and should not always be rendered by the same English or other modern-language word. There have, of course, been exceptions to such a rule, but the resulting versions have sometimes been characterized by unreadability.[1] Yet, like almost any principle of translation, this rejection of a one-for-one correspondence can be applied too woodenly and with unfortunate results. It can result, for example, in the failure to preserve in translation a wordplay that is an integral part of the text. Some such wordplays are virtually impossible to preserve without resort to extensive paraphrase: for example, the double sense of *anōthen,* meaning both "again" and "from above" in John 3:3-7, or of *diathēkē,* meaning both "will" and "covenant" in Gal 3:15-17 and Heb 9:15-18. But there are other cases in which the wordplay is easily preserved, provided its importance is recognized. Such a case is the use of *bebaioō* in the thanksgiving passage of 1 Corinthians.

The Pauline thanksgivings as a functional part of the

---

* First published in the *Harry M. Orlinsky Volume,* (Jerusalem: Israel Exploration Society—Hebrew Union College/Jewish Institute of Religion, 1982) 171*-175*.

[1]For examples in the English language tradition, see A.S. Herbert, *Historical Catalogue of Printed Editions of the English Bible* 1525-1961 (London, 1968) e.g., no. 1942.

letter have been subjected to intense scrutiny on the part of modern scholarship.[2] Without attempting to summarize the many relevant studies here, I note only two rather general and widely accepted conclusions. First, the thanksgivings are usually very carefully, often rhetorically, composed, and secondly, they contain elements that announce in advance and sometimes with delicate indirectness some of the main themes of the letter in question. 1 Cor 1:4-9 is not only no exception but is in fact an excellent example. In a carefully phrased, if not always lucid, period, it calls attention both to the presence of abundant spiritual manifestations among the community—which, as the sequel shows, are often problematic—and to Paul's eschatological perspective which will serve to keep the spiritual enthusiasm of the Corinthians in check.[3]

In the Revised Standard Version (RSV) the passage reads as follows:

> [4]I give thanks to God always for you because of the grace of God which was given you in Christ Jesus, [5]that in every way you were enriched in him with all speech and all knowledge—[6]even as the testimony of Christ was confirmed among you—[7]so that you are not lacking in any spiritual gift, as you wait for the revealing of our Lord Jesus Christ; [8]who will sustain you to the end, guiltless in the day of our Lord Jesus Christ. [9]God is faithful, by whom you were called into the fellowship of his Son, Jesus Christ our Lord.

In this translation the verb "was confirmed" in v. 6 is *ebebaiōthē,* and the phrase "who will sustain" in v. 8 is *hos kai bebaiōsei.* In choosing to vary the translation of this Greek verb the RSV committee chose to ignore the relation-

---

[2]The modern classic study is Paul Schubert, *Form and Function of the Pauline Thanksgivings* (Beiheft zur Zeitschrift für neutestamentliche Wissenschaft 20) (Berlin, 1939).

[3]For the importance of Paul's eschatological reservation as a unifying theme of the whole epistle, see the commentary of Hans Conzelmann, *Der erste Brief an die Korinther* (Meyer) (Göttingen, 1969).

ship between vv. 6 and 8 and consequently also the *kai* which, along with the repetition of the verb, links them in the text.

Many other contemporary English versions reflect a similar practice. To give only a very few examples: "the witness I bore to Christ has been so confirmed among you ... he will strengthen you to the end" (New American Bible); "our testimony about Christ was confirmed in you ... he will keep you strong to the end" (New International Version). The New English Bible, however, preserves some hint of the same verb in both verses: "in you the evidence for the truth of Christ has found confirmation ... he will keep you firm to the end."[4] This tendency to vary the rendering of the verb is a relatively modern phenomenon in the English language tradition. The Authorized Version (AV) of 1611 may have reproduced the meaning of the passage better when it translated: "the testimony of Christ was confirmed in you ... who shall also confirm you unto the end," and the nineteenth-century Revised Version (RV), which made a point of trying when possible to render the same original word with the same English word, left this translation intact.[5] It is possible to conclude, as I hope to show presently, that the tradition of translation is progressively losing sight of the meaning of these verses, even if we cannot be entirely sure how the AV understood the verses.

The problem is not in the meaning or New Testament use of the verb *bebaioō*. In general, it can bear the weight of all the translations suggested. The verb, or its noun and adjective cognates, can function as a technical legal term; the noun has this force unmistakably in Heb 6:16 and very likely in Phil 1:7. Whether this is the sense of 1 Cor 1:6, as is often

---

[4]Compare the Bible de Jérusalem: "la fermeté qu'a pris en vous ... c'est lui qui vous affermira." It is interesting to note that although the Vulgate used the verb *confirmare* in both verses, modern translations of it such as the American Confraternity version and the British version of Ronald Knox do not reflect a common verb.

[5]Cf. Millar Burrows, *Diligently Compared* (London, 1964) 38-51.

maintained, remains to be discussed.[6] In the majority of its uses in the New Testament, the word group has a non-technical sense, meaning to establish firmly, to strengthen, and the like, as is clearly the case in 1 Cor 1:8. One might raise the question whether it is likely that the verb is used in radically different senses in vv. 6 and 8, especially when they are joined by *kai.*

The main issue in the interpretation of the passage is the meaning of the phrase *to martyrion tou christou* in v. 6; Johannes Weiss remarked long ago that it was not possible to arrive at a certain understanding of this verse.[7] It is clear from the contemporary translations cited above, as well as from the majority of commentaries, that the differentiation in the rendering of *bebaioō* is dictated by the almost universal conviction that the "testimony" in question is the preaching of the gospel by Paul in Corinth, upon which the Corinthian community was founded. Just as God "confirmed" the proclamation of the gospel in Corinth by bestowing the spiritual gifts, especially of speech and knowledge, on the Corinthians, so, because he is faithful (v. 9), he will "sustain" the Corinthians until the end. This is a natural way to understand the word *martyrion* here, but it presupposes what is only an oblique reference to Paul's preaching in a context that is otherwise wholly concerned with what God has accomplished in the Corinthians themselves— which is the object of Paul's thanksgiving. It is therefore not unreasonable to examine the basis of this majority under-standing of the "testimony" with a view to suggesting, with some admitted hesitation, an alternative.

In fact, the word group *martys* and cognates is not widely used in the Pauline epistles, in contrast to its frequency in the Johannine writings, and the form *martyrion*, which refers not to the act of bearing witness but to the testimony itself, is

---

[6]Cf. Heinrich Schlier, "*Bebaios ktl.,*" *Theological Dictionary of the New Testament* I, pp. 600-3 (juridical sense); Conzelmann, 41 (non-juridical sense).

[7]*Der erste Korintherbrief* (Meyer; 9th ed.) (Göttingen, 1910) 8.

very rare in the genuine Pauline letters.[8] The decisive
evidence that it refers to the apostolic preaching, virtually
the equivalent of *evangelion* itself, would come from 1 Cor
2:1, in which Paul refers to his initial coming to Corinth
katangellōn hymin to martyrion tou theou. But this would
be an effective argument only if it is the case that *martyrion*
and not the variant *mystērion* is the correct reading. As is
well known, the issue is an extremely difficult one to decide
on grounds of textual criticism, and the commentaries are
completely divided on it.[9] The 26th edition of the Greek text
of Nestle-Aland and the 3rd edition of the United Bible
Societies' *Greek New Testament* (which are by design
textually identical) have opted for the reading *mystērion*,
largely on the ground of context, where the word is
mentioned again in v. 7.[10] The reading *martyrion* would then
be either a scribal error (the words resemble each other fairly
closely) or the influence of 1:6 understood by some scribe as
indeed a reference to Paul's preaching. If then one adopts the
reading *mystērion*, on whatever grounds, the clearest
evidence for a Pauline use of *martyrion* to refer to his
missionary preaching will have vanished.

Excluding the Pastoral Epistles, there are only two other
instances of *martyrion* to consider. In 2 Thess 1:10—if the
letter be accepted as authentically Pauline—we have an
eschatological passage referring to the coming of the Lord in
judgment: "... when he comes on that day to be glorified in
his saints, and to be marveled at in all who have believed
because our testimony to you (*to martyrion hēmōn eph'
hymas*) was believed" (RSV). Here the word may very well
be a reference to the apostle's earlier preaching in Thes-
salonica, but the construction is different: the genitive
hēmōn can hardly be anything but subjective.[11] The other

---

[8]Cf. H. Strathmann, "*Martys, ktl.,*" *Theological Dictionary of the New Testament*
IV, 474-515.

[9]Conzelmann, 69, declares it impossible to decide.

[10]Cf. Bruce M. Metzger. *A Textual Commentary on the Greek New Testament*
(London, 1971) 545.

[11]Cf. E. Best, *A Commentary on the First and Second Epistle to the Thessalonians*
(London, 1972) 266.

passage, which is certainly Pauline, is 2 Cor 1:12: "For our boast is this, the testimony of our conscience (*to martyrion tēs syneidēseōs hēmōn*) that we have behaved in the world ..." (RSV). In this case the testimony is less a public event than an internal assurance of Paul's which grounds his "boast." It is thus the case—which should not of course be overstated—that the only other certain use of *martyrion* by Paul definitely does not refer to his preaching the gospel. Of course, Paul does occasionally, though rarely, use the verb *martyreō* of his own activity, but only 1 Cor 15:15 could be construed as a reference to his preaching "... we testified of God that he raised Christ," and in this verse we are dealing with a sustained juridical metaphor.

In view of the relatively slender evidence that Paul can use *martyrion* to refer to the gospel he preached, we may be permitted to make a different suggestion for which the context of 1 Cor 1:4-9 is the best argument, there being no verbal parallels to adduce. One should bear in mind that testimony need not be a verbal message but can be an object, a condition, or an action which by its very existence as it were bears witness to a truth or a conviction, or in our case to the person of Christ. Such is the case with Paul's conscience in 2 Cor 1:12. In the Septuagint of Isa 55:4 God declares that he has made David a *martyrion* (not *martys*) "to the peoples, a leader and commander for the peoples"; David himself is thus a "testimony" to the Lord. In 1 Cor 1:16 the "testimony to Christ" may be understood as the very condition of the Corinthian community, virtually its very existence, in which spiritual gifts abound. The "testimony to Christ" is in effect not distinct from the "gift of God given to you in Christ Jesus" (v. 4). In this sense the testimony is not validated or confirmed by the spiritual gifts, but as the condition of the community itself it has been strengthened to the point where they lack no particular gift. And as the testimony has become strong, so also (*kai*, v. 8) God (or Christ) will keep the Corinthians strong until the end. This suggestion results in the supposition that the passage contains a certain amount of repetition, though the language varies, but such repetition is not untypical of the rhetorical language of the Pauline thanksgivings. In any case the suggestion has two advantages: it avoids the intrusion of a more or less gratuitous reference to the missionary preaching of Paul in Corinth—which will be mentioned in quite different terms often enough in the opening chapters of the letter—and it allows the repetition of the verb *bebaioō* full value without our having to assume a shift in its meaning.

As indicated, one cannot point to a Pauline use of *martyrion* in this sense which would be a strict parallel to 1 Cor 1:6. Nevertheless, the idea that the presence of the Spirit and miracle working activity (*dynameis*) in a community have evidential value for the Christian character of the community is not foreign to Paul. This is in fact the point of Gal 3:1-5.

Before leaving the passage, we must comment briefly on three further problems of interpretation and therefore of translation. The first is whether *tou christou* in v. 6 is best regarded as an objective or a subjective genitive. Modern commentators do not usually hesitate to affirm the former, but they also uniformly understand the testimony as Paul's preaching about Christ.[12] It is no longer possible to know how the AV and RV translators understood "the testimony *of* Christ." In the understanding of the passage proposed here it is conceivable to take the genitive as subjective and suppose that in the spiritual gifts Christ himself is giving testimony through the Corinthian community, but one would then have to ask to what this testimony is being ·rendered. It may therefore be best to accept the majority view that the genitive is objective (but on different grounds) and understand that the very lives of the Corinthians constitute a testimony to Christ, that is, in Pauline terms, that their lives are lived in him.

The second problem concerns the connective *kai* in v. 8, to which we have already given some importance in the structure of the passage. Ernst Haenchen has included this verse in a long list of instances in which *kai* following a

---

[12]Cf. e.g., C.K. Barrett, *A Commentary on the First Epistle to the Corinthians* (2nd ed.) (London, 1971) 37-38.

relative pronoun should be left untranslated.[13] There are certainly cases where the word has no real connective value in such a position beyond that already conveyed by the relative, but there are others where it is significant. For example, I would certainly exclude 1 Cor 11:23 and 15:3 from Haenchen's list; each instance must be evaluated on its own merits. In our passage, given the structure "the testimony to Christ has grown strong . . . he will keep you strong," the *kai* appears to have full value either as the connective "and" or as "also."

The third problem may be the most insoluble of all. Is the antecedent of the relative pronoun *hos* in v. 8 Jesus Christ, whose name immediately precedes it, or God, who is mentioned only in v. 4 (and again in v. 9) but may readily be thought of as the active agent in the whole passage? Once again, commentators are sharply divided. In this instance it is not essential to my interpretation to decide the issue definitively. I am, however, inclined to prefer God as the antecedent on the grounds that v. 9 (*pistos ho theos*) seems to require it and that the formulaic character of the passage might explain the distance of the relative pronoun from its antecedent.[14]

In the light of these suggestions, the passage may then be translated as follows:

> [4]I always thank my God on your behalf for the gift of God given to you in Christ Jesus, [5]that in every respect you have been made rich in him, in all speech and all knowledge, [6]since the testimony to Christ has grown strong among you [7]to the point where you lack no spiritual gift while you await the revealing of our Lord Jesus Christ. [8]He will also keep you strong to the end, blameless on the day of our Lord Jesus Christ. [9]God is faithful; by him you were called to fellowship with his Son, Jesus Christ our Lord.

[13]*The Acts of the Apostles* (Oxford, 1971) 140; cited with approval by Conzelmann, 42.

[14]See the full discussion in Rolf Baumann, *Mitte und Norm des Christlichen. Eine Auslegung von 1 Korinther 1, 1-3, 4* (Münster, 1968) 39-40.

6

Heavenly Temple and Eschatology in the Letter to the Hebrews*

It is well known to every historian of ancient religions that the existence of cultic buidings was more often than not accompanied by beliefs in cosmic or celestial cult places. Eric Burrows once stated, perhaps with slight hyperbole:

> One might almost formulate a law that in the ancient East contemporary cosmological doctrine is registered in the structure and theory of the temples. (45; cf. Widengren)

The nature of cosmic and heavenly temple symbolism is too well known to warrant a general review here. Instead, the purpose of this essay is to set forth summarily two main lines of heavenly temple symbolism reflected in Jewish texts and to apply these to the interpretation of the Letter to the Hebrews. Interpreters of this difficult New Testament book have in the past regularly recognized one or the other type of heavenly temple symbolism in Hebrews to the exclusion of its counterpart. I wish to suggest that both types are present and to offer a plausible explanation for this apparent anomaly by appeal to the eschatological orientation of the Letter, to the relationship of faith and hope in it, and, underlying all, to its peculiar literary genre.

* First published in *Semeia* 12 (1978) 179-199.

First, two preliminary observations about the temple and its symbolism are in order. The Letter to the Hebrews and the writings of Philo of Alexandria, about which we shall be speaking in a moment, do not discuss the temple of Jerusalem, as one might expect, but deal exclusively with the wilderness tabernacle or tent. I would maintain that this is so despite what some scholars regard as references to contemporary temple worship in Heb 9:6-9 and 10:1-2 (Buchanan: 257). The reason for this neglect of the temple is of course that both authors are primarily Old Testament exegetes, and the object of their exegesis is above all the Pentateuch. We may nevertheless legitimately speak of temple symbolism in discussing them, not only because the biblical accounts of the tabernacle are generally thought to reflect temple structure, but because both authors are strongly influenced by contemporary temple symbolism in their exegesis. Thus I shall not attempt to be rigorously consistent in referring to the tent or tabernacle rather than to the temple.

The second preliminary observation has to do with limiting the type of temple symbolism discussed to the notions of heavenly and cosmic temple. In ancient Judaism as well as in the New Testament, there were a variety of forms of temple symbolism. For example, in Paul the temple image is applied to the body, whether symbolizing the individual person as a temple of the Holy Spirit (1 Cor 6:19) or the community as God's temple (1 Cor 3:16-17). The latter notion was also current, and also with eschatological dimensions, among the Jewish sectarians of Qumran (Gärtner). In the Fourth Gospel the image of the temple is applied to the body of Jesus (John 2:19-22). In *Barnabas* 16:7-10 the only temple of God, the Jerusalem Temple having been destroyed, is the human heart (Barrett: 387-88). For Origen, as well as for a number of late Jewish sources, the temple, or rather tabernacle, symbolism is interpreted cosmically but extended to the human being as a microcosm (*Homiliae in Exodum* 13.3 [88]). Influenced by the kind of Hellenistic temple symbolism we shall describe in a moment, Origen also sees in the structure of the temple a symbol of the church, the outer building, and heaven, the inner

(*Homilia IX in Leviticum* 9). All these and other forms of temple symbolism in Jewish and early Christian thought we shall set aside in order to deal with the imagery used by the author to the Hebrews.

The two lines of imagery we wish to recall were clearly distinguished by George Buchanan Gray in his perennially valuable study of Old Testament sacrifice (1925:148-78) and earlier in a series of two articles (1908). Gray's interest was in investigating belief in the sacrificial service in heaven, in the course of which he brought clarity to the heavenly temple idea. Without referring to him at every step of the way, the following exposition both draws upon and sometimes diverges from his work.

The Apocalyptic Temple in Heaven

The first type of imagery we shall call the apocalyptic idea of the temple in heaven. It has its roots in the pervasive Old Testament notion that the wilderness tabernacle and various temples were constructed according to a plan revealed by God, the "pattern," Hebrew *tbnyt*, LXX *paradeigma*. Yahweh says to Moses on Mount Sinai: "According to all that I show you concerning the pattern of the tabernacle, and all of its furniture, so you shall make it" (Exod 25:9; cf. 25:40, which in the LXX uses *typos* instead of *paradeigma*). According to the Chronicler the Temple of Solomon was also constructed according to a divine plan (*tbnyt*) communicated to David in a "writing from the hand of Yahweh" (1 Chr 28:19). As Gray indicates, these references to the divine plan for the house of the Lord do not themselves presuppose the notion that there is a temple in heaven upon which the earthly one was modeled, but they no doubt formed one source of this later notion. Perhaps Ezekiel's vision (chaps. 40-48) of the restored temple of Jerusalem was also a contributing factor. It should be pointed out that the idea of a heavenly plan for a temple is by no means unique in the biblical tradition, as Mircea Eliade among others has shown (6-11). There are, for example, several ancient Near Eastern precedents.

In certain strains of Jewish thought, notably though not exclusively the apocalyptic strain, there was a tendency to "materialize" or "hypostatize" ideas in such a way that they became independent realities. Thus the notion of a divine plan for the construction of the tabernacle or temple evolved into a temple in heaven as the model for the one on earth. One can almost see the transition in a passage in the Wisdom of Solomon in which Solomon prays for wisdom to fulfill his duties:

> Thou hast given command to build a temple on thy holy mountain, and an altar in the city of thy habitation, a copy (*mimēma*) of the holy tent which thou didst prepare from the beginning. (9:8)

Here the plan mentioned in Exodus and even the "writing" of 1 Chronicles have given way to a tabernacle built by God *ap' archēs* and presumably located in heaven.

In the apocalyptic literature we find the notion of a temple in heaven full blown and even taken for granted. A few examples will suffice. In Ethiopic *Enoch* 14, Enoch enters heaven in a vision and passes through a large house, then a second house in which God is enthroned. The imagery of the passage is strongly influenced by such Old Testament texts as Isaiah 6, Ezekiel 1, and others, but it seems also to portray a temple in which God dwells in heaven (see also *1 Enoch* 90:28-29). The *Testament of Levi* is quite unequivocal: "And thereupon the angel opened to me the gates of heaven, and I saw the holy temple, and upon a throne of glory the Most High" (5:1; cf. 18:6). The most frequent references to a temple in heaven are in the visions of John of Patmos in the Book of Revelation: "Then God's temple in heaven was opened, and the ark of his covenant was seen within his temple" (11:19 and frequently). Here not merely is there a temple in heaven, but a heavenly liturgy takes place there (8:3-5). But, as is well known, in the new Jerusalem that will descend from heaven there is no temple because access to God is direct (21:22). This stands in sharp contrast to the spectacular temple that adorns the new Jerusalem of the fifth book of the *Sibylline Oracles* (lines 423-27). Among the

Qumran sectarians apparently we also have the notion of a temple in heaven in which there is an angelic liturgy, described in the fragments partially published under the title "Order of the Songs of the Sabbath Holocaust" (Strugnell). Beyond New Testament times, this apocalyptic image flourishes in rabbinic and Hekaloth Jewish sources, but further examples are not germane to our present purpose.

The Temple-Structured Universe

Quite different from this notion of the temple in heaven is that of the temple as a symbol of the structure of the universe in which the outer court or courts represent the earth and the inner sanctuary heaven. In this view there is no temple in heaven, but heaven is itself the sanctuary of a temple-structured universe. Although this theme is probably more widespread in the ancient Near East than the previous one, it is disputed whether cosmic temple symbolism is present in the Old Testament or not (de Vaux: 328-29). In any event, I shall refer to this as Hellenistic temple symbolism because it is first in Greek-writing Jewish authors that we find it developed. The presence of the idea within Judaism may indeed be the result of Hellenistic syncretism. In the use of the term "Hellenistic" for a particular type of Jewish symbolism, it is not of course my intention to minimize the extent of Hellenistic influence on all forms of ancient Judaism, including the apocalyptic tradition.

Two modalites of this imagery are current in Hellenistic Jewish sources, distinguished by Jean Daniélou in an article comparing Josephus and Philo. What may be regarded as the more traditional form of this cosmic temple symbolism is illustrated in Josephus (*Antiquities* 3.123, 180-81), for whom the tabernacle and all the elements in it exist as an "imitation and representation of the universe" (*eis apomimēsin kai diatypōsin tōn holōn*). The tripartite structure of the tabernacle corresponds to the tripartite structure of the cosmos: the two outer parts to which the priests have access are the sea and the earth, and the sanctuary is heaven, which is "reserved for God alone because heaven also is inaccessible to men" (Patai: 112-13). This traditional form of the symbolism is also known to Philo (*de Vita Mosis* 2.88; especially *de Specialibus Legibus* 1.66).

Philo, however, has other concerns and independently extends the cosmic temple symbolism to another order of reality. He interprets the pattern which was shown to Moses, the *paradeigma* in philosophical terms: Moses saw with his soul the incorporeal ideas of future corporeal realities (*tōn mellontōn apoteleisthai sōmatōn asōmatous ideas, de Vita Mosis* 2.74; cf. *Quaestiones in Exodum* 2.90). But Philo's favorite temple symbolism is an allegorical extension of the Hellenistic model of cosmic symbolism. In most of the relevant passages, the court and the outer shrine together represent the sense-perceptible (*aisthētos*) world, including the heavens, while the holy place represents the intelligible (*noētos*) world, the unchanging world of ideas which is the proper dwelling of God (see especially *Quaestiones in Exodum* 2.91-96).

The fact that these two variations on the theme of cosmic temple symbolism were recognized in antiquity is attested by Clement of Alexandria, who, when discussing "the place within the veil," i.e., the inner sanctuary, tells us that some say this is the midpoint (*mesaitaton*) between heaven and earth—the view represented by Josephus—while others say it is symbolic of the intelligible and sense-perceptible worlds— the Philonic view (*Stromata* 5.6).

Temple Symbolism in Hebrews

When we turn to the Letter to the Hebrews, we are confronted with diametrically opposing statements on the part of modern interpreters. For example, C.K. Barrett, in his essay on the eschatology of Hebrews, argues categorically that Hebrews' concept of the heavenly temple is not influenced by Philo but rather by Jewish apocalyptic; i.e., the image is that of a temple in heaven (386-89; Michel, 1966:62, 292-93). Hugh Montefiore, on the other hand, states in his commentary that Hebrews' concept of a heavenly temple is not influenced by the apocalyptic and rabbinic notion of a temple in heaven but rather by the Philonic idea of heaven as the sanctuary of a cosmic temple (136-37). Gray, in the discussion referred to above, had espoused this same position, and an inventory of interpreters of Hebrews would serve only to draw up two lists of opposing views.

The fact that such completely different interpretations are perpetuated must give us grounds for reflection. For one thing, they are symptomatic of the fundamental cleavage in the interpretation of Hebrews, namely whether the predominant background is Alexandrian/Philonic or Palestinian/apocalyptic. All too few interpreters have been able to recognize both strains in the Letter. With respect to temple imagery, it may be worthwhile to see if both conceptions are present in the work and to confront the problem of consistency only after examining the evidence.

The apocalyptic notion of a temple in heaven seems to me clearly to be the presupposition of Heb 8:1-5, despite the amount of Philonic language in these verses. Here the image is supported by the principle that things on earth have their heavenly counterparts:

> We have such a high priest, one who is seated at the right hand of the throne of the Majesty in heaven, a minister in the sanctuary and the true tabernacle which is set up not by man but by the Lord ... They (the priests on earth) serve a copy and shadow of the heavenly sanctuary; for when Moses was about to erect the tabernacle, he was instructed by God, saying, "See that you make everything according to the pattern (*typon*) which was shown you on the mountain."

The fact that everything on earth is a copy or "tracing" (*hypodeigma*) of the true, heavenly realities is expressed also in Heb 9:23:

> Thus it was necessary for the copies of the heavenly things to be purified with these rites, but the heavenly things themselves with better sacrifices than these.

Even if the word *hypodeigma* is given its normal meaning of "example"—or, as Heinrich Schlier suggests for these passages (33), "image"—the presupposition of a true tabernacle in heaven remains.

This image of a complete tabernacle in heaven seems also to underlie Heb 9:11-12, where it makes visually consistent the troublesome use of *dia* with the tabernacle. Within heaven, or better "the heavens" as in 4:14, Jesus passes through the tabernacle to enter the sanctuary:

> But when Christ appeared as a high priest of the good things that have come (reading *genomenōn*), then through the greater and more perfect tabernacle not made with hands, that is, not of this creation, he entered once for all into the sanctuary.

This is also the understanding of Otto Michel (1966:310-11); Montefiore, among others, translates *dia* as "by means of" (152-53).

In other passages, even in the same contexts, Hebrews seems unequivocally to make use of the Hellenistic notion of the temple-structured universe in such a way that Jesus' passage from earth to heaven is his entrance through the veil into the Holy of Holies. The clearest example is 9:24:

> For Christ has entered, not into a sanctuary (*hagia*) made with hands, a copy of the true one (*antitypa tōn alēthinōn*), but into heaven itself, now to appear in the presence of God on our behalf.

The imagery here demands something like the temple symbolism of Philo or Josephus, more probably the former. Michel (1966:311-12) suggests that there are different meanings of *ouranos* in Hebrews, but I find the differences hard to substantiate.

The same visual image underlies the statement about the believers' access to the sanctuary, i.e., to heaven, in 10:19-20, a *crux interpretum* on other grounds:

> Therefore, brethren, since we have confidence to enter the sanctuary by the blood of Jesus, by the new and living

way which he opened for us through the veil, that is, by his flesh. . . .

Here I prefer to understand the explanatory phrase *tout' estin tēs sarkos autou* as a reference to the way rather than to the veil, for the reasons usually adduced (Spicq). In any case entering heaven is understood as entering the sanctuary. A similar passage in 6:19-20 may be understood as reflecting the same temple imagery if we assume that the Christian's hope is to enter heaven: ". . . a hope that enters into the inner shrine behind the veil, where Jesus has gone as a forerunner on our behalf. . . ." In this instance, however, it must be acknowledged that the passage could support either type of temple imagery.

The Eschatology of Hebrews

There is in Hebrews an additional dimension of the temple imagery which is not commonly found in the Jewish types of imagery, though it is not excluded from them. That is the eschatological dimension, which mingles a time framework with the spatial images. The perspective is one of futurist eschatology with the typically Christian paradox that the future is anticipated in the sacrifice of Jesus. Christ has already entered the sanctuary, thus inaugurating the end time, which for the believer nevertheless remains future, an object of hope. Christ is seen as having bridged the gap between present and future; indeed, since the death of Jesus belongs to the past, he has also bridged the gap between past and future. "Jesus Christ is the same yesterday and today and forever" (13:18).

In this perspective, the two parts of the tabernacle can represent not only the created world and the uncreated heaven, but also the present time and the eschatological future. Heb 9:8-9 provides an explicit example of this mingling of spatial and temporal imagery. After describing the Old Testament tabernacle and the uses of its two parts, the author continues:

> By this the Holy Spirit indicates that the way into the
> sanctuary is not yet opened as long as the outer tabernacle
> (*tēs prōtēs skēnēs*) is still standing (which [*hētis,* i.e., *hē*
> *prōtē skēnē*] is symbolic [*parabolē*] for the present age).

What is striking here, and possibly quite original with the
author to the Hebrews, is the fact that he has combined an
apocalyptic time scheme with the Hellenistic mode of
heavenly temple symbolism. One may contrast Wis 3:14,
where "the temple of the Lord" is indeed an eschatological
symbol, but it does not imply cosmic imagery.

We may point out in passing that many of the other
passages dealing with the tabernacle imagery also have an
explicitly eschatological dimension, for example, the emphasis on Christ's appearing *now* before God (9:24), the
notion of hope entering beyond the veil where Jesus has
gone as a *prodromos* (6:19-20), and the believers' confidence
in entering the sanctuary by the new and living way
(10:19-20).

This emphasis on the eschatological is not merely an
added dimension of the temple imagery, however, but the
heart of it, for a primary concern of the whole of Hebrews is
with eschatology, as interpreters have often pointed out
(Barrett: 365-66). But what kind of eschatology? Some have
insisted on the futurist perspective of traditional Jewish
apocalyptic (Barrett; Michel, 1966: 58ff.). This view involves
the typical orientation to the future day of the Lord and to
judgment; it is often portrayed as linear or "horizontal," the
past leading through the present to a future yet to come.
Montefiore states (14):

> The Epistle consistently manifests a futurist eschatology,
> according to which the pilgrim People of God have drawn
> near to the Last Days but have not yet actually entered
> them.

To be sure, this concept is certainly present in Hebrews on
virtually every page. Yet other interpreters of Hebrews stress
rather the element of realized eschatology based on the
dualist or quasi-dualist perspective of the true heavenly

reality over against the imperfect earthly copy (Dey: 227). This is sometimes imaged as a "vertical" eschatology. For some interpreters what is at issue in Hebrews is the transformation of one form of eschatology into the other, with or without a polemical purpose, for example, either gnosticizing or anti-gnostic (Klappert: 14-17).

But the key to a solution, I suggest, lies in recognizing and taking seriously the literary genre of Hebrews, which is that of the homily. The author must be seen as a preacher exhorting the people to perseverance *logos parakleseōs,* 13:22). To do so, he develops a theology of hope. Indeed, his assumption throughout is that the apocalyptic eschatological scheme is that of his audience. What they need is a strengthening of their hope. This he attempts to provide by grounding hope in the Hellenistic, dualist category of the true reality located in the heavenly world of which the earthly represents only inferior copies. He uses the "vertical" eschatological perspective, in other words, neither to oppose nor to correct the "horizontal" one, but to reinforce it (Klappert).

To put the matter most simply, the apparent conflict of eschatological perspectives in Hebrews, i.e., the simultaneous presence of an apocalyptic, futurist eschatology and a realized eschatology expressed in language associated with the Alexandrian background, is to be explained by the relationship of the preacher to his audience. His own perspective, the latter one, he uses to shore up the apocalyptic hope of his hearers in the face of persecution and flagging perseverance. Dey explicitly argues that the Alexandrian perspective is that of the audience as well as of the author (123), but I believe this view ignores the literary genre of Hebrews. One need not suppose, in light of the extensive amount of attention given to doctrinal matters in Hebrews, that the preacher's aim is to alter the theological position of the hearers. Instead, as has often been pointed out, it is the paraenesis that determines the purpose of Hebrews, and the paraenetic intent is to provide some motivation for perseverance in the apocalyptically oriented Christianity of the recipients.

The homiletic intention of the author comes to its climax in the hortatory passage that follows the central section dealing with the high-priestly sacrifice of Jesus. In 10:21-23 he states:

> And (since we have) a great priest over the house of God, let us draw near with a true heart in full assurance (or: fullness) of faith.... Let us hold fast the confession of hope without wavering, for he who promised is faithful.

Faith and Hope in Hebrews

The differing but not ultimately conflicting viewpoints of the preacher and his audience may be further illustrated by comparing the roles of *pistis* and *elpis* in Hebrews. In fact, I should like to suggest that yet another center of controversy among interpreters of Hebrews can be put into focus if we interpret faith and hope respectively as the concerns of the preacher and the audience (as the author understands them, of course). In a word, the peculiar understanding of faith in Hebrews functions as a homiletic support for perseverance in hope. Some interpreters merely equate the two notions of faith and hope, but I believe a brief study of their contexts will show that such is not a sufficiently nuanced understanding of the Letter (Klappert: 47-48).

The fact that the strengthening of hope, in the face of persecution and declining enthusiasm, is the main paraenetic objective of Hebrews is widely acknowledged. For Michel, for example, *elpis* sums up the whole Christian attitude in Hebrews (1966: 347). We are God's household "if we hold fast the *parrēsia* and *kauchēma* of hope" (3:6). We have "strong encouragement to seize the hope set before us, which we possess as an anchor of the soul, sure and steadfast, and which enters into the inner shrine beyond the veil...." (6:18-19). Indeed, for the Christian "a better hope is introduced, through which we draw near to God" (7:19).

Nevertheless, if hope is the paraenetic objective of the homily, it is faith which commands much more of the author's attention, being mentioned nearly twice as often, quite apart from the massive concentration of chap. 11. But faith in Hebrews, as is widely recognized, is *sui generis:* despite the dominant christological focus of the homily, faith itself is never christologically focused, though it is clearly theological faith. What is most distinctive is that when faith and hope are related to each other, it is faith that is subordinated to hope as a means to an end, and this relationship is brought out the more clearly when the author uses his characteristic vocabulary with the conscious variation for which he is well known (Vanhoye). It will suffice to adduce two examples in paraenetic passages which the author doubtless invites us to compare.

The first is 6:11-12, in which the author desires that the Hebrews "manifest the same zeal for the *plērophoria* of hope until the end, so that you may not be sluggish, but be imitators of those who through faith and patience inherit the promises." Here it is clear that hope is the goal and faith is a means toward its full realization.

In the climactic paraenetic passage of the book, 10:22-23, the relation of faith to hope is essentially the same, though the rare word *plērophoria,* which may be taken to be merely "fullness," not necessarily "full assurance" as Gerhard Delling suggests (310-11), is here applied to *pistis* instead of to *elpis:* "let us draw near with a true heart in fullness of faith...; let us hold fast the confession of our hope without wavering, for he who promised is faithful (*pistos*)." If *plērophoria tēs elpidos* is the goal of the Christian, *plērophoria pisteōs* is the condition or means for it, and the elaborate catechesis explaining this (10:37—12:2) must not be taken out of context. It is true that both in Heb 6:10-12 and in 10:22-24 the author is using the traditional triad of faith-hope-love, but since he reinterprets it along his own lines, the occurrence of the triad does not argue against this subordination of faith to hope as a paraenetic goal. Moreover, since Hebrews' use of *homologia* is qualified only in 10:23 (with *tēs elpidos*), it may be argued that in its two absolute occurences (3:1 and 4:14), both associated with Christ's high priesthood, it is also a confession of hope, rather than of faith, that is in question.

It is not clear, contrary to the assertion of Michel (1967:215-17), that the confession should be seen as a fixed liturgical element.

Hope may be understood, quite apart from the use of the word *elpis,* for which there is no adequate Semitic equivalent, as the characteristic attitude of the apocalyptic mentality and hence the natural Christian goal of the audience of the Hebrews homily. Hope corresponds to futurist eschatology; it is hope in a future *sōtēria:*

> And just as it is appointed for men to die once, and after that comes judgment, so Christ, having been offered once to bear the sins of many, will appear a second time, not to deal with sin but to save (*eis sōtērian*) those who are eagerly waiting for him. (9:27-28)

But faith—except for the occurrence in 6:1, *pistis epi theon,* which is problematic in any case—is the peculiar contribution of the author and must be understood first and foremost against the background of Hellenistic, even typically Alexandrian, thought.

Faith provides the assurance gained from insight into the realm of true reality in heaven where Christ has already entered. As in Philo, its basis is exegetical. In his famous article on the word "faith," Rudolf Bultmann wrote:

> The paradox of hoping confidence is strongly emphasized in Rom 4:19 as well as Heb 11. It is directed to that which is invisible (v 7) or to Him who is invisible (v 27). For the sake of this paradox Heb 11 adopted the Hellenistic (Philonic) idea that *pistis* is directed to the invisible to the degree that this is not only the promised future but also the heavenly reality which cannot be perceived by the senses but can only be believed in faith. (207; Grässer: 144-46; Käsemann: 19ff.)

Without claiming any technical significance for the terms used, I should like to call *pistis* in Hebrews "insight into the heavenly world." Its relationship to hope is made quite clear in the definition (or quasi-definition, if one prefers) in 11:1: "Faith is the reality (not "assurance": Koester: 585-87) of things hoped for, the evidence of things not seen." But homiletically this reality functions as the assurance upon which hope can rest.

Because the heroes of the Old Testament possessed such insight into the heavenly world of God (note again the absence of christological claims in connection with faith), they can function as models for Christian behavior, but ultimately only when the Christians can look to Jesus as the *archēgos kai teleiōtēs tēs pisteōs* (12:2). Jesus is not the object of faith, but the supreme model of it. It is significant, however, that the first use of *pistei* in chap. 11 (v 3) is outside the series in that it relates to the subject "we" rather than to an Old Testament figure. In asserting that it is by faith that *we* know ("have insight into") the creation of the world by God's word (known from Scripture), the author illustrates what he intends his examples of faith to establish. It is only by faith in the invisible divine reality that apocalyptic hope can be sustained (see the application in 12:3ff.). The hope is the natural goal of the apocalyptically oriented addressees of Hebrews; faith is the author's peculiar argument to reinforce, not alter, that hope.

A striking parallel with this relationship of faith and hope may be found in 1 Pet 1:3-25, especially if one follows the interpretation of W.J. Dalton. Hebrews and First Peter have often been compared (Grässer: 149-54; Montefiore: 5). For our present purposes we may note that they have in common a homiletic genre with elaborately constructed passages (Vanhoye, Dalton), a context of futurist eschatology, and references to the persecution of Christians. And in both cases there is an exhortation to hope for which faith serves as the means to be cultivated (Grässer: 153): "So that your faith may also be your hope in God" (1:21; Dalton). It is faith as the author understands it—without, in 1 Peter, the clearly Alexandrian context—which shores up hope in the apocalyptic setting.

Conclusion

We may seem to have strayed far from a discussion of different forms of temple symbolism in Hebrews, but the itinerary has not really been haphazard. It was the recognition of apparently conflicting images of the heavenly temple or sanctuary in the text of Hebrews that led us to discover analogously conflicting eschatological attitudes, and then to evaluate the relationship of faith to hope in the homily. The clue, we have argued, is the literary genre. The homily demands—or at the very least permits—a situation in which the presuppositions of the preacher and those of the congregation are not necessarily identical. In the face of ostensibly irreconcilable views on the part of modern interpreters of Hebrews, we have argued that in the mixed congregations of the early church it is not unlikely that a preacher with an Alexandrian background should address an apocalyptically oriented Jewish-Christian community, not with a view to destroying its futurist eschatology, but with a view to shoring it up with his own Philonic perspective. His most concrete way of doing so was to encourage perseverance in hope, in the face of persecution and despair, with his concept of faith as insight into the heavenly world of the divine. Since he chose the vehicle of celestial priesthood and the liturgy of his specific soteriological interpretation of Christ, he mingled his Alexandrian temple symbolism with that of apocalyptic thought. The inconsistency may well be in our minds more than in his.

I have no concrete suggestion to offer with respect to the provenience of the author or the destination of his literary homily, but I should like to commend the distinction between the two as a useful interpretative tool.

Works Consulted

Barrett, Charles Kingsley, "The Eschatology of the Epistle to the Hebrews." Pp. 363-93 in *The Background of the New Testament and Its Eschatology* (C.H. Dodd

Festschrift). Eds. W.D. Davies and D. Daube. Cambridge: Cambridge University Press, 1954.

Buchanan, George W., *To the Hebrews*. Anchor Bible 36. New York: Doubleday, 1972.

Bultmann, Rudolf, "*Pisteuō, ktl.*" *TDNT* 6: 174-228, 1968.

Burrows, Eric, "Some Cosmological Patterns in Babylonian Religion." Pp. 43-70 in *The Labyrinth*. Ed. S.H. Hooke. London: S.P.C.K., 1935.

Dalton, William J., "'So that Your Faith May Also Be Your Hope in God' (I Peter 1:21)." Pp. 262-74 in *Reconciliation and Hope* (L.L. Morris Festschrift). Ed. Robert Banks. Grand Rapids: Eerdmans, 1974.

Daniélou, Jean, "La symbolique du temple de Jérusalem chez Philon et Josèphe." Pp. 83-90 in *Le symbolisme cosmique des monuments religieux*. Série Orientale Roma XIV. Rome: Istituto Italiano per il Medio ed Estremo Oriente, 1957.

Delling, Gerhard, "*Plērophoria.*" *TDNT* 6: 310-11, 1968.

de Vaux, Roland, *Ancient Israel*. New York: McGraw-Hill, 1961.

Dey, L. Kalyan K., *The Intermediary World and Patterns of Perfection in Philo and Hebrews*. SBLDS 25. Missoula, MT: Scholars Press, 1975.

Eliade, Mircea, *Cosmos and History: The Myth of the Eternal Return*. New York: Harper, 1959.

Gärtner, Bertil, *The Temple and the Community in Qumran and the New Testament*. SNTSMS 1. Cambridge: Cambridge University Press, 1965.

Grässer, Erich, *Der Glaube in Hebräerbrief*. Marburg: Elwert, 1965.

Gray, George Buchanan, "The Heavenly Temple and the Heavenly Altar." *Expositor* 8/5: 385-402, 530-546; 1908.

————, *Sacrifice in the Old Testament.* Oxford: University, 1925. Reprinted, New York: Ktav, 1971.

Käsemann, Ernst, *Das wandernde Gottesvolk.* FRLANT, NF 37. Göttingen: Vandenhoeck & Ruprecht, 1939.

Klappert, Bertold, *Die Eschatologie des Hebräerbriefs.* Theologische Existenz heute 156. Munich: Kaiser, 1969.

Koester, Helmut, *"Hypostasis." TDNT* 8: 572-89, 1972.

Michel, Otto, *Der Brief an die Hebräer.* KEK. 12th ed. Göttingen: Vandenhoeck & Ruprecht, 1966.

————, *"Homologeō, ktl." TDNT* 5: 199-220, 1967.

Montefiore, Hugh, *A Commentary on the Epistle to the Hebrews.* Harper's New Testament Commentaries. New York: Harper, 1964.

Patai, Raphael, *Man and Temple in Ancient Jewish Myth and Ritual.* London: Nelson, 1947.

Schlier, Heinrich, *"Hypodeigma." TDNT* 2: 32-33, 1964.

Spicq, Ceslas, *L'Epître aux Hébreux.* Paris: Gabalda, 1952-53.

Strugnell, John, "The Angelic Liturgy at Qumran—4Q Serek Sîrôt 'Ôlat Haššabbāt." Pp. 318-45 in *Congress Volume: Oxford, 1959.* VTSup 7. Leiden: Brill, 1960.

Vanhoye, Albert, *La structure littéraire de l'Epître aux Hébreux.* Bruges: Desclée de Brouwer, 1965.

Widengren, Geo, "Aspetti simbolici dei templi e luoghi di culto del Vicino Oriente Antico." *Numen* 7: 1-25, 1960.

7

A Kingdom that Cannot be Shaken: The Heavenly Jerusalem in the Letter to the Hebrews*

In his major work on the early Christian attitude toward the land of Jesus, *The Gospel and the Land*, W.D. Davies identified four distinct perspectives found in the various New Testament books.[1] With a great deal of simplification, especially in the examples offered, we may list these attitudes as follows: rejection, as in the overtly anti-Jerusalem and anti-Temple polemic of the Stephen speech in Acts 7; spiritualization, as in the Letter to the Hebrews and the Book of Revelation; historical concern, which is characteristic of the Gospel of Luke and at least the early chapters of Acts; and sacramental concentration, which is reflected in the nuanced and almost paradoxical attitude of the Gospel of John. In the course of his work, Davies does not analyze the spiritualization of Jerusalem in Hebrews, except in passing.[2]

(*)First published in *Tantur Yearbook* (1979-1980) 27-40.

[1] *The Gospel and the Land: Early Christianity and Jewish Territorial Doctrine* (Berkeley: University of California, 1974) 366-67. See also the summary of the argument of the book in "Jerusalem and the Land in the Christian Tradition," in *The Jerusalem Colloquium on Religion, Peoplehood, Nation and Land,* ed. Marc H. Tanenbaum and R.J. Zwi Werblowsky (Jerusalem: Truman Research Institute Publication No. 7, 1972), especially pp. 153-54.

The purpose of this article is to treat the theme of the heavenly Jerusalem in Hebrews, independently of the methods of Davies, as a theological problem in early Christian thought and spirituality. I shall try to show that the unknown author of Hebrews was aware of the problematic character of a radical spiritualizing of the land, the city of Jerusalem, and the Temple, and that he tried to compensate for the thrust of his own theology. The article will be structured in three parts: first, some observations on the nature of Hebrews itself; secondly, an exposition of the themes of pilgrimage and heavenly city; and thirdly, some more general remarks about the problem of spiritualization in early Christianity.

I

The so-called Letter to the Hebrews is by far one of the best written, most coherent and cogent documents produced by the early church. Unfortunately, it is also one of the most difficult for the modern reader to grasp without very detailed and penetrating study. It may be helpful for our access to one of the key arguments of the work to begin with several introductory observations about the nature of it—not so much the classic questions of author, date, and place, but rather issues concerning its literary character and background.

a) First, it is essential for the reader of Hebrews to be aware of its character as a work of biblical exegesis. Virtually in its entirety Hebrews derives its basic arguments from the interpretation of the Bible, using a number of different exegetical methods, but surprisingly little allegorization. A major part of its message is the one announced in the opening lines, that the word of God has the power to give meaning to life:

[2] *The Gospel and the Land,* 162-63.

> In many and various ways God spoke of old to our fathers by the prophets; but in these last days he has spoken to us by a Son...[3]

The first main division of the work, which focuses more explicitly on this power of the word of God, ends with 4:12-13, forming an inclusio to mark the division clearly. This famous passage lends itself to varying translations, of which the following (by the writer) brings out the importance of the word in the author's argument:

> God word is alive and active. It cuts more sharply than any two-edged sword and penetrates to the point of dividing between soul and spirit, joints and marrow. It provokes discernment among the longings and insights of the heart; nothing created lies hidden before it, but everything is naked and exposed in its sight. And to that word our own is directed.

Since exegesis of the Old Testament consistently underlies the argument of Hebrews, it is incumbent upon the interpreter to seek first an exegetical explanation of any passage he is dealing with. Only when no basis for the argument can be discovered in exegesis or in exegetical traditions is the interpreter entitled to see a historical or other explanation. For example, despite the persistent opinion of some modern commentators,[4] Hebrews says nothing of the Herodian Temple, and no conclusions can be drawn from his silence regarding the dating of the work before or after the destruction of the Temple in A.D. 70 or regarding the location of the author and/or original readers inside or outside Palestine. All of Hebrews' statements about the sanctuary of the Israelites are based on interpretation of the passages in the Pentateuch regarding the wilderness tabernacle.

Hebrews exhibits what one would today call a very high

---

[3]Quotations, except where otherwise indicated, are from the Revised Standard Version (RSV).

[4]E.g., George W. Buchanan, *To the Hebrews* (Anchor Bible 36; New York: Doubleday, 1972) 256-63.

view of biblical inspiration. In the Bible it is God who utters his authoritative word. It is important to realize this in order to retain some balance regarding the book. Hebrews argues in strong terms throughout for the superiority of Christ as a mediator with God, but this argument is never at the expense of the Old Testament. On the contrary, it is the inspired word of God in the Old Testament which demonstrates the truth of the claims made about Christ.

The exegetical character of Hebrews has important consequences for our examination of the spiritualization of the city and the land: it is the Bible itself, despite its focus on the land of promise and the very concrete geographical location of the holy Mount Zion, which provides the starting point for a spiritualizing and consequently a universalizing of the sacred place.

b) Secondly, we must say a word about the literary genre of Hebrews. The book entered the canon of the New Testament, after long hesitations which are well known, as a letter of Paul. It is clearly not by Paul, as was amply recognized in the earliest Christian centuries, and even more importantly, it is not a letter. But such was eventually and in certain parts of the Christian church, the authority of the Pauline letters that they were able to establish the authority of other documents which resembled them at best only superficially. Hebrews, it is now widely recognized, is in reality a homily or sermon to which in chap. 13 a quasi-epistolary ending was attached, most probably by the original author, when the homily was sent in writing to one or more Christian churches. To be sure, it may never have originally been delivered orally as a homily but have been a literary homily from the outset. But this distinction may be merely a modern one and not of great importance for understanding Hebrews.[5]

What is of importance is that the author refers to his own work as a *logos paraklēseōs,* a "word of exhortation"

---

[5]Cf. Otto Michel, *Der Brief an die Hebräer* (Meyer, 12th ed. (6th by Michel); Göttingen: Vandenhoeck & Ruprecht, 1966) 35-36.

(13:22). The only other time this expression is found in the New Testament is in Acts 13:15 in the story of Paul and Barnabas at Antioch in Pisidia. After "the reading of the law and the prophets" in the synagogue, the visitors Paul and Barnabas are asked if they have any "word of exhortation for the people." Nothing could better describe Hebrews, for its opening verses could well be the beginning of a homily immediately following the reading of the law and the prophets: "In many and various ways God spoke of old to our fathers by the prophets. . ."[6]

Structurally, Hebrews interweaves theological exposition and exhortation; as a good sermon, it both teaches and exhorts. In contemporary interpretation it is customary to acknowledge that the first twelve chapters—we shall deal with chap. 13 later—consist largely of instruction with six passages of exhortation, of varying length, interposed along the way. Though there is some debate about the extent of the latter, they are often identified as 2:1-4; 3:7-4:11; 4:14-16; 5:11-6:20; 10:19-39; and 12:1-29. These divisions are helpful, but it may be that they are still influenced by the distinction between theological instruction and paraenesis in the Pauline letters. I would like to suggest here an identification of instructional and hortatory passages based on the formal characteristics of exhortation in the context of instruction, which may provide a better understanding of the homiletic character of the work.

On the formal grounds we find sixteen hortatory passages, some of them very short, scattered throughout the homily. Each one begins with or contains a hortatory subjunctive ("let us. . .") or an imperative; the only exception, the first passage, has the form *dei . . . hēmas* ("we must. . ."). Twelve of the sixteen passages begin with a word or phrase meaning "therefore" (*dia touto, hothen, oun, dio, toigaroun*). In fifteen of the sixteen cases the expository argument is resumed with the use of the particle *gar,* "for." The hortatory passages are: 2:1-4; 3:1-2, 12-13; 4:1, 11, 14, 16; 6:1-3, 11-12;

[6]Ibid., 550-52.

10:19-25, 32-33, 35; 12:1-3, 12-16, 25a, 28.

This relatively frequent alternation between exposition and exhortation, identified by the recognition of formal elements, is precisely what one would expect of the homiletic genre. It is not necessary for the interpreter to take sides in the classic debate about whether exhortation or exposition is the more important element in Hebrews.[7] In reality both are essential to the genre of exegetical homily.

c) Our final introductory observation has to do with the religious and/or philosophical background of Hebrews. For generations modern scholars have debated whether the spiritual context of the author of Hebrews is that of Alexandrian Jewish or Jewish-Christian speculation, of the type represented by Philo, or that of Jewish or Jewish-Christian apocalypticism. The problem is that Hebrews contains abundant evidence of both. The solution to the problem again lies, I should like to suggest, in an understanding of the homiletic genre of the work.[8] We may account for the apparent conflict of viewpoints by distinguishing between the perspective of the preacher and that of the community which he is addressing. The community's understanding of Christianity is expressed in terms of apocalyptic; it is future-oriented, and the problem the church faces is one of losing hope in the future vindication. The preacher is influenced by an Alexandrian perspective, rooted in Middle Platonic speculation about the true world of heavenly realities as opposed to the material world of shadow; his perspective is present-oriented. If we use the term somewhat loosely, we may say that both viewpoints are dualistic, but only the former is conditioned by time. As a good preacher, the author of Hebrews does not attempt simply to replace the apocalyptic perspective of his hearers with something else. Instead, he attempts to shore up their

[7]See, e.g., Philipp Vielhauer, *Geschichte der urchristlichen Literatur* (Berlin: de Gruyter, 1975) 243.

[8]Cf. George MacRae, "Heavenly Temple and Eschatology in the Letter to the Hebrews," *Semeia* 12 (*The Poetics of Faith*, Essays offered to Amos Niven Wilder, Part 1, 1978) 179-99.

hope with the added assurance provided by his Platonic insight into the heavenly world of the present.

The juxtaposition of these two viewpoints can be illustrated at many points in Hebrews, but perhaps nowhere better than in the relationship between faith and hope. Readers of Hebrews have often been surprised to realize that the homily is primarily an exhortation to hope. Since hope is characteristic of apocalypticism, it should not be surprising that the preacher seeks to sustain his hearers in it. The centrality of hope emerges when the author identifies the "confession" to which he exhorts the hearers to hold fast in 4:14 as "the confession of our hope" (10:23). But despite the central importance of hope in the homily, the author gives a great deal of attention to faith which, as we shall see, is in his sense of faith the characteristic of his Alexandrian perspective. The important passage just alluded to, 10:22-23, makes it clear that faith in Hebrews is subordinated to hope, as a motivating force to the aim it motivates: "Let us draw near with a true heart in the full measure of faith . . . Let us hold fast to the confession of our hope without wavering" (author's translation).

Faith, in Hebrews, has a very special meaning which becomes apparent when compared with faith in the Pauline or Johannine writings. For one thing, it is never Christocentric but theocentric: it is not faith in Christ but faith in God and his world of reality. Indeed, Jesus himself is the supreme example of faith, "the pioneer and perfecter of our faith, who for the joy that was set before him endured the cross, despising the shame, and is seated at the right hand of the throne of God" (12:2). At the beginning of his famous list of examples of faith, of which the verse just quoted is the culmination, the author gives a definition of faith which shows more clearly its relation to hope. This famous verse should not be translated in the psychological terms that have become common in some of our well-known versions ("assurance" and "conviction" in the RSV) but in more objective terms: "Faith is what gives substance to things hoped for, evidence of things not seen." We might describe it in modern terms as insight into the heavenly world of God's reality.

Who is in need of this lesson in faith in order to motivate and sustain hope? Commentators have long discussed the issue of whether a specific community, perhaps a Jewish-Christian one, is envisioned or simply Christian communities in general.[9] In view of the fact that the Old Testament, the basis of the homily, is the common possession of all Christians, one need not think narrowly of some Jewish-Christian church in imminent danger of relapse. It may be better to take the homily as addressed to Christian communities in general at a time of a threat to their perseverance in the new way. The hortatory passages are expressed in fact in general terms throughout.

II

One of the major themes of the homily to the Hebrews— some would say the dominant theme, but I think this is exaggerated[10]—is the depiction of Christian life as a kind of pilgrimage, a wandering in search of eschatological rest, permanence, a homeland with God. The model for this pervasive imagery, like almost everything else in Hebrews, is drawn from the exegesis of the Old Testament, first from the Exodus wanderings of the Israelites in search of the promised land.[11] Just as the Exodus was a time of testing and submission to the divine discipline, so the Christian life too contains these elements. In chaps. 3 and 4 the author quotes and exegetes the Exodus story as it is recalled in Psalm 95 because he wishes to stress the failure of the Israelites to achieve the goal of their desert wanderings. They failed to enter because of their unbelief (3:19) and their disobedience (4:6), and God states in the words of the Psalm: "As I swore

[9]Cf. Vielhauer, *Geschichte*, 240-41.

[10]Cf. Ernst Käsemann, *Das wandernde Gottesvolk: Eine Untersuchung zum Hebräerbrief* (FRLANT 55; Göttingen: Vandenhoeck & Ruprecht, 1939).

[11]C. Spicq, *Epitre aux Hébreux* (2nd ed. Etudes Bibliques; Paris: Gabalda, 1952-53) vol. 1, 269-80.

in my wrath, they shall never enter my rest." The underlying presupposition of the argument is God's fidelity to his promises. Since God promised that there would be a "rest"—not merely rest from wandering toward the promised land but eschatological rest from the pilgrimage of life, as the author interprets his text—and since the Israelites failed to achieve it (4:6), it remains for "the people of God" (4:9), the Christians, to enter God's rest. The process of spiritualization of the land of promise is already visibly at work in this section of the homily.

The image of wandering in search of a homeland is used again, for example, in chap. 11, but there the model is Abraham's nomadic sojourn in the land of promise described in Genesis 12. And in this case the biblical example functions quite differently. It is faith that enabled Abraham to leave home in order to undertake a nomadic existence in Canaan, but even more importantly for the author's purpose, it is faith that enabled the patriarchs to persevere in their wanderings because it gave them insight into the true, heavenly homeland for which they were destined. In the language of Hebrews the spiritualizing of the land is expressed in strongly "dualistic" terms:

> These all died in faith, not having received what was promised, but having seen it and greeted it from afar, and having acknowledged that they were strangers and exiles on the earth. For people who speak thus make it clear that they are seeking a homeland. If they had been thinking of that land from which they had gone out, they would have had opportunity to return. But as it is, they desire a better country, that is, a heavenly one. Therefore God is not ashamed to be called their God, for he has prepared for them a city (11:13-16).

These two examples of the imagery of wandering, the Exodus and the patriarchal wanderings, are both meant to be models for Christian life, the first by contrast and the second by emulation, conceived as an earthly pilgrimage toward a heavenly homeland. In Hebrews the christological and soteriological imagery, which is really the dominant theme of the work, is carefully harmonized with the pilgrimage theme. The ultimate surety of the Christians entering the heavenly theme. The ultimate surety of the Christians entering the heavenly homeland, the city prepared by God which is the heavenly Jerusalem with its eternal sanctuary, is the fact that Christ has entered it first. And this fact enables the author to introduce a new set of christological images: Christ is the *archēgos,* the "leader" or "pioneer" (2:10 and 12:2), and the *prodromos,* the "forerunner" (6:20).[12]

In chap. 12 the author heightens even further the spiritual quality of the goal of the Christian wandering by contrasting it sharply with the external trappings of the theophany to Moses on Mount Sinai:

> For you have not come to what may be touched, a blazing fire, and darkness, and gloom, and a tempest and the sound of a trumpet, and a voice whose words made the hearers entreat that no further messages be spoken to them ... But you have come to Mount Zion and to the city of the living God, the heavenly Jerusalem, and to innumerable angels in festal gathering (12:18-19, 22).

And he concludes the formal homily (that is, apart from chap.13) with a final exhortation which is probably not to be rendered as an invitation to thanksgiving ("let us be grateful...") as many interpreters understand it, but as a final exhortation to perseverance:[13]

> Therefore, since we receive a kingdom that cannot be shaken, let us hold onto the grace (or: gift) through which we worship God in an acceptable manner with reverence and awe, for our God is indeed "a consuming fire" (12:28-29).

In this concluding section the author also heightens the confrontation between his present-oriented eschatological

---

[12]The christological title *archēgos* is also found in Acts 3:15 and 5:31 but without the context with which Hebrews invests it.

[13]Cf. Spicq, *Epître aux Hébreux,* vol. II, pp. 412-13.

perspective, nourished by faith, and the future-oriented apocalyptic imagery familiar to his hearers. The pilgrimage that is Christian life is a spiritual journey toward a radically spiritualized sanctuary, a heavenly Jerusalem, an eternal, otherwordly, unshakable kingdom, which is a present reality for the Christian because Christ has already entered it.

But we must continue to keep in mind the sermonic or homiletic character of Hebrews, which is the principal hermeneutical key to its interpretation. As a sermon it is concerned with the life of Christian communities, not merely with the eschatological goal of Christian existence. Or to put it differently, as a Christian sermon it has to do with how to live, not merely how to escape from life. Consequently, the author has scattered throughout his sermon occasional reminders of the necessity of practical Christian living in the world. For example, in 10:24-25 he exhorts: "...let us consider how to stir up one another to love and good works, not neglecting to meet together, as is the habit of some, but encouraging one another..." And in 12:14: "Strive for peace with all, and for the holiness without which no one will see the Lord." In the quasi-epistolary ending (chap. 13) the author adds a list of practical moral instructions reminiscent, perhaps intentionally, of the paraenesis of the Pauline epistles. These focus on such things as brotherly love, hospitality to strangers the imprisoned and the ill-treated, fidelity in marriage, avoidance of greed, loyalty and obedience to the leaders.

In the midst of these instructions we find a very difficult passage (13:10-16) which, taking Leviticus 16 as its background, deals with such topics as the altar and the right to partake from it, sacrificial victims consumed outside the camp and the suffering of Jesus outside the gate, and the Christian going outside the camp and offering sacrifices of praise and doing good. This is not the place to attempt a full interpretation of this complex passage, but we must consider the meaning of the exhortation contained in it.

> Therefore let us go forth to him (Jesus) outside the camp, bearing abuse for him. For here we have no lasting city,

> but we seek the city which is to come. Through him then let us continually offer up a sacrifice of praise to God, that is, the fruit of lips that acknowledge his name. Do not neglect to do good and to share what you have, for such sacrifices are pleasing to God (13:13-16).

At first sight the exhortation to go forth to Jesus outside the camp appears to mean: do not cling to the things of earth but follow Christ into the heavenly sanctuary where true reality is to be found; and some important Philonic exegesis of Exod 33:7 supports this view.[14] It is certainly consistent with the overall thought of Hebrews, but in fact it is less suitable to the particular context of this passage, which is in the midst of a series of practical ethical instructions. In view of the importance of context in interpretation, I am inclined to follow those who argue that going outside the camp means not trying to conceive of the Christian life as life lived within the shelter of a sanctuary, in imitation of either the Old Testament sanctuary or the heavenly sanctuary where Jesus' sacrifice takes place, but going out into the world itself, where Jesus suffered historically, to encounter suffering, to practice love and fidelity, to offer the sacrifice of praise and doing good.[15] It is precisely because "here we have no lasting city, but we seek the city which is to come" that Christians may not set up their own sanctuary as a privileged place to live in anticipation of heaven, but must confront God in the world.

This emphasis on practical ethical responsibility in Hebrews 13, which as we have seen is not an afterthought since it is mentioned at other points in the homily, entitles us to draw an important conclusion for our main theme regarding the spiritualization of the land and the Temple. While it is clear that the sacred places have been completely spiritualized, the author of Hebrews is aware of the danger

---

[14]Cf. James W. Thompson, "Outside the Camp: A Study of Heb 13:9-14," *CBQ* 40 (1978) 53-63.

[15]Cf. Helmut Koester, "'Outside the Camp': Hebrews 13:9-14," *HTR* (1962) 305-6.

of total otherworldliness as a possiblity for Christian life. He turns therefore to the notion that the world itself is the "sacred space" of Christian living, in the assurance that the heavenly world is both achieved and still future. In this manner he compensates for the inherent other worldliness of his own theology.

III

In what sense does the spiritualization of the land, Jerusalem, and the sanctuary, that is, the projection of them onto heavenly place, constitute a theological problem for Christianity, not only in Hebrews but throughout the early Christian movement? Before answering this question, it is important for us to realize that the tendency toward such spiritualizing was already present in both strands of the Jewish background of Hebrews. It is well known in Philo, for example, whose use of allegorical exegesis leads him consistently to regard the places of the biblical narrative as figurative references to spiritual realities of a higher order, though of course he does not deny their material existence. With a somewhat different interpretative method, Jewish apocalyptic also tends toward a conception of the new Jerusalem in increasingly otherworldly terms. For an example one might turn to the vision of the city of the Most High in 4 Ezra 10. But in the Judaism of the period, this tendency was not the dominant one and Judaism remained rooted fundamentally in the land, at least in its broadest sense.

For Christians, on the one hand, the development of this spiritualizing of the land, by means of exegesis of the Bible, made it possible to carry on the Gentile mission. It helped to provide an immediately universal appeal for the Christian message. As Christianity spread rapidly beyond the borders of Judea, Samaria, and Galilee and interacted with popular philosophy and religion in the Greco-Roman world, the land of Palestine, the city of Jerusalem, and the Temple, which was probably already destroyed by the time Hebrews was written, could not provide the basis of a universal religious appeal. But the Bible, in Greek to be sure, was not only universally available in the Greco-Roman world, but was presented as an authoritative source of religious knowledge. And it required a spiritual type of interpretation with the consequent transformation of the land into a heavenly sphere, equally accessible to all.

But on the other hand, in this process of spiritualization the Christian message itself incurred a tremendous risk, namely that of presenting Christianity as a totally disembodied, dehistoricized, radically otherworldly religion, a religion of death rather than life, or pehaps better, a religion of afterlife only. If one's true spiritual homeland was beyond history and the cosmos, in the kingdom that cannot be shaken, then the particularity of existence in the world, of history and geography, could be so relativized as to be an illusion, a matter of indifference, or an evil to be passively endured. And nothing could be further removed from the preaching of Jesus about the kingdom of God bursting in upon the world of human beings. Taken to extremes, this spiritualizing tendency could be receptive to some form of Gnosticism, and historically we know that it often was so. Hebrews itself has sometimes been interpreted in a Gnostic sense, but I do not think justifiably so.

The problematic character of this spiritualizing tendency was present in early Christianity in most of its forms at least from the outset of the Gentile mission, and various New Testament writers tried to cope with it in different ways. In the Gospel of Matthew, for example, it is the continuing validity of the law, understood according to the righteousness of Jesus rather than that of the Pharisees, which serves to root Christianity in the world of time and space. Paul confronts the spiritualizing tendency to which his theology was prone by his insistence, among other things, on the Christian community as the body of Christ with its immediate and local implications for fidelity to the law of love. For Luke the counteracting element is the notion that Christianity takes its place in human history and the geographical world, beginning from Jerusalem. The Gospel of John barely escapes capitulation to radical otherworldliness but attempts to do so by its insistence on the practice of love, which is emphasized further in the First Epistle of John as it tries to rescue the gospel message from the gnosticizing members of the community. And in Hebrews the author-preacher insists on the idea of going outside the camp to live lives of ethical responsibility and fidelity, not just of sanctuary-like symbolism, in the sure hope of entering the heavenly sanctuary, the only true one, because faith teaches that Christ the forerunner has already done so.

The temptation to spiritualize completely its historical and geographical roots is a perennial one for Christianity, and efforts to resist it will always be varied according to times and circumstances. To speak in the broadest of terms, Christianity always needs realistic contact, not only with the Bible, especially the Old Testament, which after all can always be interpreted in a merely spiritual sense, but also with the Jewish tradition and its sense of place and time and ethical responsibility. When the classic "sacred space" of the biblical tradition risks becoming wholly transmundane, then it is the world itself that must take on the character of sacred space.

Part Two

Biblical Theology

New Testament Perspectives on Marriage and Divorce*

No reader will expect to find in the New Testament a justification for or a critique of the institution of marriage tribunals. To seek one would be an exercise in anachronism, if not wrongheadedness. In addition, however, it would be theologically naive to conclude that therefore the tribunals have no justification in the life of the Church. For just as a good deal of recent theological literature has reminded us that we cannot expect to find the institution of priesthood in the New Testament and yet should not therefore regard priesthood as itself in question,[1] there is an analogy with many other features of the Church's structure, thought and practice. The Church must be constantly aware of its "home" in the New Testament communities and the teaching of Jesus; it must indeed be subject to the judgment of Scripture in all that it says and does. But even the Church "can't go home again." It cannot solve problems of its own time and culture by a flight into the past of its beginnings, which are often rather romantically portrayed.[2]

---

*First published in *Divorce and Remarriage in the Catholic Church* (New York—Paramus—Toronto: Paulist, 1973) 1-15.

[1]See, e.g., R.E. Brown, *Priest and Bishop, Biblical Reflections* (New York: Paulist Press, 1970); H. Küng, *Why Priests?* (Garden City: Doubleday, 1972).

[2]Only after writing the above paragraph did I read R.L. Wilken, *The Myth of Christian Beginnings* (Garden City: Doubleday, 1971), which develops eloquently the argument implied in the adoption of Thomas Wolfe's title.

In fact, there is a surprising amount of material in the New Testament, especially in the Pauline correspondence, which indirectly supports the development of such institutions as the marriage tribunal. St. Paul urged the Corinthian community more than once to regulate its own affairs. In the case of the incestuous man (1 Cor 5) he ordered the Corinthians uncompromisingly to take drastic action to protect the integrity—including the moral integrity—of the community by "excommunicating" the offender. In the next chapter of the same epistle he rebuked the community for its failure to deal with lawsuits in "courts" of its own making: "Do you not know that the saints will judge the world?"

The case of the lawsuits is an interesting analogy for the business of marriage tribunals, although traditionally Catholic theology has been reluctant to seek analogies to its teaching on marriage and divorce. In 1 Corinthians 6:1-11 the genuine Christian stance is not to have lawsuits with one another in the first place. But when they exist—and Paul is no less a realist than Canon Law—the community has the competence to deal with them. It is true that in the same epistle Paul also discusses marriage and divorce—and we must return to the passage presently—but in that context he makes no provision for any quasi-juridical determinations on the part of the Church. The point here is not really whether one can find some biblical precedent for the marriage tribunal, nor whether Paul would have felt more or less at home with our modern tribunals, but rather that the Pauline "Church order" allows for the Church taking the responsibility, even formally and almost institutionally, for the management of its own affairs. I should like later to suggest an analogous function for the marriage tribunals, which I do not think they now feel empowered to perform.

But the main issue I wish to raise in these pages is not whether we look to the New Testament when examining our modern ecclesiastical life. One may hope we will do so increasingly as a theology and an ecclesiastical "life-style" for our age continue to be elaborated. Rather, the issue is: What do we look for when we turn to the New Testament and the teaching of Jesus? Do we seek the formulation of an absolute, divinely revealed law or model, or do we seek a process of understanding and adaptation with which the modern Church can identify only by entering into the process and furthering it? I believe it is the latter that is the more appropriate by virtue of the nature of the New Testament materials themselves. I should like to illustrate this choice and develop the principles involved by examining the New Testament statements on the indissolubility of marriage. Obviously the example chosen is one that is of considerable concern to the marriage tribunals, though it does not directly determine their propriety or utility. As much as possible, these pages will deal with the New Testament question and the issues to which it gives rise, avoiding facile comparisons and contrasts with later Church practice. On the other hand, we will try to avoid becoming mired in exegetical detail and conjecture; in this question more than many others exegetical ingenuity has obscured what is really present in the New Testament itself.

What God Has Joined Together

Information about Jesus' teaching on the indissolubility of marriage comes to us from three main sources: (1) the Gospel of Mark, which I take to be the earliest extant example of the genre Gospel;[3] (2) Q, the sayings collection drawn upon apparently independently by both Matthew and Luke; and (3) Paul's tradition about the sayings of the Lord. These sources are preserved for us in the five New Testament passages (Mk 10:2-12 and Mt 19:3-12; Lk 16:18 and Mt 5:32; 1 Cor 7:10-16) which have always been the object of intense study on the part of theologians and biblical scholars but

---

[3]It would not be appropriate here to substantiate the use of the so-called two-source theory of Synoptic relationships, which a majority of Catholic scholars now seem to accept. For a recent discussion, see J.A. Fitzmyer, "The Priority of Mark and the 'Q' Source in Luke," in *Jesus and Man's Hope* I (Pittsburgh: Pittsburgh Theological Seminary, 1970) 131-170.

which lately have unleashed a flood of literature.[4] It is remarkable that no single interpretation of these passages has ever won what could be called the general consent of interpreters, at least of Catholic ones, and the Church has reflected this hesitancy by never attempting to define their sense. It is not the intention of these pages to survey this mass of scholarship or to build upon any argument from consensus. Instead, the very diversity of interpretation suggests a tendency to resist the obvious implications of these passages. Let us examine them in succession.

1. The Markan version of the saying of Jesus places it in the context of a challenge from the Pharisees (10:2), though a somewhat obscure one, since in asking whether divorce was allowed, they were supposedly ignoring the explicit provision of the Torah (Deut 24:1). Jesus makes them cite the Torah passage and then he interprets it as a concession to hard-heartedness. Jesus' own reflections center on the order of creation: he cites Genesis 1:27 and 2:24 and comments: "What therefore God has joined together, let not man put asunder" (10:9). Privately, as elsewhere in the Gospel,[5] his disciples question him about his statement and Jesus replies: "Whoever divorces his wife and marries another, commits adultery against her; and if she divorces her husband and marries another, she commits adultery" (10:11-12).

The original force of Jesus' encounter with the Pharisees is lost in Mark's version, and the whole passage is very typical of that Gospel in structure. Moreover, the form of Jesus' interpretation of his own words is difficult to imagine in a Palestinian-Jewish (in contrast to a Roman) setting where the concept of a woman divorcing her husband was unheard

---

[4]Much of it quite independent of the recent divorce question in Italian civil law. For bibliography see J. Dupont, *Mariage et Divorce dans L'Évangile* (Bruges: Desclée de Brouwer, 1959); B. Vawter, "The Divorce Clauses in Mt 5, 32 and 19, 9," in *CBQ* 16 (1954) 155-167; D.L. Dungan, *The Sayings of Jesus in the Churches of Paul* (Philadelphia: Fortress Press, 1971) 83-131; and for some suggestions on the most recent literature, cf. L. Sabourin, "The Divorce Clauses (Mt 5:32; 19:9)," in *BTB* 2 (1972) 80-86.

[5]Notably in the interpretation of parables: 4:10; 7:17.

of—unless we are to imagine that Jesus consciously wished to extend the individual responsibility in marriage to the wife as well.[6] In any event, the point of the saying is clear: Jesus unequivocally and unconditionally rules out divorce.

The Matthean version of this incident is much more coherent, but in view of Matthew's habitual treatment of his Markan source, it is not therefore more original, as has sometimes been alleged.[7] In Matthew the Pharisees put Jesus to the test by inviting him to take sides in a famous Jewish legal dispute: "Is it lawful to divorce one's wife *for any cause?"* (19:3). The issue is that between the school of Shammai, for whom divorce was permissible only on the grounds of adultery, and the school of Hillel, for whom divorce was permissible on many grounds. The surprising thing is that at least at first sight, after resisting the trap with his interpretation of Genesis, Jesus then seems to fall into it, for his saying on divorce is addressed to the Pharisees, not to the disciples, and it contains the famous exceptive clause: "And I say to you: whoever divorces his wife, *except for unchastity (mē epi porneia),* and marries another, commits adultery" (19:9). Perhaps it is only Matthew's concern for interpreting the teaching of Jesus within his own community that leads him to make Jesus' position seem not sufficiently distinct from that of Shammai. That is to say, the dynamic of the encounter with the Pharisees is less important to Matthew than the practical implementation of Jesus' teaching in the community. More on this in a moment. Let us forgo, at least for the present, all the philological discussion which centuries of exegetes have found irresistible. It is enough to note that no matter how the exceptive clause is to be interpreted,[8] it seems to reflect a modification within the

---

[6]Contrast Paul's conscious insistence on the equal rights of husband and wife in marriage in 1 Corinthians 7:2-4. For Paul's reciprocal formulation of the prohibition of divorce, see below.

[7]See, e.g., D.L. Dungan, 102ff.

[8]Except of course in the so-called "preteritive" interpretation, i.e., in the sense of an allusion to Deuteronomy 24:1 "notwithstanding"; this view has been most ably defended by Vawter, *art. cit.,* but few interpreters have found it a satisfactory

Matthean community of the absoluteness of Jesus' prohibition.

2. The Lukan witness to the saying (16:18) is completely independent of the discussion with the Pharisees in which Matthew and Mark place it. For convenience we regard the Lukan verse as derived from the Q source, conscious that this derivation could be challenged since the Matthean parallel in the Sermon on the Mount is not a close one. In Luke, the context contributes almost nothing to the understanding of the saying; it is best treated as an isolated element of Jesus' teaching and is often regarded as the clearest and most "primitive" form of the tradition: "Everyone who divorces his wife and marries another commits adultery, and he who marries a woman divorced from her husband commits adultery."

Another Matthean witness to the saying (5:32)—whether derived from Q or a Matthean reworking of the Markan story—presents the same problem as Matthew 19:9. Here the context is the Sermon on the Mount and specifically the list of antitheses between what was said in the Torah and the demands of Christian righteousness. In contrast to the law in Deuteronomy 24:1 Jesus says: "But I say to you that everyone who divorces his wife, *except on the ground of unchastity (parektos logou porneias),* makes her an adulteress; and whoever marries a divorced woman commits adultery."

3. For a number of reasons it may be suggested that the most important New Testament passage on the indissolubility of marriage is Paul's discussion of it in 1 Corinthians 7. This is chronologically the earliest witness both to a traditional saying of the Lord and to the practice of the early Christian communities. And like Matthew, Paul too both reiterates an absolute doctrine and introduces a qualification. And like Mark, Paul expresses the prohibition in terms of the mutual

---

explanation of the text. One would also have to except those interpretations which understand *porneia* to refer to concubinage, incestuous relationships and the like; see below.

obligations of husband and wife, though without implying complete equality. In fact, in Paul's statement there is no linguistic allusion whatever to the Synoptic sayings, but this is not surprising when we note that Paul gives this teaching as his own even though he understands it to coincide with that of Jesus: "To the married I give charge, not I but the Lord, that the wife should not separate from her husband (but if she does, let her remain single or else be reconciled to her husband)—and that the husband should not divorce[9] his wife" (7:10-11).

Having addressed "the married (Christians)," Paul immediately turns to "the rest," i.e., those in "mixed marriages," presumably marriages in which one partner has subsequently become Christian. In this instance, Paul speaks on his own authority: "To the rest I say, not the Lord ..." (7:12); but there is no indication that his strictures are less authoritative here. First, he forbids the Christian partner in such a union to initiate divorce, "for the unbelieving husband is consecrated through his wife, and the unbelieving wife is consecrated through her husband" (7:14). But secondly, he asserts the freedom of the Christian partner in cases where the non-Christian partner initiates divorce: "But if the unbelieving partner desires to separate, let it be so; in such a case the brother or sister is not bound.[10] For God has called us to peace" (7:15). This is the precedent for what became the classic case of the "Pauline privilege" in later Church practice. For our purposes it is enough to note at present that Paul on his own authority admits an "exception" to the indissolubility of marriage—which, to be sure, he understands as primarily applicable to the Christian situation, but also to the mixed as far as the Christian's initiative is concerned.

---

[9]The word for "divorce" is *aphienai*, not *apolyein* as in the Synoptics. It might be rendered "dismiss" or "put away," but the RSV (which we are citing here) is correct, since the sense is technical.

[10]Literally, the brother or sister, i.e., the Christian partner, "is not enslaved," *ou dedoulōtai*. This is generally interpreted to mean that remarriage is allowed; see below.

Let Not Man Put Asunder

What is the total impact of the New Testament evidence about the absolute indissolubility of marriage? First, all three of our sources (Mark, Q and Paul) report an unqualified prohibition of divorce as a saying of Jesus. The only reasonable conclusion is that this is what Jesus really taught. It could not reasonably be accounted for as an invention of the early Church because it so radically runs counter to the accepted practice of both Jewish and Greco-Roman society. One should note that the method underlying this conclusion is not the mathematical analogy of the least common denominator but the careful analysis of the development of the forms of dominical sayings in the Synoptic tradition.[11] In the overall context of the preaching of Jesus this radical and uncompromising assertion must be seen in relation to the eschatological urgency of his preaching: the kingdom of God is at hand!

Our second observation on the basis of the above survey of passages is that, of the four New Testament authors who deal with the teaching of Jesus about marriage and divorce, two of them make exceptions to the absolute statement. It is this fact which must be reckoned with, not by any exegetical legerdemain, but by attempting to understand the process by which the sayings of Jesus were evaluated and transmitted in the New Testament itself. That we are really dealing with exceptions on the part of Matthew (or his community) and Paul becomes clear if we allow the texts to say what they most obviously seem to say. Let us first eliminate some unsuccessful attempts to avoid this conclusion.

One cannot introduce into the New Testament the distinction between a sacramental marriage and a non-sacramental marriage. In the Synoptic passages there is no hint of the

---

[11] See R. Bultmann, *The History of the Synoptic Tradition*, rev. ed. (New York: Harper & Row, 1968) 132-136. We cannot of course repeat the details of such an analysis in this brief chapter.

possible sacramentality of marriage. On the contrary, the argument for the indissolubility of marriage in the Markan source is derived from the order of creation and thus makes no special provision for the Christian believer at all. Paul, on the other hand, seems at first sight to place Christian marriage in a separate category, but this is not really so, for the point of his concentration is the attitude of the Christian partner, not the nature of the marriage itself. From the point of view of the Christian, a marriage entered into before conversion is as "permanent" as one between Christians. It is not the nature of the marriage which determines its permanence, but the commitment of the partners. The Christian partner who is "deserted," i.e., divorced, is "not bound." It is important to emphasize the fact that it is reading Christian history backward to argue that the New Testament is even "implicitly" talking about the distinction between sacramental and non-sacramental marriage which the later Church articulated. What is most significant is that the later Church is responsible for this distinction, not any revealed divine law. And if the Church is responsible, it is our suggestion here that the Church is empowered to modify the distinction if it should see fit to do so. The nature of marriage as derived from the early Church's understanding of the order of creation is apparently not so absolute as to exclude all exceptions.

Again, one cannot argue that the exceptive clauses of Matthew or the Pauline exception have to do with separation without the right to remarry. If the context of Matthew is a Jewish (-Christian) one, such an arrangement is simply meaningless. As for the situation of 1 Corinthians 7, it is true that Paul explicitly rules out remarriage in the first case that he deals with, that of Christian partners initiating separation. It is probably also true that, given his eschatological perspective, Paul would dissuade the divorced Christian partner of a mixed marriage from remarrying (cf. 1 Cor 7:8, 27). But he makes it unequivocally clear in the same context that those who are free, i.e., widows and those who have never been married, do no wrong, even in the situation of a proximate eschatological expectation, if they choose to marry (cf. 1 Cor 7:9, 28, 39). It is very difficult to imagine him holding an unexpressed reservation for the victims of a broken marriage whom he expressly calls "not bound."

One could continue to list and criticize attempts to read the New Testament passages in such a way that they do not conflict with traditional Church practice. But the longer the list, the more uncomfortable we become about the very presupposition of such attempts. Instead, we should perhaps look to the larger contexts of the preaching of Jesus, Paul and Matthew and seek to identify the factors which the early Christians understood to authorize them to interpret the teaching of Jesus without abandoning it.

It has already been pointed out that the context of Jesus' radical reinterpretation of the law was an eschatological one. Paul had certainly not lost that sense of eschatological urgency when writing 1 Corinthians 7, but Paul confronted a new situation which had not been part of Jesus' experience. He is conscious of the newness of the situation and of the lack of direct guidance from the Lord when he points out that the instruction on mixed marriages is his own. A few verses later this consciousness is even more emphatic: "Now concerning the unmarried, I have no command of the Lord, but I give my opinion as one who by the Lord's mercy is trustworthy" (7:25). The new situation is the missionary one in which Christians are confronted with working out a way to live in the midst of pagan society. Paul does not abandon the lofty ideal of the dominical teaching about marriage; he repeats it (7:10-11). But he accommodates it to the new situation of mixed marriages, in effect introducing an exception to the absolute indissolubility of marriage. By what authority? He ends the discussion of marriage and celibacy with the remark, "And I think that I have the Spirit of God" (7:40b).

Matthew too faces a new situation with respect to the teaching of Jesus, which he too first reaffirms (19:6). The eschatological message of the pressing kingdom of heaven has now to be related to the on-going life of a Jewish-Christian Church, a Church which is confronted with solving the daily problems of its existence by exercising the powers of binding and loosing.[12] In this context Matthew—or the community he represents—is empowered by his understanding of Jesus' intentions to adapt his teaching on marriage to a situation in which a marriage broken by "unchastity" can no longer be understood as a marriage. It is of course *possible* that *porneia* in the Matthean exceptive clauses refers to a marriage within degrees of kindred which Gentiles might tolerate but Jews (i.e., Jewish Christians) would regard as incestuous (Lev 18:7-18).[13] Such a marriage would be intolerable in the eyes of Matthew's community. But that is by no means the obvious meaning of the passage since it is not clear that such a union would be regarded as a marriage in the first place. It is at least equally understandable in a Jewish-Christian context that adultery would in fact establish the situation of a ruptured marital union that was once genuine.[14]

What we must suppose in the Matthean Church is a conflict of values that has to be resolved in the on-going life of the Church and for which the tradition about Jesus' sayings provides no immediately applicable solution. The confrontation is between the principle of the indissolubility of marriage which is the tradition of Jesus' teaching and the "right" to a genuine integral marriage. The latter would no doubt be more deeply felt in a community of Jewish background where marriage was regarded as a duty.[15] If

[12]Cf. Matthew's "ecclesiological" transformation of the confession of Peter at Caesarea Philippi (16:13-19) as well as of other Markan passages such as the storm on the lake (Mt 8:23-27); for the problem-solving concern of the Church, see also Matthew 18:15-20.

[13]The principal exponent of this view was J. Bonsirven, *Le divorce dans le Nouveau Testament* (Tournai: Desclée, 1948).

[14]It is true that *porneia* is not the ordinary word for adultery, as the very context shows. But it is quite possible that *porneia* was chosen precisely to generalize the concept of the unchastity that can break a marriage. In any case, Matthew does not use the language of Deuteronomy 24:1 (LXX). On this interpretation of the exceptive clauses, see K. Haacker, "Ehescheidung und Wiederverheiratung im Neuen Testament," in *Theologische Quartalschrift* 151 (1971) 28-38, and the survey of L. Sabourin, 83-84.

[15]Q. Quesnell has very ably argued, taking up a suggestion of J. Dupont, that the eunuch saying in Matthew 19:12 refers to those who accept the separation of a

Matthew's solution falls into something like the Shammaite interpretation of the Torah which Jesus had avoided in the controversy story, we must allow that the inconsistency may mean much more to the modern interpreter than to a Jewish-Christian community of the late first century.[16] The interpretation of Shammai was not a rabbinic innovation, after all, but a strict construction of the law itself in Deuteronomy 24:1.

God Has Called Us to Peace

It is time to draw some conclusions and formulate some suggestions regarding the status of New Testament teaching on the indissolubility of marriage and the status of contemporary Church practice.

First, regarding the teaching of Jesus. We have indicated above that we can with some confidence identify what was Jesus' attitude toward divorce and what was that of some of the New Testament writers, and these are not identical. It would be false to conclude that theological judgment must rest on our ability, through historical and literary means, to isolate Jesus' teaching at the expense of that of his followers. In the light of modern New Testament scholarship, especially the methods of source, form and redaction criticism applied to the Gospels, there is widespread agreement among interpreters that we have access to the mind of Jesus primarily—indeed only—through the interpretation of the early Christian communities and their theologians. The authority of Jesus' teaching does not reach us independently

---

broken marriage without the right to remarry: "'Made Themselves Eunuchs for the Kingdom of Heaven' (Mt 19, 12)," in *CBQ* 30 (1968) 335-358. But if this is correct, the real innovation in Jesus' teaching is the notion of separation without remarriage, and this seems only very obliquely stated in the various sayings of this pericope.

[16]One must understand such a statement in the context of Matthew's presentation of the on-going validity of the law in the Jewish-Christian community even though Jesus has radicalized it; see the sayings in Matthew 5:17-20 and the essay of G. Barth in G. Bornkamm *et al.*, *Tradition and Interpretation in Matthew* (Philadelphia: Westminster Press, 1963).

of the Church. Consequently we cannot assume, in view of the role of Scripture in the life of the Church, that what scholarly research points to as Jesus' own utterance is necessarily any more determinative for the Church than what are apparently the interpretations of him by his followers. This means that we cannot regard as more authoritative for Church life the apparently "primitive" Lukan form of the divorce statement rather than the qualified Matthean form.

On another level, this observation means that we cannot rest Church practice regarding marriage and divorce upon a supposedly divine revealed law—to the extent that the New Testament serves as the vehicle of that revelation. Instead we must discern the process by which the teaching of Jesus was remembered, communicated, interpreted, adapted and enshrined in the practice of the early Christian communities. That process, we have seen, is one of accommodation to circumstances that were not the context of the preaching of Jesus himself. The Church of today must relate, not to an absolute divine law which is in practice inaccessible to our scholarly research, but to the process of identifying what is of Christ and what is Christian and entering into that discerning process for our own day. The matrix of modern discernment is, as it was in the churches of Paul or Matthew, the dwelling of the Holy Spirit among God's people.

But Jesus did teach the absolute indissolubility of marriage (note that the New Testament does not authorize us to say "of *Christian* marriage"). Was his teaching then merely an ideal from which the "realist" perceives an inevitable decline? There are modern authors who stress the nature of Jesus' matrimonial teaching as an ideal.[17] If we have in mind the formulation of Matthew 5:32, especially in the context of the antitheses of the Sermon on the Mount, there are good

[17]Cf., e.g., W.J. O'Shea, "Marriage and Divorce: The Biblical Evidence," in *Australasian Catholic Record* 47 (1970) 89-109; J.A. Grispino, *The Bible Now!* (Notre Dame: Fides, 1971) 95-107.

grounds for this view.[18] Nor does this mean the "reduction" of the Sermon on the Mount to a mere statement of an impossible ideal over against a serious program for a Christian morality.[19] The alternative of law vs. ideal is not a complete disjuction; there is also what some theologians call "Gospel," the genuine and specifically Christian challenge that can only be met by the fusion of free will and grace. But perhaps one can and even must go a step further and argue that the very preservation of the teaching of Jesus in all its eschatological and challenging purity *requires* the kind of adaptation the early Christians made.[20] The paradox is not meant to be a logical statement but an existential one. What prevents Jesus' teaching from becoming a chimera is the willingness to interpret it anew in each generation. And in this respect, is there not a serious danger that an intransigent interpretation of the indissolubility of marriage in the Catholic Church today is rapidly approaching the point of disdain for the ideal itself as a utopian one?

But are there in fact grounds for the discernment of new situations in the life of modern Christians which require new interpretation and new adaptation of the New Testament teaching on marriage? An ever growing number of serious theologians and Christian social scientists believe that there are. What is emerging is a new perception of values, and every age of creative thought must perceive its own values anew. There is a growing consciousness of the conflict of values in our Christian society over the issue of marriage, the

[18]One should compare carefully and objectively the antitheses in Matthew 5:21-48: "You, therefore, must be perfect, as your heavenly Father is perfect." In the immediate context of the divorce saying, the Church has long recognized idealistic hyperbole in the saying: "If your right hand causes you to sin, but it off and throw it away," and Jesus' absolute prohibition of oaths has not only not been taken literally as law, but has been formally contravened even by ecclesiastical practice. It is difficult to refrain from exploiting this and other examples from Jesus' teaching when discussing the divorce statements. See J.A. Grispino, 98-100 (references).

[19]For discussion of the alternatives, see J. Jeremias, *The Sermon on the Mount* (Philadelphia: Fortress Press, 1963).

[20]Cf., e.g., G. Schneider, "Jesu Wort über die Ehescheidung in der Überlieferung des Neuen Testaments," in *Trierer Theologische Zeitschrift* 80 (1971) 65-87.

conflict between a clear but inflexible matrimonial legislation which does indeed express an important part of the Christian ethical ideal, and a way of life that must reflect Christian love, pardon, dedication and self-giving in a world of loveless technocracy and existential depression.

The marriage tribunal was our starting point. What are we to conclude about it? If its principal function is a judicial one, modeled on the kind of civil judiciary that St. Paul excoriated the Corinthians for having recourse to, then it has no place in the life of the Church. The Church is a human society and its agencies are human agencies, but it is not a civil society and its courts are not civil courts. But if the tribunal can be modified so that it really enters into the process of discerning values and narrowing the perennial gap between Christian ideals and the practice of Christians, then it has an important role to play. It must arbitrate a conflict of values, not a conflict of laws. But the courts are inter-preters of the law. In that case, the Church's tribunals have but one law to serve, what St. Paul calls the "law of Christ": "If a man is overtaken in any trespass, you who are spiritual should restore him in a spirit of gentleness .... Bear one another's burdens, and so fulfill the law of Christ" (Gal 6:1-2).

9

Ministry and Ministries
in the New Testament*

One of the phenomena, among many, for which the post-Vatican II church will have its place in history is the gradual "declericalization" of ministry. This takes the form, not so much of the revival of the permanent diaconate, which is after all another clerical order, but of the public acknowledgement of multiple ministries in the church at the local and diocesan levels, many of them exercised now in an official manner by laity. I refer to ministries such as liturgy, parish council leadership, and above all—because it is so widespread—religious education, which numbers both teachers and coordinators among its practitioners.[1]

It should not be necessary, of course, to argue that these are indeed forms of ministry in the church, and one is happy to observe that increasingly they are being referred to as such. But the process of recognition, experience shows, does not always go smoothly. Conflicts among various ministers, clerical and lay alike, easily arise, and there is need not only for a common understanding and sharing of ministry, but

---

*First published in *Living Light* 14 (1977) 167-179.

[1] In a slighty different form and with a different focus, this paper was first published in Italian in a volume honoring Cardinal M. Pellegrino, *Chiesa per il mondo* (Bologna, 1974), vol. I, pp. 177-191.

sometimes even for reconciliation of ministers with one another. This essay aims to make a small contribution to this task of understanding and reconciliation by looking again, perhaps in a different way, at ministry in some of the New Testament churches.

The purpose is to argue that the increasingly diverse ministries of the contemporary church are reconciled, not in their forms, but in their internal finality. And having argued that, the essay will explore briefly the Pauline idea of the ministry of reconciliation. There is an underlying presupposition here that needs to surface at the outset. It is the presupposition that any period of theological creativity—which is what we hope our post-Vatican II age will prove to be—is also a period of rediscovery. As we strive to elaborate a theology of ministry for our own situation, we must rediscover the meaning of Christian ministry at its roots. Before looking directly at some biblical perspectives, however, let us prepare the ground by staking out some boundaries—by making a few distinctions, to use familiar theological language.

Introduction

First, let us leave out of account for the most part the largest part of the Bible, the Old Testament. The reason for such a major limitation is that the Christian ministry focuses somehow on the image we cherish of the ministry of Christ himself, which though intelligible only in the light of the Old Testament, is also a radical break with the institutionalized religion of Israel as this is understood in the first century. Whether Jesus is properly termed a "revolutionary" or not is a question we may leave to the modern christological and historical debate, but there can be no doubt that he formulated his own understanding of his mission in opposition to the cultic establishment (as incidentally did many of the prophets before him). And even if it is true, as it is often alleged, that the Christian priesthood soon rehabilitated some key elements of the Old Testament ministry, we will be justified in trying to understand the ministry of the New Covenant by staying within the framework of its own utterances. A new covenant demands a new mediator; does it also demand a new ministry?[2]

When we turn to the New Testament, what do we look for in the study of ministry? All too often, it seems to me, investigations of ministry in the Bible are in reality attempts to find in the ministry of Jesus or of the early church one's own ministry. They are searches to justify the forms or emphases of modern ministry by means of biblical precedent. Such an undertaking is doomed to fail, not only because many forms of ministry, such as priesthood, for example, are not to be discovered in the New Testament church, but also because this undertaking places a false emphasis upon the role of the Bible. Forms of ministry are responses to the needs of the Christian community, and we should not demand that the early church should have anticipated all the needs of the Christian communities throughout history. What we shall look for in the New Testament, therefore, is not a justification for any particular forms of ministry that are or have been current in the Christian churches, but rather a sense of the theological meaning of ministry in the context of the early church.

The distinction that I am making here is one between the *forms* of ministry and the *finality* of ministry. The New Testament presents to us a very considerable variety of forms of ministry, or at least of designations for ministers. These range from the specialized sense of "disciple" through presbyters, bishops, deacons, "pastors," apostles, prophets, teachers, evangelists—down even to those mysterious functionaries mentioned in the famous lists of 1 Cor 12: helpers and administrators. Clearly the variety represented in the early church was no less great than that of the Christian church today. It is not important for our present purposes to distinguish between charismatic and institutional forms of

[2]In using the language of the *Epistle to the Hebrews* it is important to recall that Hebrews itself is not concerned with the question of a Christian ministry; its scope is almost exclusively christological and soteriological.

ministry in the Corinthian and other communities, nor to determine which of the many forms mentioned in the New Testament properly constitute "offices" as opposed merely to *ad hoc* functions. Our question is rather whether there is a finality in which all these forms share.

To put it another way, given the variety of ministries in the church—ancient as well as modern—what is their unity? If I could state it as a thesis, I would suggest that the reconciliation of ministries lies in accepting the multiple forms, sometimes even in creating new forms, in response to an understanding of the relationship of ministry to the church and to the person of Jesus Christ. The emphasis of contemporary New Testament scholarship on the diversity of theologies and modes of Christian life corresponds to the trust of modern ecumenical theology which seeks to recognize a pluralism in theology and in Christian lifestyle. These two trends are not unrelated in their origins and they should inform one another in the continuing theological dialogue. It is not the goal of such a dialogue to discover unity by trying to reduce a healthy pluralism to an artificial conformity. On the other hand, it is the goal of such a dialogue to identify the purpose, the finality, the goals that unite.

Ministry in Acts

The diversity of forms depended in New Testament times on the community's perception of its needs and its purposes, and I am implying that the same process must, in the light of the Bible, of history, and of course of many other factors, determine the ministries of the modern church. St. Luke portrays the dynamic of this process vividly in the story in Acts 6:1-6 of the appointment of the "seven." The story has its problems, as every interpreter knows, not least of them the fact that two of the seven appointed to "serve tables" immediately reappear in the role of preaching missionaries.[3]

---

[3]On this point, as well as the whole passage, see the commentary of E. Haenchen, *The Acts of the Apostles* (Philadelphia, 1971) 264-268.

Without any attempt to solve the many exegetical riddles of this passage, let us make a few observations about it. Luke's intention may be simply to account for the prominent position of Stephen and the persecution that ensues, but in so doing he provides a glimpse of an important process.

First, one should note the role of conflict in this story; it is out of a crisis situation in the early church, the neglect of certain widows and the consequent divisiveness, that Luke understands the diversification of ministry to begin. This factor is all the more important in view of Luke's general tendency to suppress any trace of disharmony in the primitive community. Secondly, it is notable that the ultimate discernment of the need for a new ministry lies in the hands of the community; the Twelve function as leaders, to be sure, but the action is taken as the result of a broader process of decision-making. Finally, we observe that the language of the passage focuses on a principle of unity of ministry that overrides the diversity implied in the specialization of the Twelve and the Seven: namely that of *diakonia*, "service" or "ministry." The Seven are to "serve *(diakonein)* tables" while the Twelve continue to devote themselves to prayer and the "service *(diakonia)* of the word." Whether Luke understands the Seven as "deacons" *(diakonoi)* or not (and there are reasons to question this), he does not call them deacons, since his account interprets all ministry as "service" to the community.

The Acts of the Apostles is somewhat less direct when it relates ministry to the person of Christ, but there is some evidence that I should like to mention, always keeping in mind that for Luke the ministry of the Twelve, the "Apostles" in Luke's own restrictive use of this term, and the ministry of Paul both belong to history and are not institutionally perpetuated through successors. The unique historical perspective of Luke has been dealt with brilliantly by Hans Conzelmann, who argues that the two-volume work of Luke shows a division of salvation-history into three periods: that of the law and the prophets or the time of Israel, that of Jesus, and that of the church.[4] Whatever qualifications we

---

[4]In *The Theology of St. Luke* (New York, 1961) and in various other works.

may feel impelled to place upon this somewhat rigid scheme, the fact that for Luke the early days of the church described in Acts belong to the historical past seems unassailable. Though Paul cannot be an apostle in the eyes of Luke, his ministry shares with that of the Apostles the function of *witnessing,* a divinely commissioned function that relates the witness to Christ himself. Christoph Burchard has recently explored this issue in Acts and has demonstrated convincingly that for Luke, Paul is "the thirteenth witness."[5] What is the evidence for this? In the programmatic statement of the Book of Acts, the risen Jesus addresses the Apostles as follows: "You shall receive power when the Holy Spirit has come upon you; and you shall be my witnesses in Jerusalem and in all Judea and Samaria and to the end of the earth" (1:8). In the case of Paul, in both accounts of his conversion experience retold in his speeches, the emphasis is on his witnessing role: Ananias says to Paul, "The God of our fathers appointed you to know his will, to see the Just One and to hear a voice from his mouth; for you will be a *witness* for him to all men of what you have seen and heard" (22:14-15).

The last mention in Acts of Paul's commission to witness takes us a step further. In his speech before the Roman governor Festus and King Agrippa, Paul attributes the commission to Jesus himself in the experience on the road to Damascus: "Rise and stand upon your feet; for I have appeared to you for this purpose, to appoint you to serve and bear *witness* to the things in which you have seen me and to those in which I will appear to you, delivering you from the people and from the Gentiles—to whom I send you to open their eyes, that they may turn from darkness to light and from the power of Satan to God, that they may receive forgiveness of sins and a place among those who are sanctified by faith in me" (26:16-18). When Paul's ministry is described as opening the eyes of the blind, Luke is deliberately patterning Paul's commission on the ministry of Jesus himself which in Luke's Gospel is defined in terms of Isaiah 61:1-2, quoted in Luke 4:18-19: "The Spirit of the

[5] *Der dreizehnte Zeuge* (Göttingen, 1970).

Lord is upon me, because he has anointed me to preach good news to the poor. He has sent me to proclaim release to the captives and recovering of sight to the blind...." Throughout Acts Luke uses his consummate literary artistry to portray both Peter and Paul as leading careers in which they model themselves and their ministries on Jesus himself. They work miracles as he did, they are filled with and guided by the Spirit as he was, they move toward suffering as part of their ministries as suffering was the key to Jesus' ministry.

In his reworking of Mark, the most obvious Lukan technique of composition is the famous "travel narrative" which occupies one-third of the Gospel, Jesus' journey to Jerusalem to face his passion and death (9:51—19:27). "When the days drew near for him to be received up, he set his face to go to Jerusalem" (9:51). In Acts the journey of Paul, ultimately a journey to Rome, is patterned in some respects on Jesus' journey to Jerusalem, and of course it begins precisely as a journey to Jerusalem (19:21—28:16). At the outset of the journey, Paul's ship stops at Miletus, and he summons the presbyters of the church at Ephesus to hear his farewell address, one of the most discussed of all the many speeches in Acts. In it Paul declares to the elders: "Now, behold, I am going to Jerusalem, bound in the Spirit, not knowing what shall befall me there; except that the Holy Spirit testifies to me in every city that imprisonment and afflictions await me. But I do not account my life of any value nor as precious to myself, if only I may accomplish my course and the ministry (*diakonia*) which I received from the Lord Jesus, to *bear witness* to the gospel of the grace of God" (20:22-24).

Paul's farewell address at Miletus also contains another important link in our reconstruction of the chain of Lukan reflection on ministry. For if the ministry of the Apostles and of Paul, i.e., of the "witnesses," is modeled on that of Jesus, is not the relationship to Christ's ministry as untransferable as is the historical role of the Apostles and Paul as the foundation of the era of the church? Here precisely Luke is careful to bring out that Paul's ministry, as he sums it up in Miletus, is to serve as a model for the elders of Ephesus, i.e., for Christian ministers in the era of the church. Paul relates his own ministry and then immediately relates it, looking forward, to that of his audience: "Be alert, remembering that for three years I did not cease night or day to admonish every one with tears. And now I commend you to God and to the word of his grace. . . . You yourselves know that these hands ministered to my necessities, and to those who were with me. In all things I have shown you that by so toiling one must help the weak. . . . " (20:31-35). Though the word is not used, the theme here is the familiar one of imitation, which recurs often in the epistles of Paul himself: "Be imitators of me, as I am of Christ" (1 Cor 11:1; cf. 1 Thess 1-2 etc.). Thus the model of ministry in Lukan theology points both before and after, to Christ and to the church, passing through the generation of the "witnesses."

Let us summarize the point we have reached in this brief investigation of the Book of Acts. Christian ministry is oriented to the needs of the Christian community and it is rooted in the ministry of Christ. We may say that for Luke ministry is seen as a *relation* which points in two directions. It is service, *diakonia,* which is itself a relational concept. On the one hand, the minister carries on the work of Jesus himself, and on the other the specification of his ministry arises in the context of the community to whom he ministers. In an interesting article on "The Ministry in the New Testament" written some twenty years ago, the Swedish scholar Harald Riesenfeld chose to focus the essence of ministry on the function of representation.[6] He argued that the minister is the one who represents Jesus Christ, indeed acts as plenipotentiary in his name, and also represents human beings, gathering together their multiplicity in the unity of his own person. I do not think this particular imagery dominates in the New Testament, and I see in Riesenfeld's analysis an attempt to make the representational functions of priesthood the unifying image of ministry; I feel this goes beyond the New Testament evidence, though it is

[6] In *The Root of the Vine* (London, 1953) 96-127.

not of course alien to the Christian tradition. But I cite Riesenfeld because I think he correctly perceives the relational quality of ministry as the mediating point, as it were, between the role of Jesus and the exigencies of the community of believers in him. It is ministry understood in this way that I wish to concentrate on in the remainder of these remarks.

Images of the Church and Ministry

Perhaps the best way to do so is to acknowledge that on any analysis ministry gets its meaning from an understanding of the church, since the mission of Jesus is felt in the New Testament to be entrusted to the church, not to ministers, at least not as individuals. This is not to contradict what has just been said with respect to Lukan theology of the ministry, nor is it to contradict such statements as Paul's (to which we shall return later) that God "entrusted to us the ministry of reconciliation" (2 Cor 5:19), for Paul clearly understands the church as a whole to be involved in his own apostolate. To the Philippians he can even speak of their "partnership in the gospel" (1:5). And indeed the so-called "Great Commission" of Mt 28:18-20, though clearly addressed to the "eleven disciples," must be heard, in the context of Matthew, as addressed to the whole church. Too often the impression has been given that the task of evangelizing the world was entrusted to a group within the church and only analogously shared in by all—a form of clericalism that is easily recognizable.

One possible avenue of approach to church and ministry in the New Testament is to reflect on the implications for ministry of some of the. major biblical images of the church. Indeed several of these are most useful for seeing precisely the relational quality of ministry as its finality. In his fine book *Images of the Church in the New Testament* (1960), the distinguished biblical scholar Paul Minear catalogues no less than ninety-six analogies discussed. These are not all actually images of the church or of the ministry, but the majority of them are. In the article already referred to, Harald Riesenfeld, too, discusses a list of images of the church in the New Testament in order to bring out facets of the ministry of Jesus upon which he sees the ministry of Christians so closely patterned.

One might point out, somewhat parenthetically, that nowhere in the New Testament is the most obvious image or analogy ever drawn upon, the analogy of civil society with its structures of government.[7] This must strike us with peculiar irony when we recall the growth and organization of the church from the early patristic period down through the Middle Ages and even much later. I mention this point, not as a curiosity, but as a warning. For if a revitalization of Christian ministry in the new circumstances of modern culture and the post-Vatican II church is to be accomplished, and if indeed a fresh understanding of ministry in the New Testament is to animate this process, then we need to look very cautiously at the political models which even today enter into our discussions of the nature of the church and its ministers. In my view neither the monarchical prince-bishopric of the Holy Roman Empire nor the enlightened democratic ideals of modern civil society necessarily get us any closer to the nature of the church and its proper modes of existence. But of course, a purely otherworldly, "disembodied" understanding of the church will not help either, for it ignores the "incarnational" aspects of ecclesiology. What I am suggesting is a cautious look, not an a priori rejection.

I would like to single out a few of the more important images of the church in the New Testament, mostly Pauline ones, though they have analogies in the preaching of Jesus in the gospels, and attempt to show briefly how I think they highlight the understanding of ministry as relationship to the person of Jesus and as relationship to the Christian community. Along the way attention will be paid to some specific issues that bear on the discussion of ministry in the contemporary church.

---

[7] The use of *politeuma* in Phil 3.20 is not an image of the church, nor is "holy nation" (1 Pet 2:9) a political image.

The first image is the agricultural one: "You are God's field," says Paul to the Corinthians (1 Cor 3:9). Under this heading we might refer to all the horticultural metaphors in the New Testament such as plants, vines and branches, vineyards, grains, mustard seeds, and the like. No doubt there is a relationship between the persistence of this imagery and the preaching of Jesus himself. Compare the Matthean logion about the Pharisees: "Every plant which my heavenly Father has not planted will be rooted up" (15:13). Compare also the various parables of growth in the Synoptic tradition, which to be sure refer to the kingdom of God, not to the church, but as the complicated history of the traditions in the Synoptics themselves reveals, it was not long before such parables were being interpreted in relation to the church.

In its context in 1 Corinthians, the Pauline use of this image of the church occurs precisely in a discussion of ministry. Against the tendency of the Corinthians (apparently) to focus their factionalism on the person of various apostolic figures as mystagogues or at least as rallying figures, Paul is constrained to clarify the role of apostles: "What then is Apollos? What is Paul? Servants (*diakonoi*) through whom you believed, as the Lord assigned to each. I planted, Apollos watered, but God gave the growth. So neither he who plants nor he who waters is anything, but only God who gives the growth. He who plants and he who waters are equal, and each shall receive his wages according to his labor. For we are God's fellow workers; you are God's field, God's building" (1 Cor 3:5-9). The point is clear and needs little exegetical comment, though there are some ambiguities in the text (e.g. whether "as the Lord assigned to each" refers to the apostles or to the believers; whether *synergoi theou* is to be taken as collaboration with God or for him). Paul is quite explicit in preferring the designation "servants" (not "deacons" in any official sense); in Philippians (1:1) he can even claim the title of "slave (*doulos*) of Jesus Christ," although in the same verse he addresses the "bishops and deacons" of the Philippian church. The minister's task here is the cultivation of the community, in various ways, as the differentiation between Paul and Apollos suggests (planting and watering). The minister is a custodian of God's work; in this lies his dignity, that in some sense he collaborates in God's service. But above all, this image as Paul develops it is a reminder that the work of ministry is related to the work of grace. No theology of ministry can afford to let the total responsibility for the growth of Christian community rest on the ministers alone. God gives the growth.

In the same context Paul introduces another metaphor that is almost equally widespread in the New Testament, the building metaphor, which has given rise to one of the most familiar and most abused Christian words, "edification."[8] The Corinthians are not only "God's field," they are "God's building." Here we may refer to the variety of New Testament metaphors of the church as building, temple, and the like, to the image of the cornerstone (or keystone) and the foundation. And again the whole idea-complex reflects the parables tradition of Jesus, particularly the Q parable of the house built on rock (which in its Lukan version emphasizes the necessity of a foundation; Lk 6:47-49; Mt 7:24-27). Of course the parable does not apply to the church, neither originally nor in the gospels' application of it. Again, one can refer here to the celebrated Matthean saying of Jesus in the confession of Peter at Caesarea Philippi, "on this rock I shall build my church" (Mt 16:18). For Paul in 1 Corinthians the building image is again introduced into the context of a discussion of the apostles as ministers. "According to the commission of God given to me, like a skilled master builder I laid a foundation, and another man is building upon it. Let each man take care how he builds upon it. For no other foundation can any one lay than that which is laid, which is Jesus Christ" (3:10-11). Again the role of the minister is related to his function for the community. It can even be said that for Paul the minister *is* what he *does*. But here the relationship of ministry to Jesus is stressed.

---

[8] See G.W. MacRae, "Building the House of the Lord," in *American Ecclesiastical Review* 140 (1959) 361-376.

The image of the foundation of the building is employed in various ways in the New Testament. For Paul there is exclusive emphasis on the foundation as Christ himself, and the work of ministry is only as good as its fidelity to building on the one foundation. A minister will in fact be judged on the extent of his fidelity. For other writers this image can be adapted. The author to the Ephesians (who on this ground alone seems hardly likely to be Paul) can speak of the "household of God, built upon the foundation of the apostles and prophets, Christ Jesus himself being the cornerstone, in whom the whole structure is joined together and grows into a holy temple in the Lord ... " (2:19-21). Despite the formal difference from the Pauline passage, here too the centrality of Christ is emphasized along with the concept of apostolic tradition. In the logion of Jesus in Mt 16:18 the word "foundation" is not used, but the same image is implied though in a very different sense.

When we turn from agricultural and architectural imagery to pastoral imagery, we leave Paul but find resonances in many other New Testament writers.[9] Here we refer to the notions of shepherd, sheep, flock, fold, etc. Once again the continuity between this image and certain logia and parables of Jesus is too familiar to require citation. Moreover, like the image of planting, the pastoral image is rooted in the Old Testament, where not only is God called the Shepherd (e.g. Ps 23) but also the leaders of the people are (e.g. Jer 23:1-4), and the people themselves are the flock of sheep. This image, too, clearly connotes a set of ideals about the behavior of shepherds which become a goal for the Christian ministry, implicitly invoked when the name "shepherds" or "pastors" is given to a ministerial office (linked with "teachers") in Eph 4:11—another version of the lists of offices or gifts in 1 Cor 12. Without necessarily any explicit ecclesiological or ministerial implications, the Q parable of the lost sheep (Lk 15:3-7; Mt 18:12-14) portrays the shepherd as one totally dedicated

---

[9] 1 Cor 9:7 uses the metaphor of the flock, but only in a series of metaphors, though indeed again in the context of ministry.

to the sheep. Similarly and with similar restrictions, the Johannine "parables" of the shepherd and the sheepfold (10:1-16) establish a Christological model for the recognition of the true shepherd as opposed to the hireling: "I am the good shepherd; the good shepherd lays down his life for his sheep." Thus again the biblical imagery of church and minister places the ministry in a context of relationships to Christ and to the church.

It is quite clear from the images of the church and ministry which we have mentioned thus far that the list could easily be prolonged. But we must not leave the images of the church without a word about the most original and perhaps most beloved of all images—at least the Pauline ones—that of the body of Christ. It is worth noting that the first time this doctrine is explicitly set forth in the Pauline corpus, namely in 1 Cor 12, it is again presented in what we may understand as a discussion of ministry. The issue in 1 Cor 12 is that of the "spiritual gifts," and Paul begins by establishing the universality of the gift of the Holy Spirit to all who profess faith in Jesus as Lord. He defines the purpose of the manifestations of the Spirit, which are varied, as "for the common good" (*pros to sympheron*). Clearly in the first instance he is speaking of those gifts which we generally call charisms.

But after expounding the image of the body and astonishingly identifying the traditional metaphor with the very person of Christ—some would say after "politicizing" an image of "mystical" or spiritual identity with the body of Christ already shared with his readers—he turns to listing ministerial "offices" which God has appointed in the church: apostles, prophets, teachers, miracle-workers, healers, helpers, administrators, speakers in tongues (12:28). By placing these forms of ministry in the context of the body image as he understands it—laterally, one might say, rather than only vertically—he again defines Christian ministry in terms both of its service to the community ("for the common good") and of its relationship to Christ. Only this time the relationship to Christ is one of identity as members of the body. "Now you are the body of Christ and individually members of it" (12:27).

Even when, in Colossians and Ephesians, the body image is generalized, and complicated by the quite heterogeneous concept of Christ as the head, it is still in relation to ministry that the image is invoked. For example in Colossians: "Now I rejoice in my sufferings for your sake, and in my flesh I complete what is lacking in Christ's afflictions for the sake of his body, that is, the church, of which I became a minister according to the divine office which was given to me for you, to make the word of God fully known" (1:24-25).

The Ministry of Reconciliation

We have concentrated on an attempt to grasp the function or finality of Christian ministry rather than its diversified forms, and to do so in terms of the twofold relationship to Christ and to the community. It is not necessary to multiply examples further, but we should like to end with a brief consideration of the image of ministry that forms a central Pauline theme, the ministry of reconciliation. As one might expect, I am inclined to see in this image also an illustration of the relational nature of ministry, but this time the image is not an eccesiological one, but a soteriological one. What is the relationship between reconciliation, the ministry of reconciliation, and the message of it?

The soteriological image of reconciliation has always been a favorite of Christians because it is derived from the kind of personal experience of humanity that we know and cherish. St. Paul speaks of it twice in his major epistles: in Rom 5:10-11, where he seeks to find a multiplicity of images to show how, through the death of Christ, man though he is a sinner can still be at peace with God. In 2 Cor 5:18-19 he uses the same image in the very personal context of his own experience and his own ministry: "All this is from God who through Christ reconciled us to himself and gave us the ministry of reconciliation; that is, God was in Christ reconciling the world to himself, not counting their trespasses against them, and entrusting to us the message of reconciliation." One easily recognizes the theology of Paul in this formulation. It is always God who is active in the process of reconciliation and people who are reconciled; that is, the change takes place in people and the whole is accomplished through the work of Christ.[10] Where people become active in the process, it is in the ministry of reconciling, of proclaiming the word of reconciliation. The minister is one who somehow joins in the reconciling work of Christ (Colossians and Ephesians speak of Christ reconciling) and thus exercises a ministry that is directed from Christ to the world of people, to bring them to peace with God.

The proclamation of the message of reconciliation is not merely preaching. It can take many forms and be exercised by many different persons in the church who devote themselves to bringing about in people those changes that lead to peace with God. That is why I have argued that the reconciliation of ministries does not take place primarily in the forms of ministry but in its finality. I think it is being true to our New Testament heritage to suggest that the church must accept and create forms of ministry which will help unite us, that is, the community must perceive what ministries respond to its needs for reconciliation with God by proclaiming the message of Christ.

[10]See F. Büchsel in *TDNT*, vol. 1, p. 255.

The Gospel
and the Church*

The title is not at all original and is not meant to be. It is taken from a very famous book (first published in 1902) by a French Catholic priest, Alfred Loisy. It was a book that caused an enormous storm, so much so that within a year Loisy himself wrote another book about the book and about the reception that it got. In 1976 the English translation of Loisy's *The Gospel and the Church* was republished in a new edition with an introduction.[1] It struck me that this would be a suitable occasion to discuss the significance of this book and some of the things that have happened since. Thus my purpose in this paper is to talk about some aspects of that book when it appeared in 1902, then to follow one or two of the issues that it raised into the 1970's, and finally to focus very briefly on what I think may be one of the most central issues in Catholic theology today.

Background

In order to understand something about the storm that accompanied the publication of Loisy's book, it is worthwhile

*First published in *Theology Digest* 24 (1976) 338-348.
[1] Alfred Loisy, *The Gospel and the Church*, ed. Bernard B. Scott (Philadelphia: Fortress Press, 1976).

to review very sketchily some of the background of the situation in Catholic theology and biblical studies at the end of the 19th century when Loisy came on the scene. I will oversimplify considerably, but I hope make the point, by suggesting that at the end of the 19th century a strange reversal had taken place regarding the role of the Bible in the Christian churches. Ever since the Reformation, Catholicism found itself in opposition to Protestantism in large measure over the authority, the role, and the function of the Bible in Christian thought. Protestants had championed the Bible in opposition to the traditional Catholic reliance on the authority of the church and its traditions. In the battle over the Bible it was as though the Protestants were the defenders and the Catholics the attackers. But in the 19th century that picture changed somewhat. With the awakening and growth of scientific progress of all kinds, and more especially with the rise of rationalism which attacked the Bible as a historical document, the Catholic Church found itself suddenly become the defender of the Bible over against liberal Protestantism.

The Catholic stance of defense in the latter part of the 19th century in particular was actually against the whole spirit of the time. In 1864 Pope Pius IX published his Syllabus of Errors, which even condemned a statement like the following: "The Roman Pontiff can and should reconcile himself to and agree with progress, liberalism, and modern civilization." So strong was the antipathy of that period toward all those things represented by the so-called liberal and scientific spirit that the church found itself forced into opposition. One of the notable victims of this situation was biblical scholarship. The age was one of archaeological discovery, of linguistic breakthroughs, and of attempts to understand the ancient cultures that underlay the biblical books. In the midst of that age, because these things were allied with the spirit of progress and scientism, the church found itself continually standing in opposition.

Providentissimus Deus

By 1893 Pope Leo XIII in his famous encyclical *Providentissimus Deus* made a valiant attempt to rescue biblical studies from the negative bastion in which they were imprisoned. He tried to promote scientific biblical scholarship, to stimulate it in a variety of ways, and particularly to encourage scholars to carry it on under the aegis and in the name of the church itself. He was of course cautious in the encyclical, but I think not over cautious. But *Providentissimus Deus* may have been somewhat ahead of its time because it was soon misunderstood. Very quickly it was taken to be an attack on biblical scholarship, not an attempt to foster it. That attitude was stimulated in later years by the condemnation of Modernism; and a situation developed in 1920 wherein a subsequent Pope, Benedict XV, would issue another encyclical on biblical studies, *Spiritus Paraclitus*, in which in several paragraphs he actually undertook to refute his predecessor.

The immediate occasion for Leo XIII's encyclical had been a tempest that grew up in France over the question of biblical studies. In the newspapers and the magazines of the day it was referred to as "la question biblique." The biblical question grew up around a young professor at the Institut Catholique in Paris, Alfred Loisy. Loisy had been born in 1857, gone through a normal seminary education and showed himself particularly talented in the area of biblical languages and history. He was encouraged to go on developing himself in these areas and by 1893, the year of the encyclical, he had been teaching the Bible for several years. As a young student, he had been allowed to attend lectures at the Collège de France where he heard the famous ex-Catholic rationalist, Ernest Renan, lecturing on the Bible. The young Loisy made the resolve that he was going to learn as much as Renan knew in terms of languages, history, and all those auxiliary disciplines that are necessary for the biblical scholar, in order that he might refute Renan's position. He went at that learning with great zeal, determining that it had to consist of scientific method, a scientific knowledge of languages and an appreciation of the magnificent finds that archaeology was bringing to attention. It had to be the strict methodology of the historian as such that could be used to counteract the force of Renan's rationalism and indeed of his attacks on the church.

A Defender of the Church

Throughout all this period, however, Loisy himself in his own teaching was very ambivalent in his relationship to the church and indeed to authority in general. He regarded himself in no uncertain terms as very much on the side of the church, a defender of it and a spokesman for it, in a sense, in the world of biblical scholarship. And yet, he found it very difficult to live with church authority—a situation which of course has been known in history both long before Loisy and indeed often after him.

In 1900 the great German Lutheran historian Adolf von Harnack wrote a book that was to become one of his most famous works even though it was a slight one in comparison to some of his major scientific works. The book was called in German, *Das Wesen des Christentums* ("The Essence of Christianity.")[2] It was an attempt on Harnack's part to use strict historical methods, or so he claimed, to reduce Christianity to a very simple kind of message which could be of universal appeal and which need not end up in the elaborate kinds of organizations that churches found themselves in. Harnack's analysis of the Gospels and of the New Testament revealed that the essence of Christianity was the message of Jesus himself. The message of Jesus was simply this: God is the Father of all mankind and all mankind should be united in love for one another in brotherhood. No one could fault that ideal, but that this should be the totality, the essence as it were, of Jesus' message and consequently the message of Christians in the world, caused great scandal

[2]Adolf von Harnack, *What is Christianity?* Tr. T.B. Saunders (New York: G.P. Putnam's Sons, 1901).

and great offense particularly to many Catholics. Harnack's reduction of the message of Jesus, as Loisy saw it, left no room for a church. The church was neither needed nor indeed was it consistent with the message of Jesus. So when the book was translated into French and began to attract a good deal of attention there, Loisy, who had in fact been reading it since it first appeared in German, set out to write a kind of answer to it. His criticism of the book was to take the form of a statement of his own which would be his analysis of the message of Jesus. He called his own little book simply "The Gospel and the Church."

Loisy: Historian

What was characteristic of this book more than anything else was Loisy's firm desire that he should write solely as a historian, a historian who was in complete command of historical methods and who knew precisely how to interpret the literary monuments of the past in order to understand that past. He makes a sharp distinction in the book between the work of a theologian and the work of a historian.

> The historian as such need not constitute himself either apologist or adversary. He knows [the Messiahship of Jesus] simply as a conception or a force whose antecedents, central manifestation and indefinite progress, he can analyze up to a point, but whose deep meaning and secret power are not things that can be deduced from analysis or critical discussion of texts and facts [pp. 50-51].

The "deep meaning" and the "secret power" of Jesus as Messiah was something that Loisy relegated to the realm of the theologian. He was to be a historian and to analyze the sources in such a way as to recreate whatever one could certainly say about Jesus' message. It was his intention from the outset to show that Harnack's reduction of the message of Jesus to a proclamation of the Fatherhood of God was wrong, wrong because it was not the result of true historical method.

He states very clearly that the purpose of his book is really to examine two things. He wants to study the gospel, that is the four Gospels of the New Testament, and discover in it just what was the message of Jesus. Then he wants to examine the church and try to discover just what was its relationship to the message of Jesus. First of all, in analyzing the Gospels Loisy seeks to find the heart of Jesus' message not merely in that Jesus proclaimed the Fatherhood of God but in that Jesus proclaimed himself as the Messiah and the Son of God.

Anticipation of Form Criticism

In dealing with the Gospels Loisy put forward a method of understanding them which was somewhat novel for his own day, and it is this that I want to single out as important. He regarded the Gospels as the product of the Christian community's reflections about what Jesus said and did and was. In this sense, Loisy anticipated by about 20 years what came to be known in modern New Testament scholarship as the method of form criticism. He didn't anticipate the meticulous analysis of passages along the lines that the modern form critics use, but what he anticipated was the principle that underlies the method of the modern form critic. That principle is simply that the Gospels are not *records* of what Jesus said and did, but rather *interpretations* of what Jesus said and did, interpretations which get their form from the ongoing reflections of Christian communities in whom the memories of Jesus are lodged. But these memories are not simply kept as in a bank but rather discussed, interpreted, re-interpreted, and above all used to meet the occasions of the early Christians' lives in which they needed the insight of Jesus.

> The Gospels must be regarded as a partial expression of the great movement that proceeded from the preaching of Jesus. The literary tradition of the gospel has followed the

evolution of primitive Christianity. The two explain one another; and if the critical analysis of the Gospels necessarily precedes the reconstitution of evangelical and apostolic history, it is none the less true that, by a sort of reciprocity, it is the primitive history of Christianity that explains the composition of the Gospels, and throws light on those particular points that are most disconcerting for minds unused to criticism. Once understood and presented as a product and a witness of an ancient faith, the Gospels, however critically analyzed, will be no longer a dangerous trial to the faith of our contemporaries [pp. 35-36].

In that statement, which is made in a variety of forms throughout his discussion of the Gospels, Loisy is actually enunciating what later came to be recognized as a fundamental principle for any understanding of the Gospels.

The Church

Secondly, in the book Loisy investigated the church and concluded with Harnack that the church indeed was not established by Jesus as such but rather was formed by Jesus' followers. But for Loisy the church was just as necessary as the gospel. He saw it as essential that if the followers of Jesus were to be true to Jesus' own message, that is, the proclamation of the coming Kingdom of God and the proclamation that Jesus is the herald, the Messiah of that Kingdom, a church was absolutely indispensable. So Loisy from his analysis believed Jesus himself had preached that a society of human beings was necessary so that the Kingdom of God could come into being. And consequently, when a society of human beings organized itself after Jesus' time into a church to propagate that message, it was being true with an absolute necessity to the message of Jesus. Indeed the heart of Loisy's thinking about the church is this concept of its absolute necessity. One can question him at this point as to whether or not that is the conclusion of a historian, but nevertheless he makes it and insists upon it.

Everyone who has ever heard of Loisy's book *The Gospel and the Church* remembers this one line from it: "Jesus announced the kingdom, and it was the church that came." But that famous line is taken out of context by friend and foe alike. One can read it cynically, obviously, or one can also read it piously. This is what he really said:

> Jesus announced the kingdom, and it was the Church that came; she came, enlarging the form of the gospel, which it was impossible to preserve as it was, as soon as the Passion closed the ministry of Jesus. There is no institution on the earth or in history whose status and value may not be questioned if the principle is established that nothing may exist except in its original form. Such a principle is contrary to the law of life, which is movement and a continual effort of adaptation to conditions always new and perpetually changing. Christianity has not escaped this law, and cannot be reproached for submission to it. It could not do otherwise than it has done [p. 166].

When Loisy refers to the "law of life which is movement and a continual effort of adaptation to conditions always new and perpetually changing," he refers to a principle that lay at the heart of the movement of which he was soon to be recognized as the guiding spirit, the Modernist movement in Catholic theology.

Tradition

Now I would like to insist upon an analogy between the way Loisy recognized the Gospels as the product of the early Christian community, and therefore subject to an interpretation which comes from understanding what those communities were and how they functioned, and on the other hand his understanding of the church and the kind of pronouncements that the church has made and can make. He insists that the developmental aspect of the Gospels is also true of dogmatic pronouncements of the church. They are subject to development and reformulation because they are part of that law of life which is adaptation to continual change.

> Any one who has followed the progress of Christian thought from the beginning must perceive that neither the Christological dogma nor the dogma of grace nor that of the Church is to be taken for a summit of doctrine, beyond which no prospect opens for the believer or can ever open except the dazzling distance of infinite mystery; it is not to be expected that these dogmas will remain firmer than the rock, inaccessible even to accidental change, and yet intelligible for all generations and equally applicable without any new translation or explanation, to all states, and to every advance of science, life, and human society. The conceptions that the Church presents as revealed dogmas are not truths fallen from heaven, and preserved by religious tradition in the precise form in which they first appeared. The historian sees in them the interpretation of religious facts, acquired by a laborious effort of theological thought. Though the dogmas may be Divine in origin and substance, they are human in structure and composition. It is inconceivable that their future should not correspond to their past. Reason never ceases to put questions to faith, and traditional formulas are submitted to a constant work of interpretation wherein "the letter that killeth" is effectively controlled by "the spirit that giveth life" [pp. 210-211].

Just as here Loisy speaks of the fact that dogmatic statements, like biblical statements, are subject to the conditioning of the culture in which they are expressed, so here too he anticipates a position that was to be taken by the church only some 70 years later.

There were of course shortcomings in *The Gospel and the Church*. I have singled out only two points, neither of which I think Loisy regarded as his main points, and yet perhaps they were the ones that most frightened the traditional theology of the day. When one reads this book today one notices shortcomings in it. I would include among these what I think is his too absolute divorce between historians and theologians. I think he takes a very simplistic approach to Jesus' own messianic self-consciousness. A modern interpreter of the Gospels would be much more nuanced. I think he departs from his strict historical methods when he discusses the sacramental system of the church. And there are other failings in the book. But in terms of modern Catholic biblical scholarship and modern ecclesiology, Loisy's book was prophetic; and if Loisy played, at least in part, the role of a prophet, like most prophets he was severely criticized.

Storm of Reaction

There was a storm of reaction from Catholics over the book once it was published, and most of them ignored the fact that Loisy had set out to defend the church against Harnack. They saw his book as an insidious attack on the Church veiled in the form of a historical apologetic. Within six months the book was banned in eight French dioceses. One of the charges leveled against it, incidentally, was that the book had no imprimatur. Loisy responded that it didn't need one because it was not a theology book but a work of history.

In the midst of the storm of reaction Loisy capitulated to the church, and even though he had prepared a second edition of the book, he withdrew it before it could get into circulation. On the other hand, however, he sat down immediately to write a little book about his book which appeared one year later in 1903, called "Concerning a Little Book." It was an ironically modest title, given the storm that raged.[3] I think it was an example of his personal ambivalence that with one hand he could capitulate and withdraw the second edition, but with the other hand write a book about the book which drew even more attention to his thesis. In the latter he argued that Catholics had to get involved in

---

[3]*Autour d'un petit livre* (Paris: Alphonse Picard et Fils, 1903).

modern science, historiography, and the like

> ...under the penalty of excommunicating themselves
> from intellectual society and of preparing for the near
> future a crisis much more to be feared than all those
> which Christian faith had undergone since its beginnings
> [pp. xvi-xvii].
>
> *The Gospel and the Church* was written to explain how
> the Catholic principle, by virtue of its inexhaustible
> fruitfulness, can be adapted to all forms of human
> progress. But the adaptation, in the past, has never taken
> place without effort. And so it will be in the future
> [p. xxxvi].

Relativism?

One might think there is a prophetic tone to those remarks
also. Loisy is fair in this little book about the book because
in it he not only tries to explain himself a bit further and to
counteract the attacks made on his book, but even cites the
attacks made on his book so that his critics may have their
say. Of all the critics whom he cites, the one who was most
perceptive in my opinion was the great 20th-century Catholic
biblical scholar, the founder of the Ecole Biblique in Jerusalem and the founder of one of the great series of
commentaries and studies on the Bible, Père Lagrange.
Lagrange was to become a lifelong adversary of Loisy.
When the Modernist crisis arose in the church, Lagrange
himself was thought by many people to be tainted with the
same stamp as Loisy himself. In his criticism of Loisy there
occurs this line which I think is very central to understanding
just what Loisy was after:

> Relativism is the fundamental error of Loisy, which alone
> allows him to continue to remain within the Church
> without agreeing with it on the essential points [*Ibid.*, p.
> 293].

Aftermath

The aftermath of Loisy's little book is a well known story that I shall not go into in detail. Within a very few years when Loisy's ambivalence toward the Catholic Church was vacillating from one side to the other, he soon became the symbol and the guiding spirit of that amorphous movement called Modernism which in 1907 was decisively condemned by Pope Pius X. The condemnation did not mention specific figures like Loisy, but among the statements which were condemned there were several direct quotations from Loisy. He refused to withdraw his publication and in 1908 he was formally excommunicated.

Shortly thereafter he was invited to become professor at the Collège de France and to occupy the chair of Renan whom he had set out many years before to refute. He never became reconciled with Catholicism. He continued to be a very competent biblical scholar, exercising the critical methods of biblical interpretation which he had espoused earlier with great finesse and skill. He became increasingly rationalist, however, particularly in his attitude toward the church. In the last year of his life (1940) he stated poignantly, "Never have I realized so clearly how little a weak man, whose pen is his only weapon, can do." When Loisy died he left behind his own epitaph, which is famous for its ambiguity and perhaps for that very reason a fitting epitaph for Loisy. It is written in French except for the last line, which I shall leave in untranslated Latin: "Alfred Loisy, Priest. Retired from the ministry and from teaching. Professor at the Collège de France. *Tuam in votis tenuit voluntatem.*"[4]

The Dark Period

For nearly 40 years in the wake of the condemnation of Modernism and the rejection of Loisy's methodologies for

[4]See Alec Vidler, *A Variety of Catholic Modernists* (Cambridge: University Press, 1970) 44.

interpreting the Bible, Catholic biblical scholarship lived through and somehow survived what some people have called its darkest period in history. Its details are not part of my intention in this lecture. Everyone has heard of the role of the Biblical Commission, which was thwarted from the original plan of Leo XIII to stimulate biblical scholarship and instead was forced into the position of being a watchdog over biblical scholarship. The negativism of Benedict XV, particularly in his encyclical on the fifteen-hundredth anniversary of the birth of St. Jerome, marked the spirit of the period. In the midst of it all one might be more optimistic and look at the heroic work of Père Lagrange at the Ecole Biblique in Jerusalem, where he continued to use and refine as much as possible the methods of modern critical biblical scholarship and survived, I should say rather rose above, the debates that swirled at his feet. The slow regaining of stature of biblical scholarship in Catholicism really began in 1943 when Pope Pius XII issued his famous encyclical *Divino Afflante Spiritu*. This encyclical accepted and gave positive encouragement to the historical critical method of biblical interpretation, the method which Loisy had advocated.

Second Vatican Council

This regaining of stature on the part of modern Catholic biblical scholarship reached its culmination in the Second Vatican Council, which was made dramatic by the turbulent history of the Constitution on Divine Revelation, which talked about the role of the Bible in theology and how the Bible is to be interpreted. This Constitution was the focal point which finally crystallized the spirit of the Council when it was brought before the Council Fathers in successive versions in such wise that the last was virtually the antithesis of the first. The major importance of that Constitution for the issues that I have been raising from Loisy's book is that it formally accepted the validity and the necessity of a form critical approach to the Gospels. That is to say, that it formally and critically accepted the basic principle that the

Gospels are given their shape and form by the life of the early Christian church. They were recognized as products of the primitive Christian communities as Loisy himself had long ago insisted they were. One might say that that document accepted in principle the relativism of the biblical word and the need for hermeneutics to interpret it.

Vatican II did not extend this concept of the relativism of the biblical word to dogmatic formulations as Loisy had done, but it was inevitable that that should eventually follow. In fact, in convoking the Council, John XXIII had prophetically made a statement that was shocking then and is often repeated. He said in his opening speech, "The substance of the ancient doctrine of the deposit of faith is one thing, and the way in which it is presented is another." This led in the Constitution on Divine Revelation to seeing God's revelation primarily in non-propositional terms, to seeing God revealing himself in the person of Christ, or God revealing himself in the actions that guided Israel through the centuries. After the Second Vatican Council it was only to be expected that some of the great theologians of the day such as Rahner or Schillebeeckx, both of whom had played important roles in the Council itself, and especially the American theologian Avery Dulles,[5] should take up this point and argue the case that dogmatic statements were just as much in need of a hermeneutic or interpretive process as biblical texts were, because both of these were expressed in a human language that was subject to the conditions of the period in which it was uttered. Finally, after much discussion of these questions, in 1973 the Congregation for the Doctrine of Faith issued a document, apropos of the theological statements on infallibility by Hans Küng, in which it explicitly though hesitatingly accepted the principle that even dogmatic formulations are conditioned by the cultural factors of their time and place. This document is called *Mysterium Ecclesiae*, and the following are some excerpts.[6]

---

[5]See Avery Dulles, *The Survival of Dogma* (Garden City: Doubleday, 1971), part III.

[6]Quoted from Raymond E. Brown, *Biblical Reflections on Crises Facing the Church* (New York: Paulist Press, 1975) 116-117; see also 3-19.

The transmission of divine revelation by the Church encounters difficulties of various kinds. These arise from the fact that "the hidden mysteries of God by their nature so far transcend the human intellect that even if they are revealed to us and accepted by faith, they remain concealed by the veil of faith itself and are, as it were, wrapped in darkness" (Vatican I). Difficulties also arise from the historical condition that affects the expression of revelation.

(1) With regard to this historical condition, it must first be observed that the meaning of the pronouncements of faith depends partly on the expressive power of the language used at a certain point in time and in particular circumstances.

(2) Moreover, it sometimes happens that some dogmatic truth is first expressed incompletely (but not falsely), and at a later date, when considered in a broader context of faith or human knowledge, it receives a fuller and more perfect expression.

(3) In addition, when the Church makes new pronouncements, she intends to confirm or clarify what is in some way contained in Sacred Scripture or in previous expressions of Tradition. But at the same time she usually has the intention of solving certain questions or removing certain errors. All these things have to be taken into account in order that these pronouncements may be properly interpreted.

(4) Finally, even though the truths which the Church intends to teach through her dogmatic formulas are distinct from the changeable conceptions of a given epoch and can be expressed without them, nevertheless, it can sometimes happen that these truths may be enunciated by the Sacred Magisterium in terms that bear the traces of such conceptions.

That is rather abstract language, but the point is clear. The Congregation is acknowledging that even the dogmatic formulations of the church are the product of their time and their culture, are dependent upon the way language is understood at the time that they are uttered. They must be reinterpreted; indeed they are reformable. That is precisely the point that Loisy himself had made about dogmatic formulations 70 years before. Thus, two of Loisy's main points which in 1903 had raised such a storm have been more or less officially admitted into Catholic theology. I should call these the historical relativity of the Bible and the historical relativity of dogmatic statements. The consequences of this step, which were greatly feared in Loisy's time, now have to be faced by the church and by its theologians.

Communication and Tradition

My point has not been to suggest that Loisy was right after all. That would not be entirely correct in my opinion and certainly not historically responsible. Nor is my point to bemoan the history of 20th-century Catholic theology or Catholic biblical scholarship. Instead my point is to sharpen for us, to localize if you wish, what I consider to be at the same time the anxiety and the challenge and the opportunity of Catholic theology today. It is a theology which must ever learn an old lesson: how to speak to the modern world in a language it can understand while at the same time faithfully interpreting its traditions. For some people, to suggest that the formulations, whether biblical or dogmatic, in which revelation is enshrined are relative, poses a threat, in the same manner that it posed a threat to the church in reaction to Loisy's book many years ago. I would like in conclusion to say a word about this threat and to put it in the context of the central doctrine of Catholic Christianity.

The Incarnation

The central doctrine of Catholic Christianity is not the doctrine of the church. It is not the doctrine of the inspiration of Scripture. The central doctrine of Catholic Christianity is the doctrine of the incarnation. It is the belief that in Jesus Christ, the divine Son became truly and fully human. When one reflects on the reaction to Loisy and on some of the anxieties of modern people in the church, one has to agree that quite naturally and quite understandably the church had for a long time allowed itself to yearn for a situation in which God would provide biblical and dogmatic access to the truth about himself and his Son, would provide revelation, that is, which is exempt from the laws and the limitations of human discourse. The church had allowed itself, and many Christians still do, to yearn for that point at which God will speak directly, not through the muddled confusion of human utterance: there must be somewhere some words of God that are immune to the interpretive processes that we of necessity have to exercise when we try to understand one another.

But in that yearning the church sought a privilege that was not granted even to the Son of God. In the incarnaton, God entrusted his Son to humanity in its fullest sense. One might say that it is a consequence of the doctrine of the incarnation that God can be portrayed as taking the risk of revealing himself in the human. If all the utterances by which revelation is communicated to us are utterances in human language, that is, as is often said, if God speaks to us in the language of humanity, then we must interpret God's speech as we interpret the language of humanity. The church should not shy away from accepting that same risk which God may be said to have taken in the greatest mystery of our faith. The church can do so, and with confidence, if it does not forget the promise that God is with us.

Part Three

Gnosticism

11

Nag Hammadi
and the New Testament*

The aim of this contribution is to assess in a schematic way the impact of the Nag Hammadi library on the question of Gnosticism and the New Testament. We may begin with some observations on the state of Gnostic studies prior to the Nag Hammadi discovery.

At approximately the time the discovery was made public in 1948-49,[1] the great authority on Valentinianism F.-M.-M. Sagnard wrote an article on the "Theological Relevance of a Study of Christian Gnosis" in which he was able to mention the New Testament only peripherally and without any real contact with the Gnostic phenomenon. The origins of Gnosticism, he asserted, were impossible to ascertain, and though it had deep roots in the ancient pagan milieu before Christ, "It is at the beginning of the second century, at the moment the last of the Apostles disappeared, that it mingles closely with Christianity as though to smother it."[2] It is true

---

* First published in *Gnosis. Festschrift für Hans Jonas* (Göttingen: Vandenhoeck & Ruprecht, 1978) 144-157.

[1] One of the most significant announcements was that of H.-Ch. Puech and J. Doresse, "Nouveaux écrits gnostiques découverts en Egypte," *Académie des Inscriptions et Belles Lettres, Comptes rendus des séances de l'année 1948* (Paris, 1948) 87-95.

[2] "Intérêt théologique d'une étude de la gnose chrétienne," *RScPhTh* 33 (1949) 163.

that Sagnard's article is concerned only with Valentinianism, thus with "Christian Gnosticism" properly so-called, but this itself is indicative of the situation of the period. Too little was known of other Gnostic sects, at least first hand, to bring them into consideration.

In a similar vein the late Msgr. Lucien Cerfaux, one of the very best students of Gnosticism in the first half of the century, could also treat the subject as more or less irrelevant for understanding the New Testament. In particular in a 1940 essay he argued against the view of Harnack and others that Gnosticism contributed to the beginnings of Christian theology: "The Gnostics did not carry their stone to the edifice of Christian theology nor did they anticipate it; had it depended on them alone, Christianity would have foundered in a pagan theosophy like all those of Hellenistic syncretism."[3] When that essay was reprinted in 1954 in the first volume of his "Recueil," after the Nag Hammadi discoveries had been announced and briefly described, Cerfaux added in a note: "General studies on Gnosticism (and Valentinianism in particular) are stagnant while awaiting the publication of the manuscripts discovered at Nag Hammadi."[4]

But not all scholars prior to mid-century regarded the study of Gnosticism as more or less irrelevant to the New Testament. The views of the so-called *Religionsgeschichtliche Schule* still prevailed in some circles. We might quote as an example the late Rudolf Bultmann's short essay on Gnosticism in his "Primitive Christianity in its Contemporary Setting," which first appeared in its German original in 1949. Far from dismissing the subject, he asserts that Gnosticism is closely bound up with the earliest Christian reflections:

> It first appeared and attracted the attention of scholars as a movement within the Christian religion, and for a long time it was regarded as purely Christian movement, a perversion of the Christian faith into a speculative

---

[3]"La gnose, essai théologique manqué," *Irénikon* 17 (1940) 3-20; cited from *Recueil Lucien Cerfaux* (Gembloux, 1954) I, p. 277.

[4]Ibid., p. 278.

theology, the "acute Hellenization of Christianity." Further research has, however, made it abundantly clear that it was really a religious movement of pre-Christian origin, invading the West from the Orient as a competitor of Christianity ... In general we may call it a redemptive religion based on dualism. This is what gives it an affinity to Christianity, an affinity of which even its adherents were aware. Consequently, Gnosticism and Christianity have affected each other in a number of different directions from the earliest days of the Christian movement. True, Christianity gradually came to draw a line of demarcation in its struggle against Gnosticism, and although certain features in the Gnostic imagery claimed a rightful place within the Church, other Gnostic ideas were not only ignored, but bitterly resisted.[5]

The manner in which Bultmann himself invoked Gnostic backgrounds to explain many things in Pauline and especially Johannine theology is familiar to every student of the New Testament today. The state of the question of Gnosticism and the New Testament at mid-century can thus best be described as a stand-off.[6] And as Cerfaux remarked in 1954, only new evidence could make a contribution to the question. The evidence to which many of the History of Religions School appealed—in Bultmann's case, as is well known, the sources most often cited were Mandaean, Hermetic, even Manichean, sometimes the Odes of Solomon—was always problematic at least chronologically. The prudent position was that of the opponents, the majority of New Testament scholars no doubt, who still sought *evidence* of a pre-Christian Gnosticism. It is my contention here that such evidence as we have now in the Nag Hammadi library tends to vindicate the position of Bultmann, or perhaps more accurately that of Hans Jonas, who writes:

---

[5] *Primitive Christianity in its Contemporary Setting* (New York, 1965) 162.

[6] For a good survey of the issues see E.M.Yamauchi, *Pre-Christian Gnosticism. A Survey of the Proposed Evidence* (Grand Rapids, 1973). I would not, however, accept the conclusions of this work without qualifications.

As to the much debated question of "pre-Christian Gnosticism"—undecidable on the present evidence—I personally consider its importance overrated. What matters is that Gnosticism is roughly contemporaneous with the infancy of Christianity (certainly not later, witness Simon Magus; possibly earlier); that it is different and independent from it, but with natural points of contact, answering to the same human situation; and that from the start there was vigorous interpenetration of the two which provoked the well-known reactions in the Church.[7]

I should prefer deliberately to avoid the problem of definition and terminology to which R. McL. Wilson has given considerable attention in his book "Gnosis and the New Testament"[8] and in several articles. Whether and how one should restrict the terms "Gnosis," "Gnosticism," "Gnostic," "pre-Gnostic" and "proto-Gnostic," as the 1966 Messina Colloquium on the Origins of Gnosticism proposed, is not of course unimportant for the scholarly dialogue. But for the New Testament scholar who asks whether the topic in general is pertinent to the New Testament discipline, it is not the terminology that matters most. It is instead the issue of the originality of early Christian theology and language. Is the Christian message the product of the confrontation of Jewish and Old Testament language and imagery with Greek expression, or are there more factors involved? Is Hellenistic Christianity, in Bultmann's words, "the outcome of syncretism"[9] in which Gnosticism played a prominent role? If Gnosticism is correctly described, as I believe it is, as an essentially mythological religious phenomenon, did its myths play a creative role in the shaping of New Testament thought? It is over this issue ultimately that the scholarly

---

[7]"Delimitation of the Gnostic Phenomenon-Typological and Historical," U. Bianchi (ed.), *Le origini dello gnosticismo* (Leiden, 1967) 103.

[8](Oxford, 1968) 9ff.

[9]*Primitive Christianity in its Contemporary Setting,* 178.

stand-off was established. To what extent has the intervening quarter-century altered the picture?

Before discussing the promise and the achievement of the Nag Hammadi discovery we must call attention to one fact at the outset. The Nag Hammadi library does nothing to resolve the classic chronological challenge to Gnostic sources. That is to say that those who demand a chronologically pre-Christian Gnostic document in order to accept the argument that Gnosticism is older than the second century A.D. will not be shaken by the publication of a mid-fourth-century collection of Coptic translations. And even if we are on solid ground in some cases in arguing that the original works represented in the library are much older than the extant copies, we are still unable to postulate plausibly any pre-Christian dates.

But here is where the very methodologies of biblical scholarship should be recalled—and extended to some non-biblical literature. The biblical scholar does not call into question the existence of the sources of the Pentateuch just because he has access to no copy of the Pentateuch that antedates the Dead Sea Scrolls. Similarly the New Testament scholar does not doubt the existence of Q or the Johannine signs source solely on the grounds that no pre-Gospel exemplar of these documents has been preserved. The purely chronological challenge to the argument for a pre-Christian Gnosticism is in other words an illegitimate argument if we are to remain faithful to the very methods we use in analyzing other literature, and therefore it should be laid to rest. The interpreter's challenge is to deal with the interpretation of the texts and to draw the conclusions that best commend themselves to reason and analysis.

If the Nag Hammadi library does not give us access to any clearly pre-Christian Gnostic document, what it does do, in a variety of ways, is demonstrate a developmental model within Gnosticism itself that leads from a non-Christian Gnostic myth to a patently christianized version. If this movement corresponds to the genesis of Gnosticism itself, its importance lies in the fact that so-called Christian Gnosticism is a secondary phenomenon—secondary not only to Christianity but to Gnosticism itself. The most striking instance of this development in the Nag Hammadi collection is one in which it can be observed as a *literary* process. The collection— if we include Berlin Codex 8502 discovered by Carl Schmidt in 1896 but published only in 1955[10]—contains two copies each of two closely related documents: "Eugnostos the Blessed" (III, 3 and V, 1) and "The Sophia of Jesus Christ" (III, 4 and BG 8502, 3). The first is a treatise about "the ordering of the world" (*dioikēsis tou kosmou*) in which the author rejects the opinions of "the philosophers" that the world is governed by itself, by providence, or by destiny, and then goes on to reveal in classic Gnostic language the supreme "Father of the All" and the many spiritual beings that populate his realm. This treatise, however, contains no clear trace of Christian influence and must be regarded as an example of non-Christian Gnostic speculation.[11] "The Sophia of Jesus Christ," however, is a revelation given by the risen Jesus to his disciples in the form of answers to their questions—a literary genre frequently used by Christian Gnostics. The disciples are portrayed as confused "about the nature (*hypostasis*) of the All and the plan" (i.e. of salvation, *oikonomia*). What Jesus tells them, verbatim in most passages, is the contents of "Eugnostos the Blessed," punctuated by questions from the disciples which serve only to maintain the superficial and obviously secondary genre of the dialogue. Almost all of "Eugnostos" is contained in "The Sophia," but it is augmented by a Sophia myth and by an emphasis on Gnostic soteriology, both of which are only hinted at in "Eugnostos." Martin Krause has shown, quite convincingly, that the direction of literary dependence in this unusual case is clear: "The Sophia of Jesus Christ" is a reworking of "Eugnostos the Blessed," and not the reverse.[12]

[10]W.C. Till, revised by H.-M. Schenke, *Die gnostischen Schriften des koptischen Papyrus Berolinensis 8502* (Berlin, 1972).

[11]R. McL. Wilson, *Gnosis and the New Testament*, pp. 115f., points out some possibly Christian phrases, but they are at best doubtful.

[12]"Das literarische Verhältnis des Eugnostosbriefes zur Sophia Jesu Christi," *Mullus. Festschrift für Theodor Klauser* (Münster, 1964) 215-223.

Or to put the situation differently, "The Sophia of Jesus Christ" is the Christian appropriation of a non-Christian Gnostic work. This may, however, be a slightly oversimplified picture, since it is possible that both extant copies of "Eugnostos" are themselves dependent on a *Grundschrift* used by "The Sophia."[13] If so, the argument for christianizing remains valid. The fact that we are dealing with material that is notably older than the fourth- and fifth-century Nag Hammadi and Berlin copies is attested by the existence of a substantial Greek fragment of "The Sophia of Jesus Christ," Oxyrhynchus Papyrus 1081, certainly older than our Coptic translations and dated by its editor A.S. Hunt to the late third century.[14]

The relationship between these two of the Nag Hammadi documents affords a unique opportunity to observe the process of christianization at work. The case for non-Christian Gnosticism in the collection as a whole can be made by appealing to a number of other documents—apart from the Hermetic Tractates of Codex VI which are obviously non-Christian—some of them without any evidence of Christian reworking and others even more superficially christianized than "The Sophia of Jesus Christ." I shall mention only one further example of a pair of related tractates.

"The Apocalypse of Adam" (V, 5) has already attracted a good deal of attention and debate about its origin and character. Formally it is a revelation of gnosis communicated by Adam to his son Seth as a prophecy of the course of Gnostic salvation history from Adam himself to the final coming of the Gnostic revealer or redeemer and the triumph of the Gnostics, the descendants of Seth, over their enemies. In many respects the story covers ground familiar in a number of Gnostic tractates as well as in the patristic accounts of Gnosticism, and though the work suggests a

[13]Ibid. and see Wilson, *Gnosis and the New Testament*, 116f.

[14]The fragment has recently been republished by H. W. Attridge, "P. Oxy. 1081 and the Sophia Jesu Christi," *Enchoria* 5 (1975) 1-8.

certain primitiveness in its dissociation of the creator god
from the god of truth, even this trait corresponds to a
familiar Gnostic exegetical tradition. What makes "The
Apocalypse of Adam" controversial is the fact that it
contains no unmistakably Christian allusions, and the
ultimate revealer figure is at least not clearly portrayed as
Christ. Therefore many scholars have seen in it an example
of an early non-Christian Gnostic treatise that is neverthless
fully Gnostic even to the presence of a redeemer myth.[15]
Another Nag Hammadi work, "The Gospel of the Egyptians"
(not related to the work of the name cited by Clement of
Alexandria) or "The Holy Book of the Great Invisible
Spirit" (III, 2 and IV, 2), is closely related to "The Apocalypse
of Adam" but by no means dependent on it in a literary
sense. "The Gospel of the Egyptians" portrays Seth himself
as the Gnostic heavenly redeemer who in his final coming is
explicitly identified with Christ. This work is clearly a
product of Christian Gnosticism, but a close analysis of it
and a comparison with "The Apocalypse of Adam" suggest
that here we have another glimpse of the process by which
an originally non-Christian Gnostic myth was appropriated
and at least superficially christianized.[16] By the time one gets
to Valentinianism, for example, the christianizing process is
no longer superficial and we are dealing with an authentic
Christian Gnosticism. The important thing is that certain of
the Nag Hammadi documents tend to suggest that this
authentic Christian Gnosticism is the result of a process of
assimilating an established non-Christian Gnosticism, not a
process of heresy originating in a Christian orthodoxy.

This christianizing process has been dealt with here at
some length because to the extent that we can infer an
originally non-Christian Gnosticism, we can regard the
question of Gnostic influence on the New Testament as an
open one.

[15]See for example G. W. MacRae, "The Coptic Gnostic Apocalypse of Adam,"
Heythrop Journal 6 (1965) 27-35.

[16]See the edition of A. Böhlig and F. Wisse, *Nag Hammadi Codices, III, 2 and
IV, 2: The Gospel of the Egyptians* (Leiden, 1975).

The most fundamental issue that has dominated the study of Gnosticism in modern times, the so-called "Gnostic problem," is the question of the origin of Gnosticism. I do not intend to survey this question here except to make two observations in light of the Nag Hammadi discovery. While it may be true to say that at the present stage of analysis of the Nag Hammadi library the problem of Gnostic origins remains a problem, the range of options has at least been somewhat narrowed. For a growing number of scholars now clearly in the majority, such evidence as just observed regarding certain Nag Hammadi tractates enables us to rule out one of the oldest and most enduring options, namely that Gnosticism is to be seen as heretical offshoot from Christianity. At the same time two sets of elements in the various Gnostic treatises are becoming increasingly prominent as the documents are published and studied. These are the almost universal preponderance of Jewish influence, and not merely the use of Genesis or other biblical texts, and the central role of Greek, especially Platonic, ideas and expressions. No theory today can adequately account for the origins of Gnosticism if it does not give a prominent place— one is tempted to say the most prominent place—to Hellenistic Judaism whether in Alexandria or elsewhere in the Diaspora or even in Palestine.[17]

For my part, I believe that Gnosticism arose as a revolutionary reaction in Hellenized Jewish wisdom and apocalyptic circles. It became a rival of Christianity not only in the second century when the ecclesiastical writers such as Justin and Irenaeus identified Gnostic leaders and sects, but from the very beginnings of Christian reflection on the significance and message of Jesus. What made the rivalry the more acute—and paradoxically the more influential in shaping the formulations of some early Christians—was the natural affinity arising from a certain common parentage. The

---

[17]Among the most recent literature see for example B.A. Pearson, "Friedländer Revisited. Alexandrian Judaism and Gnostic Orgins," *Studia Philonica* 2 (1973) 23-39. See also B.A. Pearson "Biblical Exegesis in Gnostic Literature," M.E. Stone (ed.), *Armenian and Biblical Studies* (Jerusalem, 1976) 70-80.

Gnosticism of the Nag Hammadi documents is not a Christian heresy but if anything a Jewish heresy, just as primitive Christianity itself should be regarded as a Jewish heresy or set of Jewish heresies.

Thus far I have tried to suggest the way in which Nag Hammadi makes a difference for the question of Gnosticism and the New Testament by establishing the *possibility* of interaction between Gnostics and Christians during the formative period of the New Testament writings themselves. The question still remains whether it is reasonable to conclude, on the basis of analyzing both the New Testament and the Nag Hammadi library, that any interaction actually took place. But before we turn to this question, one further remark needs to be made.

If one were to single out one conclusion of modern New Testament scholarship that has drastically altered the understanding handed on from previous generations, I would point to the contemporary emphasis, fostered by the methods of historico-critical scholarship, on the diversity of early Christianity and of the various New Testament expressions of it. The New Testament is a collection, not a book, but it is a collection of very different expressions and understandings of the Christian message. To treat it as in some degree homogeneous is to misinterpret it.

Somewhat analogously, we should also avoid treating the Nag Hammadi library as a homogeneous collection. Here the issue is compounded by the fact that we really do not know the purpose of the collection in the first place. Initial archaeological investigation of the site of the find has in no sense clarified the picture, and initial examination of the documentary papyri in the bindings of the codices has in a sense actually obscured it, although these papyri have made it possible to date Codex VII with some precision to the middle of the fourth century.[18] The collection may have been the library of a group or sect of Gnostics or of an individual

---

[18]J. Barns, "Greek and Coptic Papyri from the Covers of the Nag Hammadi Codices," M. Krause (ed.), *Essays on the Nag Hammadi Texts. In Honour of Pahor Labib* (Leiden, 1975) 9-18.

Gnostic, perhaps even a monk. Or it may have been a reference collection for the use of an orthodox heresiologist or apologist, again perhaps a monk. Or it may have been simply a chance survival from a larger and even more diversified library, though I think this highly unlikely. The covers of Codex VII connect the book closely with the great Pachomian monastery at Chenoboskion, though it is difficult to place such an unorthodox set of books in that context.[19]

Whatever the purpose of the collection, its internal diversity should not be lost sight of. Not only does it contain an even greater variety of literary genres than the New Testament (gospels, acts, epistles, apocalypses, dialogues, treatises, revelation discourses, prayers, etc.), but in terms of content it embraces several different types of works both Gnostic and non-Gnostic. Of the former there are a number of Sethian works (though one should be cautious in defining Sethian Gnosticism in the Nag Hammadi collection),[20] several unmistakably Valentinian writings, and a host of others which it is not possible to classify, especially in the categories of the church fathers, which are often suspect to begin with. In Codex VI there are three Hermetic writings, two of them already known from the Corpus Hermeticum. Then there are a number of works, both previously known and new, which one would never think of as Gnostic at all. These include the passage of Plato's "Republic" badly translated into Sahidic in Codex VI, and the moralizing "Sentences of Sextus" in Codex XII which became very popular among Christians especially after Rufinus translated them into Latin. This category should probably also include "The Teachings of Silvanus" in Codex VII, which I take to be a rare example of Christian wisdom literature from a monastic milieu; part of it has been preserved in Coptic elsewhere in

[19]See T. Säve-Söderbergh, "Holy Scriptures or Apologetic Documentations? The 'Sitz im Leben' of the Nag Hammadi Library," J.-E. Ménard (ed.), *Les Textes de Nag Hammadi* (Leiden, 1975) 3-14.

[20]See F. Wisse, "The Sethians and the Nag Hammadi Library," L.C. McGaughy (ed.), *The Society of Biblical Literature One Hundred Eighth Annual Meeting Book of Seminar Papers* (Missoula, 1972) II, 601-607.

the name of St. Anthony. In addition to these one might argue the case for several other works being essentially non-Gnostic. If the purpose of the collection was to be a Gnostic library, we must suppose that there was a Gnostic tradition of exegesis of works other than the Bible. Evidence for this may be provided by "The Exegesis on the Soul" (II, 6), which interprets Homer's "Odyssey" as well as the Old and New Testaments, although the "Odyssey" was a widespread mine for allegorical exegesis throughout the period.

M. Krause somewhat differently distinguishes four categories of works in the collection: (1) non-Christian Gnostic works, e.g. "Zostrianus" (VIII, 1) and "Allogenes" (XI, 3); (2) Christian Gnostic works, which he subdivides into Christian reworkings of originally non-Christian writings, e.g. "The Nature of the Archons" (II, 4), and original Christian Gnostic writings, e.g. "The Gospel of Philip" (II, 3); (3) Hermetic texts; (4) wisdom teachings and philosophical writings, e.g. "The Sentences of Sextus" (XII, 1).[21]

We return now to the question of whether Nag Hammadi makes any difference to the arguments for actual interaction between Gnosticism and the New Testament writers. It would not be feasible to offer a broad survey of all the ways in which the Nag Hammadi documents have been brought into the exegetical discussion of the various New Testament books. Instead, I propose to mention a few examples, cursorily enough to be sure; some of them arise from unpublished research and conjectures and therefore do not represent any scholarly consensus.

To begin with the most familiar we should mention "The Gospel of Thomas" (II, 2) and the whole issue of the transmission and collection of the sayings of Jesus. In the twenty years since this collection of sayings attributed to Jesus was first published it has even won a place in our synopses of the Gospels. For much of this period the focal point of controversy has been whether "Thomas" is depend-

---

[21]"Zur Bedeutung des gnostisch-hermetischen Handschriftenfundes von Nag Hammadi," *Essays on the Nag Hammadi Texts,* 65-89.

ent on the canonical Gospels or represents an independent development of the sayings rooted in a pre-Gospel oral tradition. It now appears that a majority of scholars who have seriously investigated the matter have been won over to the side of "Thomas'" independence of the canonical Gospels, though these scholars hold a variety of views about the actual history of the composition of "The Gospel of Thomas."

This position allows for at least two important ways in which "The Gospel of Thomas" impinges upon the study of the New Testament Gospels. First, it suggests that no analysis of the sayings material in the Synoptic tradition especially can be complete without taking into account the "Thomas" version where there is a parallel. This does not mean that "Thomas" is likely to provide access to the ipsissima verba more directly than Mark or Q, of course, but it does mean that "Thomas" can contribute to discovering the history and the motivations behind the development of a particular saying. As Helmut Koester has pointed out, for example, the complete absence of apocalyptic Son of Man sayings from the Q material shared by "Thomas" gives rise to the very important possibility that this orientation was a secondary development in Q itself.[22] Secondly, the very existence of a so-called "gospel" in which there is nothing but sayings of "Jesus, the living one," that is in which there is no passion-resurrection narrative and indeed no narrative material at all, raises quetions about the theological significance of such a portrayal of Jesus. Again, as Koester has argued, such a "gospel" implies a Christology that sees Jesus as a teacher of divine wisdom—in contrast, e.g., to the suffering, dying, rising Son of Man in Mark—and this Christology has resonances in the New Testament and other early Christian literature, e.g. in Q itself or at least in its earliest stages of growth.[23]

"The Gospel of Thomas" provides a very particular kind of example of the impact of Nag Hammadi on New

---

[22]J.M. Robinson and H. Koester, *Trajectories through Early Christianity*, (Philadelphia, 1971) 186, cf. pp. 166ff.

[23]Ibid., 186f.

Testament studies. The appeal has not been to the Gnostic character of the work as such—and I believe it is a thoroughly Gnostic work though this has occasionally been challenged. Instead, the focal point here has been the process involved in the history of the traditions and the theological implications of it. Having argued for the non-Christian origin of Gnosticism and its contemporaneity with earliest Christianity, we need now to turn to an example of Gnostic influence on Christology itself. Such an example, among many possibilities, can be found in the theme of the deception of the powers. The New Testament passage in question is 1 Cor 2:6-8:

> Yet among the mature we do impart wisdom, although it is not a wisdom of this age or of the rulers of this age, who are doomed to pass away. But we impart a secret and hidden wisdom of God, which God decreed before the ages for our glorification. None of the rulers of this age understood this; for if they had, they would not have crucified the Lord of glory.

The possibility of a Gnostic background for the notion that the "powers" (i.e. spiritual powers of the universe, whether identified with human political powers or not) acted in ignorance of Jesus' true identity has often been advanced, especially be adherents of the History of Religions approach.[24] The references usually given, however, are to passages that show clear Christian influence, ones which could have been shaped by the Pauline passage itself. Thus the genesis of this rather unusual theme of the ignorance of the powers in persecuting the redeemer has remained ambiguous.

What Nag Hammadi has contributed to this situation is a number of examples—with variations of course—of the theme of the deception of the powers at the coming of the heavenly redeemer, some of them without any reference to the story of Jesus. One of the most striking examples comes from the non-Christian tractate "The Paraphrase of Shem"

---

[24]For references see H. Conzelmann, *1 Corinthians* (Philadelphia, 1975) 63.

(VII, 2) in which the heavenly redeemer is an angelic figure called Derdekeas, who descends into the lower world to save those who are related to the divine. The notion of his persecution by the "powers," here symbolized by the forces of nature, is clothed in the image of their ignorance:

> It is I who opened forever the gates that were closed from the beginning. For those who desire the height of life and those who are worthy of rest, he revealed them. I granted perception to those who perceive; I opened for them all understandings and the doctrine of the righteous, and in no respect was I hostile to them. And when I endured the wrath of the world, I was victorious. There was not one of them who knew me. The gates of fire and unending smoke opened against me. All the winds rose against me. Thunders and lightnings for a time will rise up against me. And they will bring their wrath down upon me. And on account of me they will be ruled over according to the flesh by tribes.[25]

What is most important about this example is the fact that it occurs in a Gnostic context without any reference to the passion of Jesus and indeed without any clear reference to anything Christian whatsoever.[26]

Another example of the same theme occurs in "The Apocalypse of Adam," which has already been mentioned. Here too the picture is that of the heavenly revealer or redeemer, called the Illuminator (*phōstēr*) of gnosis. At his third coming persecution results because the "powers" are unaware of his true identity:

> Then the God of the powers will be troubled, saying: "What is the power of this man, who is higher than we?" Then he will provoke a great wrath against that man. And the glory will pass through and dwell in holy houses,

[25]CG VII, 36, 2-24; text in M. Krause, "Die Paraphrase des Sêem," F. Altheim and R. Stiehl (ed.), *Christentum am Roten Meer* (Berlin, 1973) II 76-78.

[26]See F. Wisse, "The Redeemer Figure in the Paraphrase of Shem," *Novum Testamentum* 12 (1970) 130-140.

which it has chosen for itself, and the powers will not see it with their eyes, nor will they see the Illuminator. Then they will punish the flesh of the man upon whom the Holy Spirit has come.[27]

This example too is one that we encounter in a non-Christian Gnostic context. The fact that we find such examples in contexts that are not influenced by the Christian gospel suggests strongly that in 1 Cor 2:8 Paul is picking up a theme widely used in Gnosticism and applying it to the passion and death of Jesus. Christology is being expressed, as has often been asserted, in terms borrowed from the syncretistic religious milieu. The contribution of Nag Hammadi to this discussion is to illustrate the theme in contexts that are independent of the New Testament itself.

Let us turn briefly to another kind of example of Gnosticism and the New Testament and ask whether Nag Hammadi sheds any light on the alleged Gnosticism of the Fourth Gospel. In New Testament scholarship for over half a century this topic has been one of the most controversial. The Gospel of John has from time to time been identified as a thoroughly Gnostic work, a Christian revision of a Gnostic work, an anti-Gnostic polemic, a Jewish-Christian work, an anti-Jewish polemic, and of course many other things.[28] Not all of these designations, it must be added, are mutually exclusive; it is quite possible for this gospel especially to be both Jewish and anti-Jewish, and at the same time to be strongly influenced by Gnosticism and yet anti-Gnostic. Though it hardly solves the problem of the Fourth Gospel merely to assert such universality, we must be alert to the phenomenon of syncretism. C.K. Barrett in his recent lectures on the Fourth Gospel concludes that the Fourth Gospel emanates from a complex world in which both Judaism and Christianity are not only in interaction with

---

[27]CG V, 77, 4-20; translation by M. Krause and R. McL. Wilson, in: W. Foerster (ed.), *Gnosis* (New York, 1974), II, p. 20.

[28]See the survey of R. Kysar, *The Fourth Evangelist and His Gospel* (Minneapolis, 1975) especially, 102-146.

each other but are contending with Gnostic orientations that are especially congenial to the Roman Hellenistic period.[29] The problem of our attempts to sort out Jewish or anti-Jewish, Gnostic or anti-Gnostic tendencies is that we try to simplify and categorize too neatly. It is the complexity of the age, its religious syncretism, which best explains the origins of Christianity and of the Gospel of John in particular.

As long as one stays at the level of comparing the Fourth Gospel with the Nag Hammadi "Gospel of Truth," a Valentinian mediation on Christology which was one of the first Nag Hammadi documents to be published, it is relatively easy to set up a contrast in which the Fourth Gospel appears quite innocent of Gnostic influence even though both it and "The Gospel of Truth" are radical reinterpretations of the Jesus tradition with many points in common.[30] But even here caution is in order, for "The Gospel of Truth" makes obvious use of most of the New Testament, including both the Apocalypse and Hebrews, but it does not clearly cite the Gospel of John, though it may often allude to it.[31] It is possible to conclude that "Gospel of Truth" is a second-century composition which does not yet actually know John but shares with it some tendencies in the reinterpreting of the common tradition. But rather than pursue this very speculative suggestion, I wish to mention another way in which the Fourth Gospel bears comparison with the Nag Hammadi library.

The most influential of all modern commentators on the Fourth Gospel, Rudolf Bultmann, proposed as everyone knows, that among the sources of the Gospel was a revelation-discourse document, of non-Christian Gnostic provenance, which the Evangelist placed on the lips of Jesus

---

[29] *The Gospel of John and Judaism* (Philadelphia, 1975) 71-76.

[30] See the nuanced position of C.K. Barrett, "The Theological Vocabulary of the Fourth Gospel and of The Gospel of Truth," W. Klassen and G.F. Snyder (ed.), *Current Issues in New Testament Interpretation, Essays in Honor of Otto A. Piper* (New York, 1962) 210-223.

[31] See J.-E. Ménard, *L'Évangile de Vérité* (Leiden, 1972) 3-9.

in the famous discourses in the Fourth Gospel.[32] In further support of this contention, Bultmann published posthumously the dissertation of his former student Heinz Becker.[33] Few scholars indeed have accepted Bultmann's argument for such a source, and as I read the evidence the Nag Hammadi library has not vindicated him. But I believe it has placed the problem in a new and very promising light. It is not possible to demonstrate this in detail here, but only to suggest the issue.

On the basis of Mandaean, Manichean and Hermetic passages, most of them demonstrably later than the Fourth Gospel, Bultmann, and especially Becker, reconstructed a hypothetical model of the Gnostic revelation discourse which revolved often circuitously and repetitively around three points: self-predications in the "I am" style, an invitation or summons to a decision, and a promise of reward and/or threat of punishment. The pertinence of this model to the discourses of Jesus in the Gospel of John is obvious. What the Nag Hammadi library has shown is that the model of such discourses as typically Gnostic is no longer hypothetical. In many of the Nag Hammadi tractates such as "The Thunder," "The Apocryphon of John" (in the longer ending of the version in CG II and IV), "Trimorphic Protennoia," and others, we have textbook examples of such revelation discourses in both Christian and non-Christian Gnosticism. In applying this stereotyped form of revelation discourse to the lips of Jesus, the Fourth Evangelist was not using a Gnostic source, but he seems clearly to have been using a typically Gnostic literary genre.

For this and many other reasons, I believe the question of the relationship between the Fourth Gospel and Gnosticism is coming into much clearer focus at present. In my view the Fourth Gospel is neither a genuinely Gnostic work nor an anti-Gnostic one. It is rather an independent reinterpretation

---

[32] *The Gospel of John. A Commentary* (Philadelphia, 1971) 132 and passim.

[33] *Die Reden des Johannesevangeliums und der Stil der gnostischen Offenbarungsrede* (Göttingen, 1956).

of the Jesus story on the part of a gifted Evangelist who was strongly influenced by the multiple currents of his syncretistic world including Gnosticism. His Gospel represents in part a gnosticising of the tradition which, however, stops short of absolute dualism and its corollary, docetism. Thus, despite the attempt of the Valentinians to appropriate John as their Gospel because they rightly recognized its tendencies, the Fourth Gospel is not a Gnostic work.

It would be relatively easy to cite further examples of the relevance of the Nag Hammadi library for the study of the New Testament, some of them intriguing ones. One thinks of the document in Codex VII called "The Apocalypse of Peter," which contains, among other things, polemics against church officials as well as against other Gnostics. In its appeal to the authority of Peter, which may appear somewhat surprising in a Gnostic context,[34] this document appears to admit us, by the back door, as it were, to the debates about authority and legitimacy in the early second century to which Second Peter in the New Testament also gives access.[35]

This paper has tried to provide some instances of the way in which I believe the Nag Hammadi collection reopens the old question of Gnostic influence on early Christianity. Few if any problems in this area have been definitively solved by the Nag Hammadi discoveries, but we must bear in mind that so far few if any of the Nag Hammadi tractates have been submitted, as eventually they must be, to the same kind of rigorous exegesis that we lavish upon the New Testament. Once that task has been undertaken in earnest, the difference that Nag Hammadi makes to the question of Gnosticism and the New Testament may prove to be a considerable one.

[34]See P. Perkins, "Peter in Gnostic Revelation," G. MacRae (ed.), *Society of Biblical Literature 1974 Seminar Papers* (Missoula, 1974) II, pp. 1-13.

[35]The text is available in M. Krause, *Christentum am Roten Meer,* II. pp. 152-179.

12

The Jewish Background of the Gnostic Sophia Myth*

Some of the literature on Gnosticism seems to assume without discussion that the Sophia figure, from whose descent or "fall" from the Pleroma the creation of the material world ultimately results, is a Gnostic adaptation of the personified Wisdom of Jewish apocalyptic and Wisdom literature.[1] This assumption is well founded, but it has not always gone unchallenged. For example, W. Bousset argued expressly against it, holding that the Gnostic sources were in respect to Sophia influenced by a much more ancient myth of broader Near Eastern origin.[2] U. Wilckens, following Bousset in this regard, concluded his survey of Wisdom myth in Judaism and Gnosticism with the theory that both have the same *religionsgeschichtlich* background but are essentially independent traditions: in the Hellenistic period there was some Gnostic influence on the late Jewish stream, but the Jewish Wisdom tradition had no influence on the

---

*First published in *Novum Testamentum* 12 (1970) 86-101.

[1]E.g. F.-M.-M. Sagnard, *La gnose valentinienne et le témoignage de saint Irénée* (Paris, 1947) 593-598. R.M. Grant, *Gnosticism and Early Christianity*, rev. ed. (New York, 1966) 80-85, seeks to demonstrate the origin of the Simonian "First Thought" in Jewish tradition.

[2]Cf. *Hauptprobleme der Gnosis* (Göttingen, 1967) 260-273 and 335.

Gnostic Sophia myth.[3] In view of the sharply opposing views on this question—one which has an obvious bearing upon the larger problem of the Jewish factor in the origins of Gnosticism—this article will attempt in summary fashion to review some of the points of contact between Jewish Wisdom and the Gnostic Sophia and to show how the latter may have developed from the former. No effort will be made here to account for the origin of the concept of personal Wisdom within Judaism itself, but I may simply state that I believe its origin to lie in a combination of the late Jewish tendency toward the hypostatization of divine attributes[4] and the widespread ancient myths of the female deity, especially the Isis myths.[5]

In a recent article G. C. Stead has analyzed the Sophia myth in Valentinianism, tracing its inner development and suggesting an origin in currents of thought best represented by Philo.[6] The present article will not go over the same ground again, although, as will become apparent, I should give a somewhat different account of the Jewish elements in the myth. For the most part, I wish to draw on the Gnostic Sophia myth as it is found in the Coptic Gnostic writings from Nag Hammadi and to concentrate more on what we may for convenience call the Sethian-Ophite type of Gnosticism than on the Valentinian. It is clear that in some form a common myth of Sophia underlies both systems. Though it is not the purpose of this article to argue the relationship between the two types, continued analysis of the new Gnostic sources may demonstrate the more original character of the Sethian-Ophite type by virtue of its occurrence in non-Christian Gnostic contexts.

[3] *Weisheit und Torheit* (Tübingen, 1959), summary on pp. 193-197. In a later essay Wilckens modified this view enough to admit the possibility of reciprocal contact between the Jewish and Gnostic streams of development; cf. article *Sophia*, TWNT, vol. VII, p. 514.

[4] Cf. especially W. Schencke, *Die Chokma (Sophia) in der jüdischen Hypostasen-spekulation* (Kristiania, 1913) and H. Ringgren, *Word and Wisdom* (Lund, 1947).

[5] See the references in H. Conzelmann, "Die Mutter der Weisheit," *Zeit und Geschichte*, Bultmann *Festschrift* (Tübingen, 1964) 225.

[6] "The Valentinian Myth of Sophia," *JTS* 20 (1969) 75-104.

The picture of personified Wisdom in the Jewish sources is too well known to need summarizing here,[7] and especially since Bultmann's essay on the Johannine Prologue in the Gunkel *Festschrift*, the particular Jewish myth of the descent and reascent of Wisdom is also familiar.[8] Likewise it is not necessary to cite at length the Gnostic form of the myth, which occurs very frequently, with many variations, in the patristic as well as the Coptic sources. Instead, this article will first discuss a list of specific similarities between Jewish Sophia and Gnostic Sophia in the Sethian-Ophite cosmogonies, secondly present some brief reflections on the Valentinian Sophia, and finally develop an argument for the Jewish origin.

Sophia in Jewish and in Gnostic Sources

In the following list of parallels only one or two references are provided for each even where others could be cited. Discussion is furnished where the point of the parallelism needs some clarification.

(1) Sophia is personal: *passim* in both literatures. Generally the Gnostic writings have a much more exaggerated tendency to hypostatize than do the Jewish.

(2) Sophia is joined in intimate union with God: she is his breath, emanation, reflection, image (Wis 7:25-26); the first of his creatures (Prov 8:22); his companion (Prov 8:30). In the Gnostic sources we should expect Sophia to be linked with the inferior God of the OT, the Demiurge Ialdabaoth and/or his off-spring Sabaoth, also derived from the God of the OT. But characteristically of the Gnostic effort to demean the creator-God, it is not he who brings Sophia into being, but she him. She is nevertheless a "breath of the

---

[7]See especially Prov 8:12-36; Sir 24:1-22; Wis 6-10; LXX Bar 3:9; 4:4.

[8]"Der religionsgeschichtliche Hintergrund des Prologs zum Johannes-Evangelium," *Eucharistērion* vol. II (Göttingen, 1923) 3-26. See also Wilckens, *Weisheit und Torheit*, pp. 97-197. The principal passages are 1 Enoch 42; 94:5; 4 Ezra 5:10-11; Syr. Bar 48:36; Prov 1:20-23 and those in preceding footnote.

power of God," for Sophia breathing power into creation is a favorite theme of the Gnostic cosmogonies. In *On the Origin of the World*,[9] for example, the result of Sophia's abortive effort to emanate is a shapeless, lifeless mass "with no *pneuma* in it" until she breathes upon it to give it the form of the Demiurge; her breath binds him and expels him to the underworld; and finally, she breathes life into Adam.[10]

But on the other hand, there is also a sense in which the Gnostic Sophia is, at least originally, linked with the supreme Aeon, the Father, even though she appears in some versions of the myth to be the lowest of the Aeons, as distant as possible from the Father in the Pleroma. In some works, such as the *Hypostasis of the Archons*, there is no hierarchy of Aeons; only Sophia is mentioned. In others, such as the *Apocryphon of John*, Sophia is a lower Aeon, but a female figure such as Barbelo stands next to the Father as his first emanation. G. Quispel believes that it is this higher female "deity" or Aeon who corresponds most immediately to the Jewish Wisdom.[11] And H.-M. Schenke has claimed that behind the *Sophia of Jesus Christ* and the *Apocryphon of John* there is a hierarchy of three supreme Aeons, the Father, Sophia and the Son.[12] The reluctance to attribute the fall with its consequences of material creation to such a lofty Aeon—or the reluctance to admit a split within the deity itself—took two different forms. Either Sophia was placed at the bottom of the scale of Aeons, as in *Sophia of Jesus Christ*, or two female figures, both derived from Wisdom, were postulated, as in the *Apocryphon of John* (compare Sophia and Achamoth in Valentinianism).

[9]Adopting H.-M. Schenke's proposed title for the untitled fifth treatise of Nag Hammadi Codex II. In the references that follow, the Nag Hammadi works (CG) and Berlin Codex 8502 (BG) are cited by page and line (and plate number where appropriate). For the standard editions see J.M. Robinson, "The Coptic Gnostic Library Today," *New Testament Studies* 14 (1968), 380-401.

[10]On each point respectively see CG II, 99:8-100:10 (pl. 147-148); 102:32-35 (pl. 150; cf. *Hypostasis of the Archons*, CG II, 95:8-13, pl. 143); 115:11-23 (pl. 163).

[11]"Gnosticism and the New Testament," *Vigiliae Christianae* 19 (1965) 73-75.

[12]"Nag-Hammadi Studien III," *Zeitschrift für Religions- und Geistesgeschichte* 14 (1962) 352-361.

(3) Sophia was brought forth from or in the beginning (Prov 8:22 ff.; Sir 1:4; 24:9). Not only does the Gnostic myth necessarily presuppose some form of pre-existence for Sophia, but in *Sophia of Jesus Christ* the Sophia called "the great" is said to be joined in syzygy to the second Aeon, the Father, "from the beginning"—apparently an allusion to Prov 24:22 ff.).[13]

(4) Sophia dwells in the clouds (Sir 24:4; LXX Bar 3:29). In the scene of the enthronement of Sabaoth in *On the Origin of the World*, we read: "And no one was with him (Sabaoth) in the cloud except Sophia Pistis."[14] In a similar image though in a different context in the *Apocryphon of John*, Sophia conceals her monster offspring Ialdabaoth in a cloud of light.[15] In this instance "the Holy Spirit who is called the mother of the living" is within the cloud, but as we shall see this figure too may be an allusion to Sophia.

(5) Sophia attends God's throne or is herself enthroned (Wis 9:4; 1 Enoch 84:3; Sir 24:4). This image is closely bound up with the preceding in Gnostic as well as Jewish literature. In both Gnostic passages just mentioned Sophia attends the throne of the OT God; in *On the Origin of the World* there is a (possibly interpolated) passage in which Sophia is enthroned with Sabaoth on her right and Ialdabaoth on her left.[16]

(6) Sophia is identified with a (Holy) Spirit (Wis 7:7; 7:22-23; cf. 9:17). The Gnostics were prone to such an identification in part because of their fascination for the fact that *ruah* in Hebrew is feminine. They specifically identified Sophia and the Spirit of God by interpreting Gen 1:2b (the Spirit moving over the waters) as the repentance of Sophia for her fall. The *Apocryphon of John* provides an excellent example: in a "corrective" exegesis of the verse, *epipheresthai*

---

[13]BG 95, 1-3; cf. Schenke, "Nag-Hammadi Studien II," 274.

[14]CG II, 106:5-6 (pl. 154).

[15]CG II, 10:14-18.

[16]CG II, 106:11-18 (pl. 154).

is the repentant movement of Sophia.[17] O. Betz has drawn attention to the passage in the *Megale Apophasis* which explicitly interprets Gen 1:2b by means of Prov 8:22 ff., thus identifying the Simonian *hebdomē dynamis* as Wisdom.[18]

(7) Sophia was at least instrumental in the creation of the world (Prov 3:19; 8:27-30; etc.). In the Gnostic sources, this theme is the whole *raison d'être* of the Sophia myth. One should note in addition that neither in the Wisdom literature nor in Gnosticism is Sophia actually the creator, although in *On the Origin of the World* she is said to create man,[19] a statement that may have its Jewish prototype in 2 Enoch 30:8 or Wis 9:2. Both Wis 9:2 and the Gnostic passage mention man's lordship over other creatures (Gen 1:26, 28).[20]

(8) Sophia communicates wisdom and revelation to men (Wis *passim*). The parallel in the Gnostic sources is obvious in the fact that it is Sophia who is responsible for the element of light that is in man.[21] One might further compare Sophia's bringing light into creation to the statement of Wis 7:26-27 about Wisdom as the "reflection of eternal light . . . in every generation passing into holy souls." One must bear in mind that Sophia is an ambivalent figure in Gnosticism: through her fall she is blamed for the existence of evil matter, but because she belongs to the world of light as an Aeon of the Father and is sometimes in the myth reinstated to it, she is credited with the presence of the divine or of revelation in man. Creation and revelation are moral opposites for the Gnostic, the one a tragedy, the other the saving gesture. Only in an ambivalent or split personality can they be regarded as

---

[17]CG II, 13:13-23. See A. Orbe, "Spiritus Dei ferebatur super aquas," *Gregorianum* 44 (1963), 691-730.

[18]"Was am Anfang geschah," *Abraham unser Vater*, Michel *Festschrift* (Leiden 1963), 38-39.

[19]CG II, 113:12-114:15 (pl. 161-162). But in *Apocalypse of James I*, discussed below, the lower Wisdom, Achamoth, appears to create material being.

[20]CG II, 113:35; 114:19-20 (pl. 161-162).

[21]E.g. *Hypostasis of the Archons*, CG II, 94:29-31 (pl. 142).

the work of a single agent.[22] The ambivalence of Sophia— and consequently the ambivalent attitude of Gnostics toward Judaism—may be seen clearly in her role as revealer in the system described by Irenaeus, *Adv. haer.* I. 30. Here Sophia acts in opposition to Ialdabaoth and his powers by speaking through the prophets about the world above. One should compare the very common motif in which it is the voice of Sophia or Zoe which rebukes the arrogant Demiurge for his boast "I am God and there is no other."[23]

But there is another basis for associating the revealing function of Wisdom with Gnosticism, namely the various female figures, such as Ennoia, Epinoia, Pronoia, who on the one hand bring gnosis to men and on the other behave very much like the descending and reascending Wisdom of I Enoch 42 and other Jewish sources. An excellent instance is found in the hymnic ending attached to the longer version of the *Apocryphon of John*, in which "the perfect *pronoia* of the All, the richness of the light, the thought of the Pleroma, etc." describes her triple descent into the world to awaken man from his deep sleep by communicating gnosis to him.[24] This figure is not explicitly identified with Sophia, but the resemblance by way of the myth of Wisdom's descent is very striking.

(9) Sophia descends into the world of men (I Enoch 42:2; LXX Bar 3:37). This is a fixed element of the Sophia myth in all its Gnostic variations. In Irenaeus 1:30 Sophia, and in *Apocryhon of John* Pronoia, descends in order to bring revelation to men. More usually, Sophia's descent is her fall

---

[22]On the ambivalence of Sophia in Valentinianism see Stead, "The Valentinian Myth of Sophia," pp. 92-93, where *five* distinct concepts of Sophia are detected.

[23]E.g. *Hypostasis of the Archons*, CG II, 95:5-8 (pl. 143). Cf. Schenke, *Der Gott "Mensch" in der Gnosis* (Göttingen, 1962) 87-93; A. Orbe, "El pecado de los Arcontes," *Estudios Eclesiásticos* 43 (1968) 354-357; G. W. MacRae, "The *Ego*-Proclamation in Gnostic Sources," *The Trial of Jesus*, ed. E. Bammel (London, 1970) 122-134.

[24]CG II, 30:11-31:25. Cf. G. W. MacRae, "Sleep and Awakening in Gnostic Texts," *Le origini dello gnosticismo*, ed. U. Bianchi (Leiden, 1967) 496-507. There is an extensive and close parallel to this passage in the work entitled "The Triple Protennoia" in CG XIII.

from which the world results; unlike the Jewish myths, in which the descent is either unmotivated (1 Enoch 42) or is motivated by God's providence (Sir 24; LXX Bar 3-4), the Gnostic sources assign a motive for the descent which places it in the order of cosmic catastrophe. How the Gnostics could regard the descent as a fall must be discussed below.

(10) Sophia reascends to her celestial home (I Enoch 42:2). In the Wisdom literature the theme of reascent is generally absent, since the Jewish Wisdom writers wished to claim that Wisdom finds her home in Israel, sometimes by the (undoubtedly secondary) identification of Wisdom and the Law.[25] In the longer ending of the *Apocryphon of John* the Pronoia is explicitly said to reascend. In the *Hypostasis of the Archons* Sophia merely reascends to her light,[26] but in many other works such as the *Apocryphon of John* (body of the work) her reascent is narrated in terms of her repentance and eventual (at least implicit) rehabilitation into the Pleroma.[27] The latter has its nearest parallel in the theme of Sophia's repentance in Valentinianism; but we need not deal here with the element of delay in some middle region before complete rehabilitation and thus complete reascent is possible.

(11) Sophia protected, delivered and strengthened Adam (Wis 10:1-2). We have mentioned above in no. 7 the role of Sophia in the creation of Adam in *On the Origin of the World*. One may also compare the role of the Epinoia of light in protecting Adam and "delivering him from his transgression" by enlightening him about his origin and his destiny, in the *Apocryphon of John*.[28] It is of course uncertain whether one can simply identify the Epinoia and Sophia,[29] but no doubt both are inspired by the same source.

---

[25]E.g. Sir 24; cf. Wilckens, *Weisheit und Torheit*, pp. 164-169. But for traces of the reascent motif in Jewish literature see Prov 1:20-23; Job 28:12-28.

[26]CG II, 94:32-33 (pl. 142).

[27]CG II, 13:36-14:13.

[28]CG II, 20:25-28.

[29]Earlier in CG II, 9:25, however, we read: "And the Sophia of the Epinoia, being an aeon..."

(12) Sophia is referred to as a "sister" (Prov 7:4). In the *Apocryphon of John* there are several instances in which the expression "our sister Sophia" appears. These are remarkable in that they occur in different contexts in the longer and shorter versions,[30] and they do not appear to reflect any significant relationship between Aeons in the narrative. Nor is it likely that the plural "our" indicates merely the narrator, Christ, who usually uses the singular when speaking in his own person. Thus apparently this title of Sophia comes to the Gnostic author as a traditional element for which no fixed place can be found in the story. In Irenaeus I.30.11-12 Sophia is referred to as the sister of the Aeon Christ, however.

(13) Sophia is associated with a sevenfold cosmic structure (Prov 9:1). It is disputed whether or not there is any cosmic reference in the seven-pillared house of Wisdom in Prov 9:1, and it is not our purpose to discuss the question.[31] A Gnostic reader would certainly have discovered it there. *Excerpta ex Theodoto* 47:1 cites Prov 9:1 in reference to Sophia's creative role.[32] In the cosmogonic works it is conceivable that the seven Archons or planetary deities resulting from Sophia's fall are an application of the image in Prov 9:1, although the passage is certainly not the primary source of the idea of a sevenfold Demiurge.

(14) Sophia is identified with life (Prov 8:35; LXX Bar 4:14 etc.). In the Gnostic cosmogonies Sophia is intimately linked with Zoe, the celestial counterpart of Eve. In the *Hypostasis of the Archons* and *On the Origin of the World* Zoe is usually the daughter of Sophia, but in some passages of the latter we find Sophia called Sophia Zoe.[33] The background is Gen 3:20, but it is possible that the linking of Wisdom and life in the Wisdom literature facilitated the identification. We shall return below to the parallelism

[30]E.g. CG II, 23:20-21; CG III, 14:9-10; 25:20-21.

[31]For references, see R.N. Whybray, *Wisdom in Proverbs* (London, 1965) 90-91.

[32]See the notes *ad loc.* in the edition of F.-M.-M. Sagnard, *Clément d'Alexandrie: Extraits de Théodote* (Paris, 1948) 156-158.

[33]CG II, 115:12; 121:27 (pl. 163, 169).

between the Sophia myth and the story of Eve.

(15) Sophia is a tree of life (Prov 3:18; cf. I Enoch 32:3-6). In Jewish, Christian and Gnostic literature the theme of the tree(s) in Paradise is very common, but very frequently the picture is confused. In *On the Origin of the World* both the tree of life and the tree of knowledge are good (from the Gnostic viewpoint!)[34], but in the *Apocryphon of John* the tree of life is the evil instrument of the Archons.[35] In the latter work, however, the tree of the knowledge of good and evil is identified with the Epinoia of light whom we have associated with Sophia above in no. 11.[36]

Cumulatively, this long list of parallels between the Jewish Wisdom and the Gnostic Sophia makes it virtually impossible to rule out all influence of the former on the latter, and makes it at least probable that some kind of (no doubt perverse) use of the Jewish Wisdom figure lies at the source of the Gnostic myth.

Sophia in Valentinianism and the Planē Myth

Many of the preceding statements about Sophia in the works that I have lumped together as Sethian-Ophite can also be made with reference to the various strains of Valentinianism. There is no need here to sketch the Valentinian Sophia myth but merely to point out certain peculiarities. It is characteristic of Valentinianism that there are two Sophia figures, a higher and a lower, and the motivation of the fall of Sophia is sometimes different. Whereas in the other forms of the myth Sophia desired to imitate the Father by producing an emanation without the knowledge or consent of her consort, the Father himself or another Aeon, in some elaborations of Valentinianism her "fault" consisted of seeking to comprehend the Father

[34]E.g. CG II, 110:7-29 (pl. 158).

[35]CG III, 27:11-28:6; cf. CG II, 21:24-26.

[36]E.g. CG II, 22:4-5; 23:28-29.

perfectly.[37] When Sophia fell from her rank her desire (Epithymia or Achamoth) was expelled from the Pleroma and brought about the creation of the material world through her offspring the Demiurge.[38] The double Sophia functions as a device for further insulating the pleromatic world of Aeons from the sordid world of material creation.

A number of the Valentinian works from Nag Hammadi serve to corroborate the details of the myth and perhaps help understand its orientation.[39] In the *Apocalypse of James I,* for example, there is a (somewhat fragmentary) version of Valentinian teaching which provides an important independent witness for certain Valentinian formulas in Irenaeus, I.21.5).[40] Here the higher Sophia is portrayed as the revealer-redeemer of spiritual men, through the gnosis communicated by Christ, and the lower as the author of evil:

> But I shall call out to the imperishable gnosis, which is the Sophia who is with the Father, who is the mother of Achamoth.[41]

Elsewhere it is explicitly said that Achamoth is translated Sophia.[42] The process seems clear enough: it is God's Wisdom that is first hypostatized, then split, lest God's transcendence be compromised by the evil world. In the *Apocalypse of James I* there seems to be a distinction between those who are followers of the higher Sophia (the Gnostics) and those who adhere to Achamoth, and one is led to wonder whether the Hebrew name is not used to suggest that it is the Jews who are the victims of the inadequate

---

[37]Cf. Stead, "The Valentinian Myth of Sophia," p. 78.

[38]See Irenaeus' account of the system of Ptolemaeus, *Adv. haer.* I.1-8.

[39]One of the most important works is yet to be published, the Fourth Treatise of the Jung Codex (CG I). For details of its Sophia figure see J. Zandee, "Gnostic Ideas on the Fall and Salvation," *Numen 11* (1964) 13-74, especially pp. 23-27; "Die Person der Sophia in der vierten Schrift des Codex Jung," *Le origini dello gnosticismo,* 203-212.

[40]See the edition of A. Böhlig, *Koptisch-gnostische Apokalypsen aus Codex V von Nag Hammadi* (Halle, 1963) 32-33.

[41]CG V, 35:5-9.

[42]CG V, 36:5-6.

Wisdom. But in the *Gospel of Philip*, which also has close affinities with Valentinianism, there is a distinction between the two Sophia figures in which both are called by Hebrew names:

> Echamoth is one and Echmoth is another. Echamoth is simply *(haplôs)* Sophia, but Echmoth is the Sophia of death, she being the one who knows death. She is the one who is called the little Sophia.[43]

The nomenclature is obviously not in harmony with other Valentinian sources, but the distinction is clearly the same. The "Sophia of death" may be a deliberate contrast to the association of Wisdom and life in the Wisdom literature.

In the *Gospel of Truth*, which is also generally thought to be Valentinian in character, though here the case is by no means so clear, the personified Sophia does not appear at all.[44] Nevertheless essentially the same Sophia myth is in the background, although, characteristically of the work, it is recounted in terms of somewhat personified abstractions rather than in terms of the mythological personalities we have seen elsewhere. The relevant passage is the account of the origins of the human predicament at the beginning of the Gospel:

> Indeed (*epeidē*) they all went about searching for the one from whom it (pl.) had come forth, and the all was inside of him, the incomprehensible, inconceivable one, who is superior to every thought. Ignorance of the Father brought about anguish and terror. And anguish grew solid like a fog[45] so that no one was able to see. For this reason Planē became powerful; she fashioned her own matter (*hylē*) in emptiness, not having known the truth. She set about

---

[43]CG II, 60:10-18 (pl. 108; omitting a dittography in line 13). See the commentary of J.-E. Ménard, *L'Evangile selon Philippe* (Paris, 1967) 155-156.

[44]Sophia is mentioned in CG I, 23:18, but this is very probably not a reference to the celestial Aeon.

[45]The role of the fog here may be an allusion to the sort of self-assertion of Wisdom we find in Sir 24:3.

making a creature (*plasma*), virtually preparing, in beauty,
a substitute for the truth.[46]

The motivation of the process here is essentially the same as
in one of the types of Valentinianism: a disordered attempt
to comprehend the Father from which ignorance results.
Here no individual Aeon is said to fall, but the process of a
fall is set in motion, enabling Planē (Error)—of whose origin
nothing is clearly stated—to counterfeit a world of matter
superficially resembling the true world of the Pleroma. Thus
although neither Sophia nor the Demiurge is mentioned, the
Sophia myth seems to underlie this account, and Planē, as
Betz has remarked,[47] seems to do double duty for both
Sophia and the Demiurge.

Because this account is of itself not readily intelligible
without a knowledge of the Sophia myth, one may conclude
that the *Gospel of Truth* is a later formulation which
presupposes the earlier, perhaps less sophisticated, myth.[48] It
is difficult to decide on internal grounds whether Planē is
merely a personification of error in the abstract or is a
mythological personality.[49] But the supposition that the
Sophia myth underlies this account may provide an indication of the author's intention. He does not abandon the
myth; he merely tries to express it in rather more "philosophical" terms. His effort results in an emphasis on the
opposition truth-error which more clearly than the original
myth poses the conflict between the spiritual and the
material worlds. But in introducing a personification, Planē,
whose origin is left unexplained, the systematic background
of the *Gospel of Truth* is more frankly dualistic than even

[46]CG I, 17:4-20.

[47]"Was am Anfang geschah," p. 42.

[48]See H. Jonas, *The Gnostic Religion*, 2nd ed. (Boston, 1963) 313-319.

[49]See R. Haardt, "Zur Struktur des Plane-Mythos im Evangelium Veritatis des
Codex Jung," *Wissenschaftliche Zeitschrift für die Kunde des Morgenlandes* 58
(1962) 24-38.

the extravagant mythology of the Sethian-Ophite cosmogonies.[50]

To adopt a mythological interpretation of the *Gospel of Truth* does not mean to turn a blind eye to its effort to relate the cosmic drama to human experience of truth, error, anguish, fear, hope and the other attitudes mentioned in the work. At the bottom of the Gnostic myth itself is the projection of the human predicament onto a "pleromatic" scale in a sense that differs fundamentally from the Jewish Wisdom speculation. No doubt some of the Gnostic writers lose sight of the motivation of Gnosticism itself in their preoccupation with myth-making. The genius of the author of the *Gospel of Truth* was to return to this motivation without abandoning the mythic structure, but by restating it in other terms.

The Jewish Origin of the Sophia Myth

The Jewish contribution to the myth is already clear from the large number of points of contact between the two traditions, especially when these are considered in the larger context of the numerous Jewish elements scattered throughout the Gnostic mythologies. But can the Jewish background explain the basic spirit of the Gnostic myth? The Jewish attitude was one of confidence in Wisdom, resulting from the conviction that God had made his Wisdom dwell in Israel. How then explain the Gnostic hostility, or at least ambivalence, toward the personified Wisdom? Although in some accounts Sophia is both the good revealer and the hapless originator of material creation, in others she is frankly despised as the source of all that is evil. She falls, repents and is readmitted to the Pleroma in some accounts, and in others her place is simply taken by error or deception.

The answer to the question must lie in the realization that

---

[50]The radical dualism of the *Gospel of Truth* is emphasized by Ménard, "La planē dans l'Évangile de Vérité," *Studia Montis Regii* 7 (1964) 3-36; but Ménard offers a very different interpretation of the passage in question.

the essence of the Gnostic attitude, as has often been stated, is one of revolt, and it is a revolt against Judaism itself.[51] Yet somehow it must be conceived as a revolt *within* Judaism. The poignancy of the expression of it indicates this: the Wisdom of Yahweh has been a deception.[52] Moreover, the familiarity which Gnostic sources show toward details of Jewish thought is hardly one that we could expect non-Jews to have. In this notion of the deception, the disillusionment, that Jewish Wisdom proved to be, lies in my opinion the key to the Gnostic attitude toward Judaism. There is still place for a foreign element—indeed without it the whole phenomenon is inexplicable—and that is the fundamental attitude of anticosmicism, the loss of confidence in the created world. Whence the latter comes is still an unsolved problem, and it is not my intention to discuss it here. Whether of Orphic or Neo-Platonist or Iranian or other origin, it must arise from the confrontation of religious and philosophical ideas in the syncretistic process. But whatever the precise origin of this anticosmicism, it is a foreign element that intrudes upon a form of Jewish thought and expression to drive it toward what we know as Gnosticism.[53]

But there is a further question yet to be answered. If the Jewish Wisdom can offer a satisfactory medium for explaining the *descent* of Sophia from above, can the Jewish sources explain the notion of a *fall* of Sophia? Here we must stress the complexity of the notional background of the Gnostic myth. No single form of Jewish tradition can account for the pre-cosmic fall, nor indeed can any single line of non-Jewish thought account for it. Betz has for-

[51]E.g. see H. Jonas, "Response to G. Quispel's 'Gnosticism and the New Testament,'" *The Bible in Modern Scholarship*, ed. J.P. Hyatt (New York, 1966) 286-293. Jonas stresses the aspect of revolt, but for him it is not a revolt *within* Judaism.

[52]Zandee, "Gnostic Ideas on the Fall and Salvation," pp. 23-25, interprets the myth as a revolt against the wisdom of "the philosophers."

[53]On the question of the origin of the Gnostic spirit, see *Le origini dello gnosticismo, passim*, and my report on the Messina Colloquium, "Gnosis in Messina," *CBQ* 28 (1966) 322-333.

mulated the difficulty and enumerated some of the elements from various Jewish traditions which conspire to make possible the theme of the fall of Sophia,[54] but I believe he stops short of the principal link in the chain. Some of these elements of Jewish speculation (not all enumerated by Betz) are the following. First, the fact that the Jewish tradition had already associated Wisdom with the act of creation and had already "put Sophia into the Genesis *Urgeschichte*" in the exegesis of Gen 1:1 and even of Gen 1:2b.[55] Second, the fact that Sophia in the myth of 1 Enoch 42 and of the Wisdom literature is represented as descending into the world; it is a short, though vital, step to having the world result from this descent once the descent itself is placed before the world came into being. Third, the idea of the fall of celestial beings is well known in Jewish apocalyptic literature as the result of interpretation of Gen 6:1-4; moreover, the view of this event reflected in apocalyptic literature is that it caused the evil upon the earth.[56] All of these elements may be said to enter into the Gnostic myth of the fall of Sophia, but they do not yet suffice to account for it.

The principal source of the fall, I suggest, is the Genesis account of the fall of Eve. One would miss an essential insight into the Gnostic myths if he failed to realize that a close correspondence is intended there between the celestial world of the Pleroma and the material world of men. The Gnostic revelations of the higher world are after all projections of human knowledge and experience onto another plane, and the primary source of this knowledge in the Gnostic works we have been dealing with is the Genesis story. In a sense we may say that the very intention of the Gnostic myth is to provide a "true," esoteric explanation of

[54]"Was am Anfang geschah," pp. 38-42.

[55]Betz, p. 39, calls attention to Wis 6-7, from which the role of Sophia in Gen. 1:2b could easily be deduced.

[56]See 1 Enoch 6-16; Betz, p. 40. On the direct Gnostic use of this theme see Y. Janssens, "Le thème de la fornication des anges," *Le origini dello gnosticismo*, pp. 488-494.

the Genesis story itself.[57] Therefore, if the events of earth are held to be but shadowy copies of the realities above, we must expect to find at least some of the characters and actions of Genesis translated to the pleromatic level. We may not be able to recognize them easily, but that is merely a consequence of the estoteric intentions and often inept craftsmanship of the Gnostic mythologizers. As examples of this correspondence one might mention the First Man as a name for God, or in more Christian contexts the Aeon Christ over against the human Jesus.

Jewish tradition from biblical times onward had a keen sense of the disorder in the world resulting from the fall of the first couple from the state in which they had originally been constituted. Now the Gnostic, who began with the more radical notion that the world itself was disorder, would seek to explain this situation by postulating a fall in the Pleroma of which the fall of man is but an inferior copy. But the correspondence is not quite as straightforward as this statement implies, for often the Gnostic "midrash" perverts the whole intention of the biblical story, as it does in this instance in the *Apocryphon of John* and other works, by showing that the fall of man from Paradise was actually beneficial for man, at least in its intent, since it was an attempt to liberate him from the power of the Archons. Man could only begin to rise to the supreme God when he had left the clutches of the Jewish creator-God.

What internal evidence is there for suggesting that the fall of man in Gen 3 is, partially at least, the real prototype for the fall of Sophia? First of all, there is the fact that the sin in Gen 3 is primarily that of the woman. Adam may bear the weight of responsibility in Jewish and Christian theology (e.g. the Epistle to the Romans), but in the myth of Genesis it is the woman who initiates the wrong and transmits it to

---

[57]"Die werdende Gnosis wollte nicht mehr und nicht weniger sein als richtige Auslegung des Alten Testaments," D. Georgi, "Der vorpaulinische Hymnus Phil. 2, 6-11," *Zeit und Geschichte*, p. 269. See also Betz, pp. 24-28; S. Giversen, "The Apocryphon of John and Genesis," *Studia Theologica* 17 (1963) 74-76.

her husband.[58] And in the Gnostic myth it is likewise a female Aeon Sophia whose disgrace initiates the creation process. Secondly, the motivation of the fall in Gen 3:5 is to "be like God" and this is precisely how we must understand the motivation of Sophia's fall.[59] In the Sethian-Ophite form of the myth she seeks to emanate another being without the collaboration of her male partner-Aeon, or merely "alone," and this is the divine prerogative. In a form of the Valentinian myth she seeks to comprehend the unknowable God, and this too is not granted to lower Aeons. Thirdly, as already mentioned above, there is in many forms of the Sophia myth a close association of Sophia and "her daughter" Zoe, i.e. Eve; sometimes the two are even identified in the name Sophia-Zoe. This shows the correspondence of Eve and the celestial being of which she is a copy, in this case Sophia or some other Aeon closely linked with her. Lastly, there is an explicit allusion to the sin of Eve in the *Sophia of Jesus Christ* in the context of the fall of Sophia. There it is said that the cosmic veil came into existence so that, among other reasons, "the fault of the woman should live and she should combat error."[60] In the context this can only refer to Sophia and the phrase "the woman" strongly suggests Gen 3:15, interpreted gnostically.

These details may not establish a perfect parallelism between the fall of Sophia and the sin of Eve, but they are enough to suggest that the Jewish myth of the descent of Wisdom could be transformed by the Gnostic into a cosmic catastrophe when combined with the mythical precedent for

[58]Even within Jewish-Christian tradition, however, there are instances of attributing the sin to Eve; cf. E. Peterson, "La libération d'Adam de *Anagkè,*" *RB* 55 (1948) 210.

[59]Betz, p. 40, alludes to this correspondence but does not draw the conclusion from it.

[60]BG 118:15-17.

the fall of Eve. But once more it must be stressed that this explanation is meant to account only for the materials out of which the myth was made, not for the basic anticosmic attitude that inspired the making of it. That at least was an element for which nothing within Judaism itself can adequately account.

13

The Ego-Proclamation
in Gnostic Sources*

A number of modern interpreters propose that the crucial moment in the Jewish trial of Jesus according to Mark is reached with Jesus' use of the absolute form of the *egō eimi* proclamation (14:62). Against a background of Old Testament usage this formula is taken to be a divine self-revelation which constitutes the blasphemy for which Jesus is condemned (14:64).[1] It is not the purpose of this paper to determine whether such an acknowledgement in Mark of what is undeniably a common Johannine usage provides a correct exegesis of the trial scene.[2] Instead, we wish to investigate the extent to which Gnostic sources made use of the *egō* formulas and to inquire both about the origin of the Gnostic usage and its relationship to the New Testament.

In his study of the *egō* proclamaton in the New Testament, Stauffer has drawn attention to the way in which Mark 14:62 serves as a model for a scene in the life of the Gnostic

---

*First published in *The Trial of Jesus: Cambridge Studies in Honor of C.F.D. Moule* (London: SCM Press, 1970) 122-134.

[1]See, e.g., E. Stauffer, *Jesus and His Story* (London, 1960) 100, 150 ff.; H. Zimmermann, "Das absolute 'Ich bin' in der Redeweise Jesu," *Trierer Theologische Zeitschrift* 69 (1960) 1-20.

[2]It is noteworthy that Stauffer in his TWNT article on *egō* had at first regarded Mark 14:62 as an "ordinary" use of *egō eimi* in contrast with Mark 13:6 or John 8:28: TDNT II, p. 352.

leader Simon Magus in the Pseudo-Clementine *Homilies*. To the words of Dositheus, *ei sy ei ho hestōs, kai proskynōse*, Simon replies simply, *egō eimi*, and thus wins the adoration of his rival.[3] In reality, the Pseudo-Clementine passage is as ambiguous as its Marcan model: in both cases it makes good sense to see in the use of *egō eimi* more than a mere affirmative response, "I am," but in neither case is one compelled to do so.[4] It is therefore of interest to inquire whether Gnostic sources in general recognized and used either an absolute or a predicative form of *egō eimi* as a claim to divine or transcendent identity. The following investigation is based in particular on some of the Coptic Gnostic sources from the Nag Hammadi library. It will study first the "I am God" formula and secondly the use of "I am" with a variety of predicates in the manner of the Fourth Gospel.

I

To begin with, we do not find any other instances in the Gnostic sources of the absolute *egō eimi* to parallel the Marcan and Johannine ones. Instead, there is an extremely common Gnostic parallel which also alludes to the Deutero-Isaian background from which the New Testament *egō eimi* very probably springs. This usage is the boast of the Demiurge in the Gnostic creation myths, "I am god and there is no other." The saying of the creator-God in Second Isaiah so fascinated the Gnostic mind that it is almost

---

[3]*Hom.* II. 24.6, ed. B. Rehm, *Die Pseudoklementinen* I (GCS), 1953, p. 45; cf. Stauffer, article *egō*, p. 354. In *Jesus and His Story*, p. 153, the same author suggests that Simon adopted this usage as a result of hearing Jesus use it in Samaria, but this suggestion involves a series of historical judgements about both the Fourth Gospel and the Pseudo-Clementines that are difficult to maintain. A similar reserve must be mentioned, it seems to me, about Stauffer's main point, that the use of *egō eimi* goes back to Jesus himself.

[4]In his famous classification of the I-sayings, R. Bultmann, *Das Evangelium des Johannes* (KEKNT, 19th [=10th] ed.), 1968, pp. 167-8, regards *Hom.* 2.24.6 as a genuine revelation-formula of the *Rekognitionsformel* type..

endlessly repeated in the sources as an empty boast of the inferior Jewish creator. And it is easy to see why, for it was precisely the heart of the Gnostic revelation to show that this statement was wrong. The God of Israel was deluded; worse, he was a deceiver. There is another God, the ineffable, unnamable Deity of the Pleroma whose light is shared by the immortal spark dwelling in pneumatic (i.e. Gnostic) man. And the ultimate Gnostic refutation of the exclusive claims of Judaism lay in the persuasion that the boast of the Demiurge Yahweh was an empty lie.[5] It is paradoxical, part of the very paradox of Gnosticism itself, that whereas the Deutero-Isaian "I am God" formula was primarily a polemic against polytheism, the Gnostics should have borrowed this very formula in the service of a cosmic dualism.

The context in which the boast occurs is very similar in all the Gnostic works in which the statement occurs. As a typical example it will be enough to cite merely one instance, from the Apocryphon of John, in which the allusion to Isa 45:5 (etc.) is combined with a reference to Ex 20:5 or Deut 5:9 (*theos zēlōtēs*):

> But when [Ialdabaoth] saw the creation that surrounded him and the crowd of angels who were about him, who had come into being from him, he said to them, "I, I am a jealous God and there is no other God but me." But in uttering this he indicated to the angels who were beside him that there was another God, for if there were no other, of whom would he be jealous?[6]

H.-M. Schenke has assembled some of the Gnostic instances of this boast of the Demiurge for the purpose of distinguishing between Gnostic allegorical exegesis and Gnostic myth.[7] Several additional passages can now be added to his list, but what is primarily intended here is to

---

[5] Cf. Irenaeus, *haer.* II. 9.2 (ed. Harvey, vol. I, p. 272).

[6] Codex II, 13.5-13; M. Krause and P. Labib, *Die drei Versionen des Apokryphon des Johannes* (Wiesbaden, 1962) 145.

[7] *Der Gott 'Mensch' in der Gnosis* (Göttingen, 1962) 87-93; see also A. Orbe, "El pecado de los Arcontes," *Estudios Eclesiásticos* 43 (1968) 354-7.

make a few observations on the Gnostic use of the Old Testament citations as well as of the *egō* proclamation.

The possible Old Testament passages alluded to, in addition to Ex 20:5 and/or Deut 5:5-9, are the following: Deut 4:35 and 32:39; Hos 13:4; Joel 2:27; and especially Second Isaiah 43:10-11; 44:6; 45:5-6, 18, 21-2; 46:9.[8] Apart from the specific allusions to the "jealous God," it is very difficult to assert categorically which other passages are being cited in the Gnostic documents. It is true that some citations are closer in form to one passage than to another, but we cannot be sure that we have accurate citations in any case. It is most unlikely, as the variations between different versions of the same work, e.g. the Apocryphon of John, would suggest. There is at least one reason, however, to think that the Gnostic citations are derived from Second Isaiah, and that is the fact that the boast of the Demiurge regularly occurs in a creation context. Very often it is precisely at some critical stage of his creative work that the archon asserts his pretended divinity, and the Gnostic cosmogonies have woven the claim into their midrashic treatment of the Genesis creation story.

Most authors who have commented on the Gnostic sources point out the allusions to Isa 45:5 or 46:9, but the fact that Deutero-Isaiah itself may have enjoyed some special prominence in the circles in which Gnosticism arose has for the most part gone unnoticed. For one thing, it is widely held that certain aspects of Deutero-Isaiah exercised a special influence on the development of Jewish apocalyptic thought.[9] Its insistence on universalism and its open conflict

---

[8]I would regard it as unlikely (against Stauffer, *Jesus and His Story*, p. 145) that the presence of the formula in Deut 32:39-40 is due to Deutero-Isaian influence. The Song of Moses is certainly pre-exilic and doubtless very ancient; cf. G.E. Wright, "The Lawsuit of God: a Form-critical Study of Deuteronomy 32," in *Israel's Prophetic Heritage*: Essays in honor of James Muilenburg, ed. B.W. Anderson and W. Harrelson (London, 1962) 26-67. Similarly, it is not clear that Hos. 13:4 is a post-exilic interpolation. Though typically exploited by Second Isaiah, the formula may be much older.

[9]It is not, of course, presumed that the book of Isaiah was divided in antiquity in the manner in which modern commentators treat it, but because of the radical

with the claims of polytheistic paganism made it especially
welcome to both apocalyptic and Hellenistic Judaism.[10] The
Servant Songs themselves may have been influential in the
development of the apocalyptic Son of Man concept as well
as in the self-consciousness of the Qumran sectarians.[11] Thus
if Gnosticism is particularly indebted to Jewish apocalyptic,
as a detailed study of its imagery and attitudes would lead
one to believe, some preference for Second Isaiah, along
with the much more obvious dependence on Genesis, is only
to be expected.

But is there anything more or less peculiar to Second
Isaiah that would appear attractive to the Gnostic mentality
itself? Here we may mention the theology of creation, the
explicit insistence on monotheism (which the Gnostic would
wish to "correct"), certain references to the role of wisdom
and knowledge (e.g. in Isa 53:11), and the use of Sabaoth as
a proper name, in the LXX virtually confined to Isaiah.[12]
The fact that Second Isaiah actually did influence Gnostic
sources in a special manner would have to be brought out by
a number of detailed references in the Coptic Gnostic works
such as the Untitled Work of Nag Hammadi Codex II and
the Gospel of Truth, and in the patristic sources, such as
Hippolytus's account of the Naassenes, which contains
many citations from Isaiah.[13] Finally, there seems to be very

change of tone and subject, ancient readers would naturally have recognized some
distinction. Such elements as the theology of creation, the polemical insistence on
monotheism, the role of the servant, etc., belong to one part of the book only.

[10]Cf. W. Bousset, *Die Religion des Judentums im späthellenistischen Zeitalter,*
3rd ed., by H. Gressmann (Berlin, 1926) 243, 304-7. The influence of Second Isaiah
on the wisdom literature, especially the Wisdom of Solomon, has been pointed out
by D. Georgi in *Zeit und Geschichte: Dankesgabe am Rudolf Bultmann,* ed. E.
Dinkler (Tübingen, 1964) 266. It may be argued that the wisdom tradition played a
significant role in the development of Gnostic mythology (e.g. the Sophia myth),
and thus we may have another link between Second Isaiah and the Gnostics. The
wisdom literature is also interested in the theology of creation.

[11]For a summary of the arguments alleged, see D.S. Russell, *The Method and
Message of Jewish Apocalyptic* (London, 1964) 338-40. Stauffer, *Jesus and His
Story,* p. 145, remarks that Isaiah seems to have enjoyed special favour at Qumran.

[12]Cf. C.H. Dodd, *The Bible and the Greeks* (London, 1935) 16-17.

[13]See, e.g., the indexes of the various editions.

definite influence of the Servant Songs and of the whole context of Second Isaiah on the portrayal of the redeemer or revealer figure in the Coptic Gnostic Apocalypse of Adam.[14]

In particular the context of some of the Deutero-Isaian monotheistic claims would prove especially suggestive for the irreverent setting into which the Gnostics place the citation. For example, Isa 45:18-19:

> I am the Lord, and there is no other. I did not speak in secret, in a land of darkness; I did not say to the offspring of Jacob, "Seek me in chaos,"

or in a different vein, Isa 47:10:

> You felt secure in your wickedness, you said, "No one sees me"; your wisdom and your knowledge led you astray, and you said in your heart, "I am, and there is no one besides me."

In both cases one would have to suppose a Gnostic exegesis at work, but it is significant to note that both contexts would be less suggestive for the Gnostic mind in their LXX form than in their Hebrew form: e.g. *mataion zētēsate* instead of *tohû baqqešunî* in 45:19, whereas it is precisely out of the primordial chaos that the Demiurge utters his boast. Thus if passages such as this did influence the Gnostic usage, it must not readily be assumed that they were known to the early Gnostic myth-makers in Greek, but rather in the Hebrew or perhaps in a Targumic version.

But even though the likelihood of a special Gnostic predilection for Second Isaiah is established, perhaps we must avoid overstating the case with regard to Gnostic use of the "I am God" formulas, for there is some reason to think

---

[14]Cf. A. Böhlig and P. Labib, *Koptisch-gnostische Apokalypsen aus Codex V von ivag Hammadi* (Berlin, 1963) 86-117; G.W. MacRae, "The Coptic Gnostic Apocalypse of Adam," *Heythrop Journal* 6 (1965) 33-4. Is there an allusion to the prominence of Isaiah in Jewish apocalyptic and/or in Gnosticism in John's statement that Isaiah "saw his glory" (12:41)? R.M. Grant, "Gnostic Origins and the Basilidians of Irenaeus," *VC* 13 (1959) 123, suggests that in their use of the Caulacau formula from Isa 28:10 some Gnostics may have taken this statement literally.

that this statement had become almost a commonplace in some late Jewish circles.[15] Moreover, there are non-Gnostic examples in which it is used specifically in a pejorative setting, such as the idle boast of Babylon in Isa 47:10 cited above. In Sir 33:1 (36:10) God is called upon to avenge his people: "Crush the heads of the rulers of the enemy, who say, 'There is no one but ourselves'" (*ouk estin plēn hēmōn*), but in this instance the main part of the formula is merely implied. A Gnostic reading of such a passage is easy to imagine, however. Finally, two passages from the Christian sections of the Ethiopic Ascension of Isaiah attribute the same boast to the evil angel Beliar (referring to Nero) and to the "princes of this world":

> And all that he had desired he will do in the world: he will do and speak like the Beloved and he will say: "I am God and before me there has been none." And all the people in the world will believe in him. And they will sacrifice to him and they will serve him saying: "This is God and beside him there is no other."
>
> For they have denied Me and said: "We alone are and there is none beside us."[16]

In discussing the significance of the first of these passages, Stauffer draws attention to the support it gives for the use of the "I am" formula by Jesus, "the Beloved" whose speech Nero emulates.[17] But since neither the canonical sources nor any other early Christian works ever attribute to Jesus the words of Isa 43:10 or of any similar Old Testament passage, except the absolute use of *egō eimi*, Stauffer is forced to conclude that the Ascension of Isaiah draws upon an independent tradition. Whether or not there was such a

---

[15]See, for example, the use of '*ny hw' wl' 'hr* in the Passover Haggadah in explanation of "I am Yahweh" in Ex 12:12, pointed out by D. Daube, *The New Testament and Rabbinic Judaism* (London, 1956) 325-9; Stauffer, *Jesus and His Story*, 147.

[16]Trans. R.H. Charles, *The Ascension of Isaiah* (London, 1900) 27 (4.6-8), 71 (10.13). Schenke, p. 93, notes these passages also.

[17]*Jesus and His Story*, 150-1.

tradition must remain a matter for conjecture, but for Jesus ever to have applied to himself explicitly any of the Isaiah statements such as "I am God and there is no other besides me" would be incongruous both with the indirect nature of his self-revelation in Mark and John and with the exigencies of his mission among the Jews in general. On the other hand, the author of this section of the Ascension of Isaiah may be drawing simply on a familiarity with the canonical tradition of Jesus' absolute use of *ego eimi* and on an apocalyptic familiarity with the Deutero-Isaian statement repeated in other contexts. At any rate, there is some witness to the currency of the statement as a blasphemous expression of arrogance in Jewish sources. But merely because the Coptic and other Gnostic works use the citation in a parallel sense, we are not obliged to conclude that they owe it to apocalyptic sources rather than to Isaiah itself, since Gnostic exegesis of the Old Testament is generally perverse in any case, arising from an anti-Jewish bias. And the creation context of the Gnostic cosmogonic myths still seems to favor direct use of Deutero-Isaiah.

The *ego eimi* statement is spoken by the inferior creator-God in a wide variety of Gnostic sources,[18] and always with

---

[18]Valentinians: Irenaeus, *haer.* I.5.4 (Harvey I, pp. 46-7); Hippolytus, *ref.* VI.33 (W. Völker, *Quellen zur Geschichte der christlichen Gnosis*, Tübingen 1932, p. 132); see also *haer* II.9.2 (Harvey I, p. 272). Basilides: *ref.* VII.25.3 (Völker, p. 52). Justin's *Baruch: ref.* V.26.15 (Völker, p. 29). Barbelognostics: *haer.* I.29.4 (Harvey I, p. 226). Ophites: *haer.* I.30.6 (Harvey I, p. 232). Apocryphon of John: codex II: 11.20-1; 12.8-9; 13.8-9 (Krause-Labib, pp. 140-5); BG 43.2-3; 44.14-15 (W. Till, *Die gnostischen Schriften des koptischen Papyrus Berolinensis 8502*, Berlin 1955, pp. 126-8). Hypostasis of the Archons: 134.30-1; 142.21-2; 143.5 (P. Labib, *Coptic Gnostic Papyri in the Coptic Museum at Old Cairo*, Cairo 1956). Untitled Work of Codex II: 148.32-3; 151.11-13; 155.30-1; 160.28-9 (A. Böhlig and P. Labib, *Die koptisch-gnostische Schrift ohne Titel aus codex II von Nag Hammadi*, Berlin 1962, pp. 42, 48, 58, 70). Apocalypse of James II: 56.26-57.1 (fragmentary and conjectural; Böhlig-Labib, *Apokalypsen*, p. 78). Apocalypse of Adam: 66.28-9 (conjectural; *ibid.*, p. 98). Egyptian Gospel: 58.24-6 (J. Doresse, "Le livre sacré du grand Esprit invisible," *Journal Asiatique* 254, 1966, pp. 386-7). Also the unpublished Paraphrase of Shem (Codex VII, Tractate I; cf. J. Doresse, *The Secret Books of the Egyptian Gnostics*, ET London 1960, p. 149). Other examples of the theme may be found in: C.S.C. Williams, "Eznik's Résumé of Marcionite Doctrine," *JTS* 45, 1944, pp. 65-73; and in the Cathar work republished by R. Reitzenstein, *Die Vorgeschichte der christlichen Taufe*, Leipzig and Berlin, 1929, p. 309.

the same intention on the part of the writer: to demonstrate that gross ignorance which the creator-archon possesses and transmits to his followers. Generally the author points out how mistaken the claim is, sometimes by merely calling it a lie or ignorance,[19] sometimes by the logical argument in the Apocryphon of John passage quoted above, and sometimes by a rebuke from Sophia or from a voice out of the pleromatic region, reminding the Demiurge that a higher God exists.[20] With rare exceptions, the Gnostic writers do not themselves refer to the Demiurge as "God," but only represent him as making this false claim for himself.[21]

To sum up, the boast of the Demiurge in the form "I am God and there is no other" is a fixed element of the Gnostic creation myth which recurs in numerous Gnostic sources. It provides an excellent example of the use of *egō* in divine self-proclamations and is rooted in the usage of Deutero-Isaiah or at least in the Jewish apocalyptic application of the Old Testament monotheistic utterance. There is no positive indication in this Gnostic mythologoumenon that the Gnostics were aware of the absolute use of *egō eimi* as a claim to divinity, nor is there any reason to suggest that this Gnostic usage is indebted to the Christian use of Deutero-Isaiah or to the claims of Jesus.

II

A second form of the *egō* proclamation in Gnostic sources as well as in the New Testament is the use of "I am" with a variety of predicates. In this instance, the comparison to be drawn is with the Fourth Gospel. In the Coptic Gnostic

---

[19]E.g. *Apocryphon of John*, Codex II, 11.20-1 (Krause-Labib, p. 140).

[20]E.g. Irenaeus, *haer.* I.30.6 (Harvey I, p. 232).

[21]The Apocalypse of Adam is a notable exception to this general rule, when Adam refers to the lower deity as "the God who made us"; cf. Codex V, 64.17, etc. The Sophia Jesu Christi (BG 104.4-7; Till, p. 248) apparently refers to the boast of the Demiurge and his assumption of the name God: "on account of the pride and the blindness and the ignorance [of the Demiurge], for a name was given to him."

library there are several important instances of this usage which may be briefly described here.

The first is found in Tractate 2 of Codex VI, a codex which contains several Hermetic works. Tractate 2 is entitled "The Thunder: Perfect Mind." This work is a proclamation entirely in the first person, spoken by an apparently female figure who is probably meant to be the figure named in the title. In fact, the word "thunder" does not recur in the work (apparently, for there are lacunae), and *nous teleios* recurs only once and only if a probable reconstruction is correct. In the latter case the speaker specifically says, "I am the [perfect] mind." The name "thunder" suggests a divine or quasi-divine voice and reminds us of a usage very frequent in many ancient literatures: e.g. the *Juppiter tonans* of classical literature, the magical papyri, the God of the Old Testament, John 12:29, Rev 10:3-4, etc. In particular one may call attention to the epithet of Isis, in the Kyme aretalogy, 42: "I am the mistress of the thunder."[22]

In its content the tractate consists of three types of statement, more or less intermingled throughout: self-proclamations in the first person singular ("I am the first and the last," etc.), exhortations to heed the speaker ("Look upon me. . .?" etc.), and reproaches ("Why have you hated me. . .?" etc.). These are addressed to "hearers" (*akroatēs*), "you who know me," etc., and to "Greeks" as opposed to "barbarians": "For I am the wisdom (*sophia*) of the Greeks and the knowledge (*gnōsis*) of the barbarians." This may, however, be a purely conventional designation; compare Kyme aretalogy 31: "I appointed languages for Greeks and barbarians."[23] Perhaps a similar caution has to be made with regard to the possible mention (the reading is uncertain) of Egypt.

What is particularly distinctive about this document is the fact that the numerous "I am" proclamations contained in it

---

[22]J. Bergman, *Ich bin Isis. Studien zum memphitischen Hintergrund der griechischen Isisaretalogien* (Uppsala, 1968) 302.

[23]*Ibid.*

are for the most part either sharp antitheses, e.g. "I am the mother and the daughter," or outright paradoxes, e.g. "I am the mother of my father and the sister of my husband, and he is my offspring," or "I am knowledge and ignorance; I am shame and boldness."

Any attempt to classify this work in terms of the types of literature represented in the Nag Hammadi collection may be premature until it can be studied in detail and compared with the entire corpus. There is nothing at all specifically Christian in it and very little that is Jewish, although the style is occasionally reminiscent of the wisdom hymns. On the other hand, the work does not appear to be especially "Gnostic" either. One recognizes such passages as the following:

> What is within you is what it outside you, and the one who fashioned the outside of you shaped the inside of you. And what you see outside of you you see inside of you; it is revealed and it is your garment.[24]

But it is not clear that even such a popular Gnostic image is originally Gnostic. Nor does The Thunder appear to be related to the Hermetic works in the same codex.

The closest analogies are to the Isis hymns which have been studied most recently by J. Bergman, who traces the origin of the aretalogy hymns to Egyptian soil.[25] It seems highly likely that The Thunder owes its use of the first-person style to the aretalogy form, which, of course, had spread far beyond Egypt. But except for occasional indirect allusions such as those mentioned above, this work does not have the same predications as the aretalogies do. Notably, the aretalogies predicate a wide variety of things about Isis, but they do not use the forms of antithesis and paradox found in The Thunder. We shall return momentarily to what may be a possible significance of this difference.

---

[24]Cf. Gospel of Thomas, logion 22 (A. Guillaumont et al., *The Gospel according to Thomas,* Leiden 1959, p. 16); Gospel of Philip 116.4-6. (J.-E. Ménard, *L'Evangile selon Philippe* (Paris, 1967) 80 and references, 188).

[25]See n. 22 above.

M. Krause has pointed out a parallel to this work in a short, probably hymnic passage attributed to Eve, the first virgin, in the Untitled Work (Tractate 5) of Codex II which reads as follows:[26]

> I am the part of my mother, and I am the mother; I am the woman, I am the virgin; I am she who is pregnant; I am the physician; I am the comforter of birth-pangs. It is my husband who begot me, and I am his mother and he is my father and my lord; he is my power; whatever he wishes he says. I come into being reasonably (*eulogōs*). But I have begotten a lordly man.[27]

In its setting in the Untitled Work this pasage has all the marks of a citation of traditional material, and though it is not a direct quotation, we doubtless have a more ample witness to the same tradition in The Thunder.

We find what is a somewhat different use of the predicative *egō eimi* proclamation in two other works from the Nag Hammadi collection, which can be dealt with only very briefly here. The first is the main work of Codex XIII, "The Triple Protennoia,"[28] a narrative composition in three parts, told in the first person by the revealer figure. Besides containing the classic account of creation and the pre-creation drama familiar from many of the Nag Hammadi works, it describes the triple descent of the revealer into the world to save the divine spark in mankind. The work is filled with proclamations in the I-style, some of which are antithetical, but not in the paradoxical style of The Thunder. It may be noted that this work contains the name Christ and a few other Christian allusions, but it is at best only very superficially Christianized.

There is a close parallel to this work in the longer ending of the Codex II version of the Apocryphon of John.[29] This is

---

[26]Cf. *Le origini dello gnosticismo*, ed. U. Bianchi (Supplements to *Numen*, 12, (Leiden, 1967) 82.

[27]162.7-15 (Böhlig and Labib, *Schrift ohne Titel*, p. 74).

[28]Cf. J. M. Robinson, "The Coptic Gnostic Library Today" *NTS* 14 (1967-8) 401.

[29]30.11—31.25 (Krause-Labib, pp. 195-8).

also a first-person narrative of the triple descent of the Pronoia into the world to awaken the dormant gnosis in men. The parallel here also extends to the frequent use of the first-person style of proclamation: "I am the perfect Pronoia of the all. . .; I am the richness of the light, I am the remembrance of the Pleroma."[30] In a study of this passage I have suggested that this ending was a hymnic, probably cultic summary of a narrative recital of the Gnostic "salvation history."[31] It is now apparent from Codex XIII that we have an extended narrative of the same material with which to compare the hymnic summary.

Finally, in surveying the use of the *egō*-proclamation in Gnostic sources, we should call attention briefly to two sayings of the Gospel of Thomas which also contain "I am" proclamations attributed to Jesus: "I am the one who exists out of that which is the same" and "I am the light which is above them all; I am the all."[32] It is easy to recognize the Gnostic coloring of the Thomas saying "I am the light *which is above*" as opposed to the Johannine "I am the light *of the world."* If it is not actually independent of the New Testament usage—and I think that it is—the Thomas use of the "I am" style is different, and it may be another instance of an already traditional form.

To conclude this brief survey of the predicative use of *egō* proclamations in the Gnostic sources, I should like to suggest possible lines for comparison with the Fourth Gospel. Two observations will be made without detailed development; they are intended merely as suggestions for further research.

First, it has often been objected to Bultmann's commentary on the Fourth Gospel that his derivation of the Johannine use of the "I am" style from Mandaean sources is questionable, not least because of the doubtful antiquity of the Mandaean materials. Sometimes a compromise is reached in

[30]30.11-12, 15-16.

[31]*Le origini dello gnosticismo*, p. 502.

[32]Logia 61 and 77 (Guillaumont, pp. 34, 42).

the proposal that both John and the Mandaean writings shared a common source in this respect.[33] With such abundant evidence of the Gnostic use of predicative *egō eimi* proclamations, one can shift the focus of the discussion away from Mandaeism, and it may be found that the Gnostic sources—whose antiquity is still, of course, uncertain—offer an even closer parallel.

Secondly, it has already been observed that the predicative "I am" proclamations found in these Gnostic sources may have originated in the syncretistic form of the Isis aretalogies, but that The Thunder adds a new element in its use of antithesis and paradox. I would suggest the following brief analysis of this difference. In the Isis hymns the purpose of the many "I am" sayings is to state the *universality* of the goddess Isis: she is known by many names, she is the source and origin of the manifold religious aspirations of men. In a word, Isis corresponds to all that men worship and think and long for. But the paradoxical form of the "I am" sayings in The Thunder seems to me to have as its goal a statement of the *transcendence*, not merely the universality, of the revealer, perfect mind. She is not simply the truth or reality of all men's aspirations, but she is of a higher order than the moral, conventional and rational standards of the world. She is both the saint and the prostitute, both peace and war, both innocence and sin, both law and lawlessness, both master and slave, both silence and word, both hidden and revealed, both wise and foolish. In the face of divine revelation no human values are adequate.

Now, of course, the Fourth Gospel does not use this paradoxical form in the *egō* proclamations of Jesus. Nevertheless, it may be that the Fourth Gospel, taking into consideration its over-all structure and its techniques, uses the form of *egō* proclamation not merely to assert that Jesus must be recognized as or identified with[34] the variety of human religious symbolism: bread, light, shepherd, life,

---

[33]See, e.g., E. Schweizer, *EGO EIMI* ... (FRLANT 56, 1939).

[34]Using the classification of Bultmann, *Das Evangelium des Johannes*, 168.

etc.,[35] but that Jesus in his truest reality *transcends* all of this and is revealed only in the moment of his return to the Father, through death and resurrection, as the love of the Father for men. This suggestion is based on the view that the Fourth Gospel means to pass a negative judgment, as ch. 12 explicitly does, on the success of Jesus' self-revelation through sign and symbol. In effect it would suppose that the evangelist is not merely influenced by a complex and syncretistic religious background, but that he deliberately makes use of such a background for his interpretation of the meaning of Jesus.[36] This view cannot be substantiated in detail here, nor has it been the intention of this paper to do so, but if it is tenable, it points to a parallel between some of the Gnostic sources in which the *egō* proclamation appears and the Fourth Gospel—a parallel not so much in words or explicit allusions, as in religious outlook and religious discourse.

[35]Compare the remarks of Stauffer, article *egō* TDNT II, 350; Schweizer, *op. cit.*, p. 122.

[36]Cf. e.g., E. Fascher, "Platon und Johannes in ihren Verhältnis zu Sokrates und Christus," *Das Altertum* 14 (1968) 83; Schweizer, 167.

14

Prayer and Knowledge
of Self in Gnosticism*

I

In his famous book on prayer, which is so often cited in
any discussion of the topic, Friedrich Heiler begins his
Introduction with a paragraph entitled "Prayer as the
Central Phenomenon of Religion."[1] In it he quotes with
approval a statement of Adolf Deissmann to the effect that
"for students of religion and religions there are no more
instructive sources than prayers and testimonies concerning
prayer. They characterize a religion, a religious level, a
devout person better than mythology, legends, dogmas,
ethics or theology." One could actually "write a history of
religion by writing a history of prayer."[2]

The question to which this article is addressed is whether
or not such an assessment of the centrality of prayer can be
applied to that unconventional religion of the early centuries
of our era which interacted in various ways with Christianity,
the Gnostic religion. The issue is problematic because at first
sight both the Gnostic writings themselves and the patristic

---

*First published in *Tantur Yearbook* (1978-1979) 97-114.

[1] *Das Gebet. Eine religionsgeschichtliche und religionspsychologische Untersuchung* (reprint of 5th ed.; Munich: Reinhardt, 1969) 1.

[2] *Evangelium und Urchristentum* (Munich, 1905) 95-96, cited by Heiler, 2.

descriptions of Gnosticism give us conflicting signals about the practice and even the possibility of prayer among Gnostics. The procedure that we shall follow in this exposition of the question will be first to sketch the problematic character of Gnostic prayer, and then to present and briefly discuss examples of two types of prayers found in Gnostic literature.

It may be advisable, however, to call attention first to some limits of this inquiry. Thanks to important recent discoveries and publications in Gnosticism (the Nag Hammadi documents), Manicheism, Mandaeism, and Hermetism, there is an extensive new wave of scholarly study of the Gnostic religion in its various manifestations.[3] For the purposes of this lecture our investigation will be confined to what is generally called Gnosticism in the narrow sense, namely those individuals and groups of the second to the fourth centuries who were opposed by the Christian heresilogical tradition and many of whose writings are now available to us. This area of Gnosticism is far from homogeneous, however, for it includes both Christian and non-Christian Gnostics and their works. For purposes of comparison, we shall mention briefly some prayer practices in the contemporary pagan Gnosis of Egypt, Hermetism.

It is customary in discursive treatments of prayer to set forth a number of distinctions that help to define categories of prayer. Already we find Origen in his treatise on prayer (14.2-6) exegeting 1 Tim 2:1 in this vein: "I urge that supplications (*deēseis*), prayers (*proseuchai*), intercessions (*enteuxeis*), and thanksgivings (*eucharistiai*) be made for all people." Without trying to be exhaustive, or even properly systematic, we may mention some of the customary distinctions as a way of narrowing further the scope of the present discussion.[4]

First, prayer may be either vocal or mental. We are

---

[3]Rather than cite the literature here, one may refer to the excellent recent survey of Kurt Rudolph, *Die Gnosis. Wesen und Geschichte einer spätantiken Religion* (Göttingen: Vandenhoeck & Ruprecht, 1977).

[4]Compare the survey of categories in Heiler's concluding section, pp. 486-87.

concerned here mainly with the former. In fact, mental prayer—meditation, contemplation, the "prayer of silence"— as it has been known and written about for centuries in the Christian and of course the Far Eastern traditions is not as prominent in the early centuries of our era in the West as one might expect, nor is it referred to by the usual words for prayer. Since our Gnostic sources rarely discuss prayer but usually only give examples of it which are, as prayers embedded in narratives, dialogues, or treatises, essentially vocal prayers, we shall be mainly limited to them. But, as we shall see, there is some evidence for a kind of mental prayer also.

Secondly, prayer may be individual or corporate, the latter often taking the form of liturgical prayer. There are some instances of corporate or liturgical prayer formulas in descriptions of Gnostic sects and their rites in Irenaeus and Epiphanius, for example, but we shall avoid here the difficult question of Gnostic liturgical practice and concentrate on the prayers of individuals or small groups such as the apostles. If logical consistency were an operative principle in the development of religious practices, and it certainly is not, one would expect of Gnostics only individual prayer if any at all. It is the practice of corporate worship, however inadequate our evidence for it, that is the more surprising.

Thirdly, vocal prayer, individual or corporate, may be expressed either in prose or in hymnic form. Important as this distinction is in the study of many religious traditions, it is not as helpful as one might think in the analysis of Gnostic, or for that matter, very early Christian sources. That hymns were used in earliest Christianity is not in question, for they are attested not only by the mention of them in such passages as Col 3:16 (*psalmoi, hymnoi, ōdai*), but also by widely acknowledged examples such as Phil 2:6-11. And in Gnostic sources we know of such famous examples as the "Hymn of the Pearl" in the Acts of Thomas or the so-called "Naassene Psalm" attached to Hippolytus' account of the Naassene Gnostics. But these Gnostic examples, though they may of course have had a function as prayer, are of a narrative that does not readily fit the model of prayer as address to God. The main problem with the distinction between prose and hymn in the early period, however, lies in the fact that both early Christian and Gnostic hymns were written in a form of stylized prose that blurs the distinction, especially when one realizes that there is an inherent tendency in the language of formal prayer itself toward exalted and poetic forms of expression. Metrical hymnody is known in Christian texts only from the third century on. For this reason, therefore, we shall not be concerned with identifying hymns as such in our Gnostic sources.

Finally, there are the various distinctions made among prayers by virtue of their content, for example between prayer of petition, which may be personal or intercessory, and prayer of praise and/or thanksgiving. In this regard we shall deal with prayers of various types, sometimes in combination, as is often the case with Christian prayers, and we shall observe one possibly significant division between prayers of petition and prayers of praise.

Christian church writers contemporary with the Gnostics, and often their bitter opponents, have left us a number of treatises on prayer such as the *De oratione* of Tertullian or the *Peri euchēs* of Origen. These are informative both for the practice and for the theology of prayer. They have in common a predilection for commenting in some detail on the Lord's Prayer as the example par excellence of Christian prayer, so much so that Cyprian, who depends to some extent on Tertullian, wrote a treatise called simply *De dominica oratione*. The Gnostics, however, whether Christian or not, have not left us anything quite like a treatise on prayer,[5] and we are compelled to deduce their practice and understanding of it from more casual sources. Though the Christian Gnostics made extensive use of the New Testament, they do not seem to have followed the practice of commenting on the Lord's Prayer.

---

[5]On the Hermetic tractate *The Discourse on the Eighth and Ninth* see below.

II

What makes prayer, at least theoretically, problematic in Gnosticism is the nature of the saving *gnōsis* itself, which is essentially knowledge of self, that is, knowledge of the divine as constitutive of the true being of the knower.[6] In its now famous attempt to provide a generally agreed-upon definition of Gnosticism, the Messina Colloquium of 1966 spoke of the particular understanding of *gnōsis* in Gnosticism as involving "the divine identity of the knower (the Gnostic), the known (the divine substance of one's transcendent self), and the means by which one knows (gnosis as an implicit divine faculty . . .)."[7] It is this emphasis on self-knowledge which is reflected in the widely quoted Valentinian formula in the *Excerpta ex Theodoto* 78, 2:

> It is not the bath alone which liberates, but it is also the knowledge of who we were, what we have become, where we were, into what we have been cast, whither we are hastening, whence we have been redeemed, what birth is, what rebirth is.

The Gnostic texts from Nag Hammadi provide numerous examples which confirm the centrality of this self-knowledge and sometimes make it even more explicit. The *Gospel of Truth*, which is in all likelihood also a Valentinian work, echoes Theodotus when it says: "He who is to have knowledge in this manner [i.e., by having his 'name' called by the Father] knows where he comes from and where he is going."[8] The *Gospel of Thomas* even more clearly states the importance of knowing oneself when Jesus says:

[6]Cf. Eric Segelberg, "Prayer Among the Gnostics?" in Martin Krause, ed., *Gnosis and Gnosticism* (NHS 8, Leiden: Brill, 1977) 55-69. I acknowledge my debt to this pioneering article on prayer in Gnosticism.

[7]Ugo Bianchi, ed., *Le origini dello gnosticismo* (Supplements to *Numen* XII; Leiden: Brill, 1967) XXVII.

[8]CG I,3: 22, 13-15. References to the Nag Hammadi works are by codex, tractate, page, and lines. For convenience all translations are taken from James M. Robinson and Marvin W. Meyer, eds., *The Nag Hammadi Library in English* (San Francisco: Harper & Row, 1977).

When you come to know yourselves, then you will become known, and you will realize that it is you who are the sons of the living Father. But if you will not know yourselves, you dwell in poverty and it is you who are that poverty.[9]

The Gnostic use of the ancient Delphic maxim *gnōthi sauton*, "know thyself," is also reflected in another work connected with the name of Thomas, the *Book of Thomas the Contender*, a radically ascetical statement of Christian Gnosticism. At the beginning of his revelation dialogue with Thomas, Jesus says:

Now since it has been said that you are my twin and true companion, examine yourself that you may understand who you are, in what way you exist, and how you will come to be. Since you are called my brother, it is not fitting that you be ignorant of yourself. And I know that you have understood, because you had already understood that I am the knowledge of the truth. So while you accompany me, although you are uncomprehending, you have (in fact) already come to know, and you will be called "the one who knows himself." For he who has not known himself has known nothing, but he who has known himself has at the same time already achieved knowledge about the Depth of the All.[10]

In its long history the Delphic maxim assumed, in light of the context in which it was used, many different meanings, some of them diametrically opposed to one another.[11] One might contrast, for example, the Greek iconographical use of the formula as a caption for a representation of a skeleton, with the emphasis on the immortality of the soul in other

---

[9]Logion 3; CG II, 2: 32, 26-33, 5.

[10]CG II, 7: 138, 7-18.

[11]Cf. Hans Dieter Betz, "The Delphic Maxim *Gnōthi sauton* in Hermetic Interpretation," *HTR* 63 (1970) 465-84, and the major study of Pierre Courcelle, *Connais-toi toi-même, de Socrate à Saint Bernard* (3 vols.; Paris: Etudes Augustiniennes, 1974-75); on the Gnostic usage see vol. I, pp. 69-82.

strains of Greek tradition: "Know that thou art immortal." For the Gnostics "know thyself" meant to know one's divine origin, nature, and destiny as being a particle or seed of the divine provisionally imprisoned in the human condition.

This aspect of the Gnostic discovery of the divine within the human minimizes if not eradicates the "otherness" of God upon which the fundamental experience of prayer depends. It therefore would seem at least at first sight to render prayer superfluous or even meaningless. Such a conclusion is confirmed by some of the patristic accounts of Gnosticism as well as by some Gnostic texts. Hippolytus quotes a letter from the Gnostic Monoimus the Arabian to a certain Theophrastus in which he says:

> Cease to seek after God and creation and things like these, and seek after yourself, and learn who it is who appropriates all things within you without exception and says, "My God, my mind, my thought, my soul, my body," and learn whence comes grief and rejoicing and love and hatred, and waking without intention, and sleeping without intention, and love without intention. And if you carefully consider these things, you will find yourself within yourself, being both one and many..., and will find the outcome of yourself.[12]

In his long discussion of the necessity and manner of prayer for the "true Gnostic," Clement of Alexandria says of the followers of the libertine Gnostic Prodicus that they teach that one should not pray.[13] A similar attitude is reflected in several sayings in the *Gospel of Thomas*. In a rejection of the classic forms of Jewish and Jewish-Christian piety—fasting, prayer, and almsgiving—Jesus says: "And if you pray, you will be condemned." And in an enigmatic

---

[12]*Refutatio* VIII. 15.1, trans. Werner Foerster (English trans., ed. R. McL. Wilson), *Gnosis. A Selection of Gnostic Texts, I. Patristic Evidence* (Oxford: Clarendon, 1972) 250.

[13]*Stromata* VII.7 (41, 1). Origen in his treatise on prayer (5-8) also argues against those who say that one should not pray, but without explicitly identifying them as Gnostics or suggesting that self-knowledge is the obstacle to prayer.

saying, he responds to the invitation of the disciples, "Come, let us pray today and let us fast":

> What is the sin that I have committed, or wherein have I been defeated? But when the bridegroom leaves the bridal chamber, then let them fast and pray.[14]

However one should interpret the reference to the bridegroom, the saying suggests a negative attitude toward prayer on the part of Jesus himself and thus also of those who would be like him. This negative attitude seems also to appear in the *Gospel of Philip* in such passages as the following, which rejects prayer as a proper mode of behavior for the Gnostic living in this world:

> Those who sow in winter reap in summer. The winter is the world, the summer the other aeon. Let us sow in the world that we may reap in the summer. Because of this it is fitting for us not to pray in the winter. Summer follows winter. But if any man reap in winter he will not actually reap but only pluck out, since this sort of thing will not provide [him] a harvest.[15]

But the evidence of this Gnostic gospel is very mixed; elsewhere, for example, it speaks positively of "the cup of prayer" with reference to the Eucharist.[16]

These passages are enough to show that there did exist among some gnostics a disdain for prayer that was probably rooted, as the letter of Monoimus and the *Gospel of Thomas* imply, in the Gnostic perception of saving *gnōsis* as knowledge of self. But if we are to judge by the body of Gnostic literature now available to us, the rejection of prayer was the exception rather than the rule, for there are many examples of prayer and even exhortations to pray in the Nag Hammadi corpus. We shall next turn to some selected examples in

---

[14]Quotations from Logion 14, 35, 16-17, and Logion 104, 50, 10-16. See also Logion 6. Cf. Segelberg, 58-60.

[15]CG II, 3: 52, 25-33.

[16]75, 14-15. Cf. Segelberg, *art. cit.*, pp. 56-58.

search of a preliminary understanding of Gnostic prayers. It will be important to observe that despite their notion of self-knowledge as knowledge of the divine, the Gnostics are rarely so radically consistent as to identify themselves purely and simply with the highest God. They belong to him, are indeed a part of him, but there remains enough awareness of his otherness as the totality of the divine to make possible and even necessary prayer to the Father and indeed to his emissary the Son. The *Testimony of Truth*, for example, can insist as much as any Gnostic document on self-knowledge as redemptive: "[This] is the perfect life, [that] man know [himself] by means of the All." But it can also use a more accurate formulation in its classic summary statement of the Gnostic message:

> This, therefore, is the true testimony: when man knows himself and God who is over the truth, he will be saved, and he will be crowned with the crown unfading.[17]

III

The first example of Gnostic prayer consists of two short prayers taken from the *Letter of Peter to Philip*. This tractate is not really a letter, though it begins with one, but a brief apocryphal acts of apostles consisting of a reinterpretation of certain passages in the canonical Book of Acts. It is designed to show how the apostles were emboldened to confront the dangers of their mission in a hostile world dominated by demonic powers once they had received the communication of saving knowledge from the risen Jesus. They pray for strength in the following manner:

> Then, when the apostles had come together and thrown themselves upon their knees, they prayed, saying, "Father, Father, Father of the Light who possesses the incor-

---

[17]CG IX, 3: 36, 26-28 and 44, 29-45, 6.

ruptions, hear us just as [...] in thy holy child Jesus Christ. For he became for us an illuminator in the [darkness]. Yea hear us."

And they prayed again another time, saying, "Son of life, Son of Immortality who is in the light, Son, Christ of Immortality, our Redeemer, give us power, for they seek to kill us."[18]

The first of these prayers, addressed to the Father, the most common name for the supreme God of Gnosticism, is very unspecific in its petition (the lacuna not being large enough to add much to the content). It serves mainly as an introduction to the second prayer, which is highly specific in its petition for power to resist the hostile forces. But the very fact that the first prayer is merely conventional in content may be an indication of the role played by prayer in some Gnostic circles, namely that it is taken almost for granted.

In what follows these prayers the voice of Jesus comes to the assembled apostles and seems at first sight to rebuke them for praying: "Listen to my words that I may speak to you. Why are you asking me? I am Jesus Christ who is with you forever." But the document is not in fact negative with regard to prayer, for the voice later instructs the apostles: "Gird yourselves with the power of my Father, and let your prayer be known."[19]

These two prayers introduce us to a characteristic, almost distinctive, formal element of Gnostic prayers, the use of a triple form of address and sometimes of statement in the prayers: for example, "Father, Father, Father of the Light," or "Son of Life, Son of Immortality, Son, Christ of Immortality." Among the many examples, there is a prayer to twelve heavenly powers in the unfortunately rather fragmentary work *Melchizedek*, which contains a repeated refrain of which the following is a reconstructed typical element: "Holy are you, holy are you, holy are you, Mother

[18]CG VIII, 2: 133, 17-134, 9.

[19]134, 15-18 and 137, 26-28.

of the aeons, Barbelo, for ever and ever. Amen."[20] This example suggests that the triple form is merely an extension of the Trishagion well known already in Christian usage. But the majority of examples of the form do not connote the Trishagion. To give another illustration, we find in the Nag Hammadi work called by modern scholars *A Valentinian Exposition* a number of prayers including the following:

> And we [glorify] thee: [Glory] be to thee, the Father in the [Son, the Father] in the Son, [the] Father [in the] holy [Church and in the] holy [angels]! From now on he abides forever [in the fellowship] of the Aeons, [until] the eternities, until the [untraceable] Aeons of the Aeons. Amen.[21]

One would hesitate to suggest that this triple invocation is significantly characteristic of Gnostic prayers were it not for the fact that, apart from the use of the Trishagion, it is significantly absent from Christian prayers preserved from the first few centuries of our era. There are traces of a triple invocation in one or two prayers attributed to early martyrs, but in general it is very rare. What is found in Christian prayers are the use of the Trishagion in various forms and the triple Agnus Dei.[22]

Not all the prayers in the Nag Hammadi codices may properly be classified as Gnostic prayers. For example, there is the prayer of the martyr James which concludes the (*Second*) *Apocalypse of James*. It is worth quoting in full here because it is a little-known example of a fine martyr's prayer. Neither formally—it has no triple invocation nor any appeal to heavenly beings other than God—nor in content is it typically Gnostic. It probably represents part of the Jewish-Christian tradition upon which the *Apocalypse*

[20]CG IX, 1: 16, 16-18, 7.

[21]CG XI, 2: 40, 20-29. This tractate contains other prayers which do not have the triple structure.

[22]Cf. A. Hamman, *Prières des premiers Chrétiens* (Paris: Fayard, 1952). Relevant examples of the martyrs' prayers are found on pp. 97, 102 (?), and 95, the prayer of Agathonica: "Lord, Lord, Lord, come to my aid; to thee I have recourse."

draws. It is interesting to note that the author of the work, who presents James clearly, though with restraint, as a Gnostic initiate, may be aware of the non-Gnostic character of the prayer when he introduces it as "this prayer—not that (one) which it is his custom to say":

> My God and my Father,
>> who saved me from this dead hope,
>> who made me alive through a mystery of what he wills,
>
> do not let these days of this world be prolonged for me,
> but the day of your [light . . .] remains
>> in [. . .] salvation.
>
> Deliver me from this [place of] sojourn!
> Do not let your grace be left behind in me,
>> but may your grace become pure!
>
> Save me from an evil death!
> Bring me from a tomb alive,
>> because your grace—love—is alive in me
>> to accomplish a work of fullness!
>
> Save me from sinful flesh,
>> because I trusted in you with all my strength!
>> Because you are the life of the life,
>
> save me from a humiliating enemy!
> Do not give me into the hand of a judge
>> who is severe with sin!
>
> Forgive me all my debts of the days (of my life)!
> Because I am alive in you, your grace is alive in me.
> I have renounced everyone,
>> but you I have confessed.
>
> Save me from evil affliction!
> But now is the [time] and the hour.
> O Holy [Spirit], send [me]
>> salvation [. . .] the light [. . .]
>> the light [. . .] in a power [. . .].[23]

---

[23]CG V, 4: 62, 16-63, 29. For a different interpretation of the prayer see Wolf-Peter Funk, *Die zweite Apokalypse des Jakobus aus Nag-Hammadi-Codex V* (TU 119; Berlin: Akademie-Verlag, 1976) 179-91 and 211-20. Funk's discussion calls attention to several Gnostic and Manichean prayers not dealt with here.

For another example of an unmistakably Gnostic prayer, it may be instructive to quote in full what survives from the *Prayer of the Apostle Paul,* which is inscribed on the front flyleaf of the Jung Codex from the Nag Hammadi collection. Some brief comments will follow the citation:

> [. . . your] light, give me your [mercy]!
>
> [My] Redeemer, redeem me, for [I am] yours: from you have I come forth.
>
> You are [my] mind: bring me forth!
>
> You are my treasure-house: open to me!
>
> You [are] my fullness: take me to you!
>
> You are [my] repose: give me [the] perfection that cannot be grasped!
>
> I invoke you, the one who is and preexisted, by the name [which is] exalted above every name, through Jesus Christ [the Lord] of Lords, the king of the ages: give me your gifts which you do not regret through the Son of Man, the Spirit, the Paraclete of [truth].
>
> Give me authority [when I] ask you; give healing for my body when I ask you through the Evangelist, [and] redeem my eternal light-soul and my spirit.
>
> And the [First]-born of the pleroma of grace—[reveal] him to my mind!
>
> Grant what no angel-eye has [seen] and no archon-ear [has] heard and what [has not] entered into the human heart, which came to be angelic and (came to be) after the image of the psychic God when it was formed in the beginning, since I have faith and hope. And place upon me your beloved, elect, and blessed greatness, the First-born, the First-begotten, [. . .] and the [wonderful] mystery of your house; [for] yours is the power [and] the glory and the blessing and the [greatness] for ever and ever. [Amen.(?)][24]

Because the opening lines of the prayer are lost, it is not possible to observe whether it contained the triple invocation

[24]CG I, 1: A, 1-B, 10.

found in many other Gnostic prayers. Perhaps more importantly, it is not quite clear to whom the prayer is addressed if one thinks in Christian Trinitarian terms, though it is probably to the Father. The title "Redeemer" does not appear to be addressed to Jesus. Such ambiguity about the God addressed in Gnostic prayer, however, would seem to be consistent with the underlying Gnostic emphasis on *gnōsis* as self-knowledge. The prayer is obviously dependent on the New Testament in its language, and it ends with a common form of doxology. Its Gnostic theology is equally unmistakable and can be perceived in the interpretation of the saying in 1 Cor 2:9 in which the negative role of angels, archons, and the "psychic God" presupposes a typically Gnostic creation myth.

The prayer is exclusively a prayer of petition for redemption, perfection, spiritual gifts, revelation, and the like. It clearly shows that the principle of self-knowledge was for some Gnostics no obstacle to prayer of petition for enlightenment and salvation. Further, it suggests that the patristic heresiologists' indignation that the Gnostics considered themselves as *physei sōzmenoi*, saved by their (divine) nature and not by God's gracious gift, was not pertinent in all cases.

For purpose of comparison, one may cite the Hermetic *Prayer of Thanksgiving* which is preserved in Greek in the magical Papyrus Mimaut and in Latin as the conclusion to the *Asclepius* in the Corpus Hermeticum. In the Nag Hammadi corpus we now have a Coptic version which is placed immediately after the Hermetic *Discourse on the Eighth and Ninth* and is thus perhaps intended to illustrate the prayer of which the *Discourse* speaks. The following translation is from the Coptic version:

> We give thanks to Thee! Every soul and heart is lifted up to Thee, O undisturbed name, honored with the name "God" and praised with the name "Father," for to everyone and everything (comes) the fatherly kindness and affection and love and any teaching there may be that is sweet and plain, giving us mind, speech, (and) knowledge: mind, so

that we may understand Thee, speech, so that we may expound Thee, knowledge, so that we may know Thee. We rejoice, having been illumined by Thy knowledge. We rejoice because Thou hast shown us Thyself. We rejoice because while we were in (the) body, Thou hast made us divine through Thy knowledge.

The delight of the man who attains to Thee is one thing: that we know Thee. We have known Thee, O intellectual light. O life of life, we have known Thee. O womb of every creature, we have known thee. O womb pregnant with the nature of the Father, we have known Thee. O eternal permanence of the begetting Father, thus have we worshipped Thy goodness. There is one petition that we ask: we would be preserved in knowledge. And there is one protection that we desire: that we not stumble in this kind of life.[25]

This prayer is mainly one of thanksgiving, and thus quite different from the preceding, but it too contains at the end a prayer of petition for preservation in knowledge and perseverance in the Hermetic way of life. Like the Christian gnostic documents already cited, it refers to the divinity of the self: "Thou has made us divine through Thy knowledge." Evidently the process of Hermetic divinization through *gnōsis* is one that requires divine assistance to sustain.

Our final example of Gnostic prayer introduces us to a quite different type of prayer and even a different type of Gnosticism. It is taken from the Nag Hammadi work entitled *The Three Steles of Seth*, which consists almost in its entirety of three prayers, supposedly written by the eponymous hero of Sethian Gnosticism and inscribed on steles. The opening lines introduce the work as follows:

---

[25] CG VI, 7: 63, 34-65, 2. The three versions are presented in Douglas M. Parrott, ed., *Nag Hammadi Codices V, 2-5 and VI with Papyrus Berolinensis 8502, 1 and 4* (NHS 11: Leiden: Brill, 1979) 378-87, and in Jean-Pierre Mahé, *Hermes en Haute Egyptè Les textes hermétiques de Nag Hammadi et leurs parallèles grecs et latins,* Tome I (Bibliothèque Copte de Nag Hammadi, Section Textes 3; Quebec: Université Laval, 1978).

> The revelation of Dositheos about the three steles of Seth,
> the Father of the living and unshakable race, which he
> (Dositheos) saw and understood. And after he had read
> them, he remembered them. And he gave them to the
> elect, just as they were inscribed there.
> Many times I joined in giving glory with the powers, and I
> became worthy, through them, of the immeasurable
> majesties.[26]

The prayers are notably different from those we have seen so
far in that they are almost exclusively prayers of praise,
although there is an occasional element of petition in them,
for example: "Unite us as thou hast been united. Teach us
[those] things which thou dost see. Empower [us] that we
may be saved to eternal life."[27] Secondly, they are different
in that they show no Christian elements nor even any
evidence of contact with Christianity. They represent, as do
several other related works in the Nag Hammadi collection,
a form of non-Christian Sethian Gnosticism. The three
prayers are addressed to the heavenly Father of Seth, to
Barbelo, and to the supreme Father. The following selection
of passages, which is quite indicative of the genre, is taken
from the third "stele":

> We rejoice! We rejoice! We rejoice!
> We have seen! We have seen! We have seen the really
> preexistent one (masc.) really existing, being the first
> eternal one.
> O Unconceived, from thee are the eternal ones and
> the aeons, the all-perfect ones who are established, and
> the perfect individuals.
> We bless thee, non-being existence which is before
> existences, first being which is before beings, Father of
> divinity and life, creator of mind, giver of good, giver of
> blessedness!
> Present a command to us to see thee, so that we may be

[26]CG VII, 5: 118, 10-23.
[27]123, 30-124, 1.

saved. Knowledge of thee, it is the salvation of us all. Present a command! When thou dost command, we have been saved! Truly we have been saved! We have seen thee by mind! Thou art them all, for thou dost save them all, he who was not saved, nor was he saved through them. For thou, thou hast commanded us.

Thou art one, thou art one, just as there is one (who) will say to thee: Thou art one, thou art a single living spirit. How shall we give thee a name? We do not have it. For thou art the existence of them all. Thou art the life of them all. Thou art the mind of them all. [For] thou [art he in whom they all] rejoice.

As what shall we bless thee? We are not empowered. But we give thanks, as being humble toward thee. For thou hast commanded us, as he who is elect, to glorify thee to the extent that we are able. We bless thee, for we were saved. Always we glorify thee. For this reason we shall glorify thee, that we may be saved to eternal salvation. We have blessed thee, for we are empowered. We have been saved, for thou hast willed always that we all do this.[28]

In a preliminary study of this prayer, James M. Robinson has shown its relationship to other works of the Nag Hammadi collection, chiefly *Zostrianos* and *Allogenes*, which together undoubtedly represent the writings of Gnostics which Porphyry tells us were read and refuted by Plotinus.[29] Robinson has clearly demonstrated that the three prayers represent the utterances of the Gnostic as he ascends spiritually to the three levels of Mind, Life, and Existence—a triad characteristic of later Neoplatonic thought and mentioned also in the selection just quoted. The ascent is described in *Zostrianos* and especially in *Allogenes* with only fragments of prayers extant, but enough to make the

---

[28]124, 17-126, 32.

[29]James M. Robinson, "The Three Steles of Seth and the Gnostics of Plotinus," *Proceedings of the International Colloquium on Gnosticism, Stockholm August 20-25, 1973* (Stockholm: Almqvist & Wiksell, 1977) 132-42.

association unmistakable. *Allogenes* refers to the ascent in terms such as the following:

> When [I] was taken by the eternal Light out of the garment that was upon me, and taken up to a holy place whose likeness cannot be revealed in the world, then by means of a great blessedness I saw all those about whom I had heard. And I praised all of them and I [stood] above my knowledge and [I inclined to] the knowledge [of] the Totalities, and Aeon of Barb [elo].
>
> And I ascended to the Vitality as I sought it, and I joined it in entering in and I stood, not firmly but calmly. And I saw an eternal, intellectual, undivided motion that pertains to all the formless powers, (one which is) unlimited by limitation.
>
> And when I wanted to stand firmly, I ascended to the Existence, whom I found standing and at rest like an image and likeness of what is conferred upon me by a revelation of the Indivisible One and the One who is at rest.[30]

At the peak of the ascent there is the silence of mystical contemplation. The conclusion of *The Three Steles of Seth* refers to the process in these terms:

> He who will remember these and give glory always will become perfect among those who are perfect and unattainable from any quarter. For they all bless these individually and together. And afterwards they shall be silent. And just as they were ordained, they ascend. After the silence, they descend. From the third they bless the second; after these the first. The way of ascent is the way of descent.[31]

What we have in these prayers is a psychodrama in which the prayers are a vehicle of mystical ascent to the contemplation of the divine. But even this understanding of prayer

[30]CG XI, 3: 58, 26-59, 3; 60, 19-39.
[31]CG VII, 5: 127, 6-21.

is not inconsistent with the fundamental principle of *gnōsis* as self-knowledge. At the peak of the ascent, Allogenes says: "I knew the One who exists in me."[32] Such mystical prayer of praise reminds us of the prayer that forms the main topic in the Hermetic dialogue *The Discourse on the Eighth and Ninth*: "O my son, what is fitting is to pray to God with all our mind and all our heart and our soul . . ."[33] And here too at the summit of the ascent, there is only silence.

IV

We have seen that the Gnostics were not of one mind on the subject of prayer. Some seem undoubtedly to have rejected it and probably because of its seeming incompatibility with the Gnostic principle of self-knowledge. But there was no consistency, and those Gnostics who practiced and valued prayer may have been the more numerous. In general terms, the Gnostic religion too can be studied from the point of view of its use of prayer.

Two principal forms of prayer emerged from the Gnostic texts. One was a prayer of petition for the light to have knowledge and for perseverance and protection in it as the sole way to salvation. This form of Gnostic prayer is particularly characteristic of the Christian Gnostic texts examined. A second form was principally a prayer of praise constituting a mystical experience of ascent to the divine which is at the same time the divine within the Gnostic, and this form of prayer is particularly characteristic of non-Christian Gnostic texts.

What the student of Jewish and Christian prayer observes as missing from both forms is the starting-point in the consciousness of human sinfulness before God and the consequent plea for forgiveness that are characteristic of prayer in the biblical tradition.

[32]CG XI, 3: 61, 5-6.
[33]CG VI, 6: 55, 10-14.

15

Apocalyptic Eschatology in Gnosticism*

1. Apocalyptic Eschatology

There is growing agreement among contemporary scholars that the phenomenon of apocalyptic cannot be understood or defined by the exercise of cataloguing elements or characteristics found in apocalypses or in literature that is widely acknowledged to contain apocalyptic features.[1] What is at issue is not merely a matter of proper definition but, as Hans Dieter Betz makes clear, the fact that most of the "apocalyptic" characteristics usually listed are common features of religious literature in the Hellenistic world.[2] Attempts to circumvent the practice of listing and to define the phenomenon by what is distinctive of it are more difficult. One such attempt looks for "the pattern of these elements in combination,"[3] and as long as this is not the sole criterion for coming to grips with apocalypticism, it may be acknowledged as a useful one. At some point, even when consciously dealing with patterns of elements, most scholars

---

*First published in *Apocalypticism in the Mediterranean World and the Near East* (Tübingen: Mohr-Siebeck, 1983) 317-325.

[1]Hanson 1976, 28; Betz 1969, 136; Smith 1975, 132.

[2]Betz 1969, 136.

[3]Smith 1975, 132.

do not totally abandon the practice of compiling descriptive lists of them.[4]

For a recent example, one might look at the list of "points of contact" between apocalyptic and Gnosticism with which Carl-A. Keller begins his study of the problem of evil:[5]

> a. Apocalyptists and Gnostics use the same forms of literature (apocalypses, dialogues, etc.).
> b. Both groups of texts are permeated with Old Testament citations and reminiscences.
> c. In both there is the communication of a knowledge that is revealed, essentially secret, and necessary for salvation (also with similarities in content).
> d. Both literatures teach that there is a split or conflict in the celestial world that is determinative of certain aspects of human life on earth.
> e. In both cases knowledge leads into a clearly circumscribed ethic of ascetical stamp.[6]
> f. Apocalyptic and Gnostic writings have in common an expressly polemical attitude against those who live in error and are destined to be lost.

On the surface, such a list might provide a starting-point for a discussion of apocalyptic and Gnosticism, but one would have to ask precisely whether the points listed are in every case distinctive characteristics of either apocalyptic or Gnosticism. To be sure, Keller's intention is quite different: he uses the list merely to show that there are enough obvious points of contact between the two to justify a more penetrating comparative study of the problem of evil, making use of the categories of the sociology of religion. But there is another problem in the compilation of a list such as this, namely that although it ostensibly concentrates on the

---

[4]Hanson 1976, 31.

[5]Keller 1977, 70-72, briefly summarized here.

[6]Keller rightly observes that extant Gnostic literature advocates asceticism; whether "Gnostic libertinism" is excluded or not deserves further discussion. See also Kippenberg in the present volume; for an opposing view see Schmithals 1975, 108.

characteristics of apocalyptic literature, it does not clearly distinguish among literary, theological, and social dimensions of either apocalyptic or Gnosticism.

It is useful, therefore, to be guided by the kind of basic distinctions in definition advocated by Paul D. Hanson, who urges clarity in the discussion of three terms.[7] (a) The first is the literary genre of *apocalypse*, which is properly described by a listing of its formal elements and material contents. That there were Gnostic apocalypses is not in doubt, and the nature of them is discussed elsewhere in this volume.[8] It is important to remember that the presence of apocalyptic thought is by no means conterminous with the use of the literary genre of apocalypse. Indeed, it might be observed that the most characteristically apocalyptic passages in the Gnostic literature of Nag Hammadi do not occur in works labeled (in antiquity) apocalypses—but this may be part of the modern scholar's problem: Is "apocalyptic" an ancient or a modern concept?[9] (b) The second of Hanson's categories is that of *apocalyptic eschatology*, the broadest of the three, which is closely identified with the continuation and transformation of the prophetic eschatology of the Old Testament. Surprisingly, apocalyptic eschatology is the most easily verifiable in the literature of Gnosticism. It is surprising because at first sight one would expect Gnostic literature to so emphasize a totally realized eschatology as to exclude the future-oriented apocalyptic perspective. But that is not the case; a certain apocalyptic perspective remains, as we shall see below, and may be fundamental to the Gnostic world-view. (c) Thirdly, Hanson defines *apocalypticism* as "the symbolic universe in which an apocalyptic movement codifies its identity and interpretation of reality." This category implies certain sociological and anthropological criteria which will not be the subject of the present paper but which

[7]Hanson 1976, 29-31.

[8]See Krause in *Apocalypticism in the Mediterranean World;* see also Fallon 1979a, 123-158; Ménard 1973, 300-323.

[9]Vielhauer 1975, 486.

are essential to an investigation of the relation between apocalyptic and Gnosticism.[10]

This third category gives rise to a fundamental question with which the Colloquium inevitably is concerned, but to which the present paper alone cannot give a definitive answer. The question is whether the Gnostic movement is properly understood as an apocalyptic movement. Hanson expressly denies that the abandonment of the mundane concepts of space and time, typical of Gnosticism, is properly regarded as a manifestation of the "symbolic universe of apocalypticism."[11] On the other hand, Walter Schmithals, in a very provocative essay, citing with approval the dictum of Rudolf Otto, "Gnosis is of the very spirit of apocalyptic teaching," even asserts that the statement may be made conversely as well.[12] To a limited extent, the present paper will attempt to take a stand upon this issue, not by exploring the nature of Gnostic apocalypticism with the tools of the social sciences, but rather by seeking evidence of apocalyptic eschatology in Gnostic texts.

There is one perhaps obvious and in any case much-traveled approach to the question which we may set aside at the beginning, important as are its conclusions. That is the question of the role of Jewish apocalyptic in the *origins* of Gnosticism. The fact that Gnosticism arose out of Jewish apocalyptic (and wisdom) tradition, however radical the revolt against the Jewish matrix may have been, is now very broadly acknowledged, especially in view of the prominent Jewish elements in the Nag Hammadi Gnostic texts.[13] One must not too quickly polarize the discussion by trying to distinguish between what is Jewish and what is Hellenistic. These categories overlap in the Greco-Roman period, but the evidence of Jewish traditions in every known form of

[10]Hanson 1976, 30-34; Keller 1977, 75-90; Kippenberg in the present volume.

[11]Hanson 1976, 31; MacRae 1966, 302-303 (which needs to be modified in light of Gnostic literature now available).

[12]Schmithals 1975, 93.

[13]Grant 1966, 27-38; Rudolph 1977, 294-299; MacRae 1966; Fallon 1978; and many other contemporary works.

Gnostic thought in that period is too overwhelming to be ignored. But the historical influence of Jewish apocalyptic on the origins of gnosticism is also not the subject of this paper. Our question is rather, to what extent is Gnosticism itself a manifestation of apocalyptic eschatology?

2. Gnostic Apocalyptic

At first glance and a priori, the question might seem otiose. Gnosticism is after all the supreme example of realized eschatology, and for a rational understanding of it, it must be so. It is knowledge of self in the present that is the saving principle, even if that knowledge can deal with past and future in its content. Once one knows one's (divine) self, one is already liberated and the future is radically relativized. The celebrated definition of Theodotus is evidence of this:

> It is not the bath (washing) alone that makes us free, but also the knowledge: who were we? what have we become? where were we? into what place have we been cast? whither are we hastening? from what are we delivered? what is birth? what is rebirth?[14]

Yet, while emphasis on the realized eschatological dimension is not misplaced, the Gnostic texts themselves remind us that future eschatology is not completely set aside.[15] Perhaps early Christian Gnosticism is not theoretically consistent— what form of early Christianity, except perhaps Marcionite, is after all consistent?

Instead of listing elements of apocalyptic eschatology in gnostic texts, we shall cite some examples of passages that are unmistakably apocalyptic in language as well as in perspective. Such passages are not numerous in the texts, but they are sufficiently frequent as to comprise a regular dimension of the gnostic myth. In the untitled cosmogonic

---

[14]*Excerpta ex Theodoto* 78.2 (Foerster [ed.] 1972, 230).

[15]Peel 1970, 155-159.

tractate of Nag Hammadi Codex I, commonly called by modern scholars *On the Origin of the World*, we find the following description of the end time:

> Before the consummation [of the aeon], the whole place will be shaken by a great thunder. Then the rulers will lament, [crying out on account of their] death. The angels will mourn for their men, and the demons will weep for their times, and their men will mourn and cry out on account of their death. Then the aeon will begin to (...and) they will be disturbed. Its kings will be drunk from the flaming sword and they will make war against one another, so that the earth will be drunk from the blood which is poured out. And the seas will be troubled by that war. Then the sun will darken and the moon will lose its light. The stars of the heaven will disregard their course and a great thunder will come out of a great power that is above all the powers of Chaos, the place where the firmament of woman is situated. When she has created the first work, she will take off her wise flame of insight. She will put on a senseless wrath. Then she will drive out the gods of Chaos whom she had created together with the First Father. She will cast them down to the abyss. They will be wiped out by their (own) injustice. For they will become like the mountains which blaze out fire, and they will gnaw at one another until they are destroyed by their First Father. When he destroys them, he will turn against himself and destroy himself until he ceases (to be). And their heavens will fall upon one another and their powers will burn. Their aeons will also be overthrown. And his (the First Father's) heaven will fall and it will split in two. Likewise (the place of) his joy, [however], will fall down to the earth, [and the earth will not] be able to support them. They will fall [down] to the abyss and the [abyss] will be overthrown.
>
> The light will [cover the] darkness, and it will wipe it out. It will become like one which had not come into being. And the work which the darkness followed will be dissolved. And the deficiency will be plucked out at its

root (and thrown) down to the darkness. And the light will withdraw up to its root. And the glory of the unbegotten will appear, and it will fill all of the aeons, when the prophetic utterance and the report of those who are kings are revealed and are fulfilled by those who are called perfect. Those who were not perfected in the unbegotten Father will receive their glories in their aeons and in the kingdoms of immortals. But they will not ever enter the kingless realm.[16]

For the Gnostic the material world, which came into being through the tragic fault of the cosmic drama, is perishable and must perish. It is characteristic of Gnostic eschatological passages such as this to emphasize the totality and the finality of the destruction by pointing out that the agent of the final destruction ultimately destroys itself as well. In the Valentinian description of the eschaton according to Ptolemy, the agent of destruction is fire:

When this has taken place, then (they assert) the fire that is hidden in the world will blaze forth and burn: when it has consumed all matter it will be consumed with it and pass into non-existence.[17]

In Valentinian eschatology there is no absolute dichotomy between the reintegration of the spiritual elements into the divine and the total destruction of the material cosmos. Influenced by their position within—or on the margin of—Christianity, the Valentinians allow a place of intermediate repose or salvation, often called "the Middle," for the "psychic" class of people who are other, non-Valentinian Christians.[18] This place, which is also the repository of the psychic element of the highest class of people, the "pneum-

[16]CG II, 5: 125, 32-127, 14. All translations of Nag Hammadi texts are from Robinson (ed.) 1977. On this passage see Tardieu 1974, 74-83; Rudolph 1977, 216-217; Böhlig/Labib 1962, 104-109; Haardt 1964, 315-336; van Unnik 1970, 277-288.

[17]Irenaeus, *Adversus haereses* 1.7.1 (Foerster [ed.] 1972, 139).

[18]*Ibid.*, 1.6.1 and 7.1-5.

tics," is at the same time beyond the cosmos—and thus not subject to the destruction of the latter—and yet not a part of the divine Pleroma. A similar distinction of eschatological places of rest is made at the end of the passage cited from *On the Origin of the World*: some will enter "the kingdoms of immortals," but the "kingless realm"[19] is reserved for the true Gnostics.

The futurity of the apocalyptic eschatology in *On the Origin of the World* is unmistakable, but there is usually no suggestion of the immediacy of the final events such as is often found in apocalyptic thought, eloquently phrased, for example, in 4 Ezra 14:10: "For the age has lost its youth, and the times begin to grow old" (RSV). We find an indirect reference to such immediacy in the *Trimorphic Protennoia*, where hostile powers, once the revelation has come into the world, are represented as saying:

> As for the future, let us make our entire flight before we are imprisoned perforce and taken down to the bosom of the underworld. For already the slackening of our bondage has approached, and the times are cut short and the days have shortened and our time has been fulfilled, and the weeping of our destruction has approached us so that we may be taken to the place we recognize.[20]

In this document there is clearly apocalyptic language in the distinction of the present age and the age to come. The revealing Voice states:

> I shall tell them of the coming end of this Aeon and teach them of the beginning of the Aeon to come, the one without change...[21]

But the same Voice also proclaims: "I am the Aeon to [come. I am] the fulfillment of the All."[22] Thus the language

---

[19]Fallon 1979b, 285.

[20]CG XIII, 1: 44, 12-19.

[21]*Ibid.*, 42, 19-21.

[22]*Ibid.*, 45, 8-9.

of apocalyptic eschatology is sometimes appropriated in the service of an essentially realized eschatology, and this phenomenon is quite common in many Gnostic works.[23]

On the Origin of the World and *Trimorphic Protennoia* are Christian Gnostic works, or, perhaps better, christianized versions of Gnostic myths, but one should observe how little the apocalyptic language of them is influenced by New Testament apocalyptic texts. To have some sense of contrast, one needs only turn to *The Dialogue of the Savior* where, despite the fragmentary character of the work, there are clear examples of Jesus reinterpreting apocalyptic sayings from the Gospel tradition.[24] But the apocalyptic eschatology of Gnostic sources does not originally stem from contact with Christianity. One of the most graphic apocalyptic passages in the Nag Hammadi texts, which also deserves to be quoted at length, is in a totally non-Christian context. It is from *The Paraphrase of Shem,* and the speaker is Shem:

> After I cease to be upon the earth and withdraw up to my rest, a great, evil error will come upon the world, and many evils in accordance with the number of the forms of Nature. Evil times will come. And when the era of Nature is approaching destruction, darkness will come upon the earth. The number will be small. And a demon will come up from the power who has a likeness of fire. He will divide the heaven, (and) he will rest in the depth of the east. For the whole world will quake. And the deceived world will be thrown into confusion. Many places will be flooded because of envy of the winds and the demons who have a name which is senseless: Phorbea, Chloerga. They are the ones who govern the world with their teaching. And they lead astray many hearts because of their disorder and their unchastity. Many places will be sprinkled with blood. And five races by themselves will eat their sons. But the regions of the south will receive the Word of the Light. But they who are from the error of the

[23]Rudolph 1977, 214-215.
[24]CG III, 5 :122, 1 ff.

world and from the east—. A demon will come forth from (the) belly of the serpent. He was in hiding in a desolate place. He will perform many wonders. Many will loathe him. A wind will come forth from his mouth with a female likeness. Her name will be called Abalphe. He will reign over the world from the east to the west.

The Nature will have a final opportunity. And the stars will cease from the sky. The mouth of error will be opened in order that the evil Darkness may become idle and silent. And in the last day the forms of Nature will be destroyed with the winds and all their demons; they will become a dark lump, just as they were from the beginning. And the sweet waters which were burdened by the demons will perish. For where the power of the Spirit has gone there are my sweet waters. The other works of Nature will not be manifest. They will mix with the infinite waters of darkness. And all her forms will cease from the middle region.[25]

To be sure, there are elements in this vivid apocalyptic description which can be compared with elements in, for example, Mark 13—earthquakes, darkness, stars falling from heaven, false leaders appearing with miracles to lead the world astray—but these are what one might call standard materials of apocalyptic and no more original in Mark 13 than in *The Paraphrase of Shem*. In their non-Christian context in the latter work they merely illustrate the independence of the Gnostic apocalyptic development from the Christian sources.

To the extent that apocalyptic eschatology is characterized by a periodization of history leading into the end time, we should expect to find examples of such periodization in the Gnostic texts. And there are many such examples, often built on the Jewish apocalyptic scheme involving the flood and the fire and the end time, for instance in *The Apocalypse of Adam*.[26] There is another example in *The Concept of Our*

---

[25]CG VII, 1: 43, 28-45, 31.

[26]CG V, 5: 64, 1-85, 32. See Perkins 1972, 591-599; Perkins 1977, 387-389.

Great Power, a not entirely coherent Christian Gnostic work which, if it does indeed contain a reference to the Anomoean heresy (at 40, 7) may be as late as the mid-fourth century, or if the reference is a gloss or simply to "dissimilar things," may be a much earlier work.[27] Here the scheme of periodization is developed into what the author calls "the aeon of the flesh," "the psychic aeon," and "the aeon of beauty."[28] Here too the flood and the fire and the eschaton are the basis of the scheme, but the development of it is not clear.

What is of course most distinctive of the apocalyptic eschatology of Gnosticism is the total absence of any new creation. Given its radically dualist perspective, expressed in the concept of creation as error, Gnosticism can see the end time only as the dissolution of the created world. Even though the Gnostics can speak of "the aeon to come," there is strictly speaking no age to follow the destruction, and such language is but another illustration of the well known ambiguity of the Gnostic use of the word "aeon." Ultimate destiny is the reintegration of the divine particles into God, the dissolution of multiplicity in the restored unity. And with that the whole cosmos disappears. The *Endzeit* is indeed the restoration of the *Urzeit*, but the result is as timeless as the unknown God himself.[29] Gnosticism may thus be described as the ultimate radicalizing of apocalyptic eschatology.

3. Conclusion: Present and Future

One of the elements most characteristic of apocalyptic eschatology is the conviction that salvation lies in the future, indeed in a future beyond the history of the cosmos.[30] Because of its basic doctrine that it is knowledge that saves, Gnosticism at first sight might seem to be in conflict with

[27]Parrott (ed.) 1979, 292 and 304.
[28]CG VI, 4: 26, 1-48, 15.
[29]Schmithals 1975, 106.
[30]Hanson 1976, 30.

this futurity. But in reality both apocalyptic and Gnosticism center on the acquisition (by revelation) and the communication of a knowledge that exercises saving power in the present by its future-oriented content.[31] It is true that the vast bulk of Gnostic revelations are much more obviously centered on the origins of humanity and world, but the perspective is future nevertheless: it is in the return to the precosmic that human destiny lies. And the presence of explicit passages of apocalyptic eschatology in Gnostic revelations is further evidence that the categories of apocalyptic and Gnosticism should not be too sharply divided. The latter is one manifestation of the former, albeit in extreme form.

Bibliography

Betz, Hans Dieter 1969: "On the Problem of the Religio-Historical Understanding of Apocalypticism," in: *JTC* 6 (1969) 134-156 (German original: *ZThK* 63 [1966] 391-409).

Böhlig, Alexander/Labib, Pahor 1962: *Die koptisch-gnostische Schrift ohne Titel aus Codex II von Nag Hammadi* (Berlin, 1962).

Fallon, Francis T. 1978: *The Enthronement of Sabaoth: Jewish Elements in Gnostic Creation Myths* (NHS X, Leiden, 1978).
-1979a: "The Gnostic Apocalypses," in: John J. Collins (ed.),

---

[31]Schmithals 1975, 95.

Apocalypse: The Morphology of a Genre (Semeia 14 [1979]) 123-158.

-1979b: "The Gnostics: the Undominated Race," *NT* 21 (1979) 271-288.

Foerster, Werner (ed.) 1972: *Gnosis. A Selection of Gnostic Texts*, Vol. I (Oxford 1972).

Grant, Robert M. 1966: *Gnosticism and Early Christianity* (rev. ed., New York, 1966).

Haardt, Robert 1964: "Das universaleschatologische Vorstellungsgut in der Gnosis," Kurt Schubert (ed.), *Vom Messias zum Christus* (Vienna, 1964) 315-336.

Hanson, Paul D. 1976: "Apocalypticism," in: Keith Crim et al. (ed.), *IDBSup* (Nashville, Tenn, 1976) 28-34.

Keller, Carl-A. 1977: "Das Problem des Bösen in Apokalyptik und Gnostik," in: Martin Krause (ed.), *Gnosis and Gnosticism* (NHS VIII, Leiden, 1977) 70-90.

MacRae, George 1966: *Some Elements of Jewish Apocalyptic and Mystical Traditions and Their Relation to Gnostic Literature*, diss. Cambridge University 1966.

Ménard, Jacques E. 1973: "Littérature apocalyptique juive et littérature gnostique," *RevSR* 47 (1973) 300-323.

Parrott, Douglas M. (ed.) 1979: *Nag Hammadi Codices V, 2-5 and VI with Papyrus Berolinensis* 8502, 1 and 4 (NHS XI, Leiden, 1979).

Peel, Malcolm L. 1970: "Gnostic Eschatology and the New Testament," *NT* 12 (1970) 141-165.

Perkins, Pheme 1972: "Apocalyptic Schematization in the Apocalypse of Adam and the Gospel of the Egyptians," in: Lane C. McGaughy (ed.), *The Society of Biblical Literature: One Hundred Eighth Annual Meeting. Book of Seminar Papers* (1972), Vol. 2, 591-599.

-1977: "Apocalypse of Adam: The Genre and Function of a Gnostic Apocalypse," *CBQ* 39 (1977) 382-395.

Robinson, James M. (ed.) 1977: *The Nag Hammadi Library in English* (San Francisco, 1977).

Rudolph, Kurt 1977: *Die Gnosis. Wesen und Geschichte einer spätantiken Religion* (Göttingen, 1977).

Schmithals, Walter 1975: *The Apocalyptic Movement. Introduction and Interpretation* (Nashville, 1975) (German original: *Die Apokalyptik. Einführung und Deutung* (Göttingen, 1973).

Smith, Jonathan Z. 1975: "Wisdom and Apocalyptic," Birger A. Pearson (ed.), *Religious Syncretism in Antiquity: Essays in Conversation with Geo Widengren* (Missoula, Mont, 1975) 131-156.

Tardieu, Michel 1974: *Trois mythes gnostiques: Adam, Eros et les animaux d'Egypte dans un écrit de Nag Hammadi (II, 5)* (Paris, 1974).

van Unnik, W.C. 1970: "The 'Wise Fire' in a Gnostic Eschatological Vision," Patrick Granfield/ Josef A. Jungmann (ed.), *Kyriakon. Festschrift für Johannes Quasten* (Münster, 1970) Vol. I, 277-288.

Vielhauer, Philipp 1975: *Geschichte der urchristlichen Literatur* (Berlin, 1975).

16

Why the Church
Rejected Gnosticism*

In discussing the history of his interest in the study of
Gnosticism, the philosopher, and acknowledged master of
Gnostic studies, Hans Jonas has remarked: "I wanted to
take up the question: Why did the Church reject Gnosticism?
Apart from the obvious reason that many of its teachings
were fantastic and not in agreement with the Gospels, why
was *Gnosis as such* from Paul on rejected as a possible
option? Why was Pistis chosen instead?"[1] As every student
of Gnosticism knows, Jonas began his investigation with a
brilliant study of the meaning of *gnōsis* and never really
confronted the broader question that first interested him.
And, somewhat surprisingly, no one else has systematically
taken up this challenging question.

On the contrary, scholarship throughout the twentieth
century has preferred to concentrate on what is virtually the
opposite of this question, namely, to what extent has
Gnosticism influenced the shaping of Christianity itself?[2]

---

*First published in *Jewish and Christian Self-Definition: Volume One: The
Shaping of Christianity in the Second and Third Centuries* (Philadelphia: Fortress,
1980) 126-133, 236-238.

[1]"A Retrospective View," *Proceedings of the International Colloquium on
Gnosticism, Stockholm, August 20-25, 1973* (Stockholm, 1977) 6.

[2]For a survey of the literature see Edwin M. Yamauchi, *Pre-Christian Gnosticism.
A Survey of the Proposed Evidences* (Grand Rapids, 1973).

Efforts to detect Gnostic influence have concentrated on the gospel of John, the epistle to the Ephesians, certain passages in the Pauline correspondence, the letters of Ignatius, the development of the doctrine of the Trinity, the origin of Christian asceticism, and many other documents and doctrines. It is thus at least possible that Gnosticism, far from being rejected universally by the church, was a formative element in the evolution of Christianity itself.[3] But this is not our question, and we must leave it; yet we cannot leave it totally out of account.

Before attempting to identify some of the reasons why the church rejected Gnosticism—an enterprise which must remain very tentative at least at the outset—we must state several presuppositions and limitations of our inquiry, without taking the time to justify them in detail.

(1) We shall assume that Gnosticism is non-Christian in origin, leaving aside the question of a chronologically pre-Christian origin of it, and that it is more or less as old as Christianity. One cannot assume that the venerable controversy about the origins of Gnosticism has been settled, but the weight of evidence from Nag Hammadi has come down solidly on the side of those who argue against the classical Christian heresy theory.[4] In consequence, it will be possible to suggest that New Testament writers, including even Paul, are already in dialogue, not to say competition, with at least "incipient" Gnosticism.

(2) It is essential to bear in mind that one cannot meaningfully speak of "Christianity" or "the church" as a monolithic entity in the early centuries of its existence. Not only the study of the New Testament, but the history of early post-apostolic Christianity abundantly affirms the essential diversity of forms of Christianity. It is now as much a dogma

---

[3]See, e.g., the summary statement of Rudolf Bultmann, *Primitive Christianity in its Contemporary Setting* (New York, 1965) 162-71.

[4]For a brief summary of the argument, see George W. MacRae, "Nag Hammadi and the New Testament," *Gnosis. Festschrift für Hans Jonas* (Göttingen, 1978). See also the essays of Jacques-E. Ménard and Birger A. Pearson in the present volume, pp. 134ff. and 151ff.

of scholarship as its opposite used to be: orthodoxy is not the presupposition of the early church but the result of a process of growth and development.[5] It is this very situation which poses the intricate challenge to which the McMaster Project is in part addressed and which justifies the efforts of the Project. In consequence of it, one can expect that not all of the early church rejected Gnosticism, but some branches of Christianity were indeed informed by it.

(3) It may be necessary, though difficult, to distinguish between early Christian polemic aginst Gnosticism and the "real reasons" why early Christians rejected it. Polemic is in many contexts a conventional exercise, with rhetorical rules to guide it.[6] It was fashionable, for example, to charge an opposing philosophical school with venality, various forms of immorality, and logical absurdity, merely because they were opponents.[7] If they were wrong, their behavior must have reflected their errors. The consequence of this caution is that one must do more than accept the arguments of the heresiological literature at face value.

(4) Finally, since another contribution to this volume deals with the anti-heretical argument of Irenaeus's *Adversus haereses*,[8] the earliest extant clear and explicit exposition of the church's case against the Gnostics, the present essay will assume some practical limitations. For the most part it will concentrate on arguments against Gnosticism, explicit and more often implicit, prior to Irenaeus, on the grounds that the post-Irenaean heresiological tradition is largely dependent on Irenaeus himself. In fact, we shall concentrate mainly on New Testament evidence.

---

[5]Walter Bauer, *Orthodoxy and Heresy in Earliest Christianity;* James M. Robinson and Helmut Koester, *Trajectories through Early Christianity.*

[6]See Pheme Perkins, "Irenaeus and the Gnostics. Rhetoric and Composition in Adversus Haereses Book One," *VC* 30 (1976) 193-200.

[7]Cf. Robert J. Karris, *The Function and Sitz im Leben of the Paraenetic Elements in the Pastoral Epistles,* dissertation Harvard University 1971.

[8]Cf. Gérard Vallée, "Theological and Non-Theological Motives in Irenaeus's Refutation of the Gnostics."

Non-Conformist Ethical Behavior

One constant element of Christian anti-Gnostic polemic is the charge of libertinism, especially prominent in Irenaeus and Epiphanius.[9] To what extent is this charge based on empirical evidence? Or is it a typical example of conventional polemic? I propose to address these questions at first not by analyzing the arguments of the patristic heresiologists, but by returning to the Christianity of Corinth in the time of Paul. The implications for the case made by the Fathers will become apparent.

Whether we should properly speak of Gnosticism already present in the Corinthian community when Paul wrote 1 Corinthians continues to be disputed.[10] The "enthusiasm" that is generally agreed to characterize at least one element of the community is in any case well on the way to becoming a form of Gnostic theory and practice. The esteem of the Corinthians for *gnōsis* is clearly at the root of the problems which Paul regards as a fundamental challenge to his gospel (1 Cor 8:1). In this light the problem of *porneia* in 1 Cor 5, the case of the incestuous member of the community, merits a second look. It is increasingly recognized by interpreters that the text of 1 Cor 5:3-5 must be read in its natural order, repressing as much as possible the reservations of modern translators: "As for me, absent in body but present in spirit, I as one who is present have already judged the *one who has done this thing in the name of the Lord Jesus....*"[11] The incestuous man is best understood as one who flouts the morality that is customary "even among pagans" on religious grounds based on a Gnostic or quasi-Gnostic scorn for material existence. He believes that he is asserting his true spiritual identity, and thus his fidelity to the Lord Jesus, by

[9]Even in cases where Irenaeus describes *egkrateia*, as in that of Saturninus, AH 1.24.1-2, he is at pains to say it is "feigned" (*peripoiētos, ficta*).

[10]For the extreme affirmative position see Walter Schmithals, *Gnosticism in Corinth* (Nashville, 1971).

[11]Translation of Jerome Murphy-O'Connor, "1 Corinthians, V, 3-5," *RB* 84 (1977) 245 (emphasis added).

showing that he transcends such merely material, bodily concerns as sexual morality. The traditionally alleged Gnostic libertine stance is perfectly illustrated not only in his behavior, but in the community's proud tolerance of it—which is more properly the object of Paul's indignation. And what Paul objects to is a Gnostic-like disdain for a morality that is ultimately conventional. Perhaps the church's objection to Gnosticism really did lay considerable emphasis on its inability to tolerate such radical non-conformity in ethical behavior.

Yet we must consider another trend in current scholarly assessment of anti-Gnostic polemics. The evidence that Gnostics did in fact behave in an antinomian manner is virtually confined to the Christian polemical literature. Of the Valentinians Irenaeus says, in the famous passage about the gold in the mud, "For this reason the most perfect among them freely practice everything that is forbidden."[12] And of the Carpocratians he reports: "They live a dissipated life and hold an impious doctrine, and use the name [of the church] as a cloak for their wickedness."[13] The original Gnostic writings from the Nag Hammadi library, however, have contributed little or nothing to support these allegations of libertinism. To the extent that they deal with ethical practices directly, they uniformly advocate extreme asceticism. As a result, scholars have called into question the patristic charges of antinomian behavior; if these are merely conventional polemics, then non-conformist ethical behavior is not a reason for the rejection of Gnosticism but at most a consequence of such a rejection.

Irenaeus bases his assessment of the libertine behavior of the Carpocratians, however, on a principle of their own which is not unlike the slogan "all things are lawful for me" of the Corinthians: " ... they claim to have in their power and to be able to practice anything whatsoever that is ungodly and impious. They say that conduct is good and evil

---

[12]AH I.63; tr. Werner Foerster (ed.), *Gnosis* (Oxford, 1972), vol. I, p. 313.
[13]Ibid., I.25.3; tr. Foerster, p. 37.

only in the opinion of men."[14] I have not found this statement as such in the Nag Hammadi writings, but a different type of formulation of the principle is to be found there, and it is quite likely that Irenaeus' observation was indeed an accurate one. *The Gospel of Philip*, for example, contains an important doctrine of the radical relativity of names and categories, including moral categories, which might serve as the justification for an ethic of at least indifference: "In this world there is good and evil. Its good is not good, and its evil not evil."[15] I believe a similar implication can be drawn from the identification of the divine voice of the thunder with opposites of every sort of category, including the ethical, in the Nag Hammadi work called *The Thunder: Perfect Mind*. There we find, for example: "For I am knowledge and ignorance. I am shame and boldness . . . I, I am sinless, and the root of sin derives from me. I am lust in (outward) appearance, and interior self-control exists within me."[16] One could hardly expect to find Gnostic documents openly advocating libertinism, but in statements like these we may have examples of Gnostic authors' own formulations of a principle underlying such conduct.

Both Paul and Irenaeus, and of course many others, rejected Gnosticism in part on the grounds that it led to forms of ethical behavior that were perceived as unacceptable. Whether the Gnostics actually flouted the laws of ethical behavior to any considerable extent, as the incestuous man of 1 Corinthians apparently did, or were merely indifferent to ethical behavior, as some other Corinthians were (e.g. 1 Cor 6:12-20), the church saw the danger of libertinism inherent in Gnostic language and speculation.

[14]Ibid., I.25.4; tr. Foerster, p. 37. See also I.25.5 and, of the Simonians, I.23.3.

[15]CG II. 66.10-13; tr. James M. Robinson (ed.), *The Nag Hammadi Library in English*, p. 140. See also *Philip* 53.14-54.5.

[16]CG VI. 14.16-28 and 19.15-20; tr. Robinson, p. 272, 276. See George W. MacRae, "Discourses of the Gnostic Revealer," *Proceedings of the International Colloquium on Gnosticism*, pp. 111-12, especially p. 122.

The God of This World

An almost ubiquitous charge brought against the Gnostics by the ecclesiastical writers is the blasphemy of denigrating the God of creation as an inferior, or an evil, demiurge. They interpret this basic Gnostic doctrine as an attack on monotheism, a repudiation—or at least an unacceptable interpretation—of the Bible, and an affront to reason itself. All of these interpretations, and doubtless more, were reasons why Christians rejected the Gnostics. But we may look again to Paul for a hint of a particular perspective on the anti-dualist argument that underlies a good deal of later Christian polemic as well.

The setting for Paul's argument against a duality of gods is again Corinth, and it may be more than coincidental that it is in such a context that he perceives the danger of dualistic language. In his defense of his ministry in 2 Corinthians, following upon the celebrated discussion of letter and spirit, Paul speaks of the devil with unusual boldness as "the god of this world (or age)." Referring apparently to Jews who reject the gospel and therefore "are perishing," he says, "In their case the god of this world has blinded the minds of the unbelievers, to keep them from seeing the light of the gospel of the glory of Christ, who is the likeness of God" (2 Cor 4:4). After a statement that the gospel he preaches concerns Jesus Christ and not himself, Paul apparently sees the danger of his own language when heard by persons inclined toward a Gnostic view of a lower "god of this world."[17] In verse 6 he then refutes any such interpretation of his own language by a statement which in form closely parallels verse 4 and in content offers a decisive argument against any Gnostic doctrine of a demiurge: "For it is the God who said, 'Let light shine out of darkness,' who has shone in our hearts

---

[17]Cf. Rudolf Bultmann, *Theology of the New Testament* (London, 1952) vol. I, p. 173: "It is Gnostic language when Satan is called 'the god of this world.'"

to give the light of the knowledge of the glory of God in the face of Christ."[18]

If I am correct in interpreting the passage in this manner, it can be seen to contain a number of allusions which would be significant in the debate with Gnostic dualism: e.g. the light-darkness contrast, the language of *doxa*, "glory," and *eikōn*, "image," the mention of *gnōsis*. But the crucial argument against a Gnostic dualist interpretation of Paul's own language about "the god of this world" is allusion to Gen 1:3, "the God who said, 'Let light shine out of darkness.'" Paul is at pains to make the point—incisively, since Gnostic exegesis of Genesis is embarrassed by the creation of light in 1:3—that the creator God is the God of enlightenment and thus of salvation. The chasm between the Old Testament and the New created by the Gnostic interpretation of Yahweh as the inferior demiurge is as abhorrent to the Christian Paul as it is to Irenaeus and others.[19] Paul's reply is to assert the continuity of salvation history, the identity of the God of creation with the God of salvation.

It is precisely this denial of identity which offends the Christian opponents of Gnosticism. That there should be a lower spiritual being who is inimical to humanity is not itself at issue. In a sense Paul is a "dualist" of sorts in that he believes in Satan and evil spiritual powers; he can even call Satan "the god of this world." But he cannot tolerate a radical rupture of the salvation-historical process which is based on Scripture. It is important, it seems to me, to note that the Gnostics, unlike Marcion, did not simply repudiate the scriptures of the old covenant. Instead, they derived much of their mythology from exegesis of the scriptures. And it was not simply a matter of methods of interpretation of the scriptures to which the churchmen objected. Even Paul was capable, in Galatians, for example, of methods of interpretation no less daring than those of the Gnostics. But

[18]For a more detailed discussion see George W. MacRae, "Anti-Dualist Polemic in 2 Cor. 4, 6?" *Studia Evangelica IV* (TU 102; ed. F.L. Cross, Berlin, 1968) 420-31.

[19]See the anti-Marcionite interpretaton of 2 Cor 4.6 on the part of Tertullian, cited ibid., p. 420.

any interpretation which disrupted the continuity of the history of salvation, that it, which denied that the God of Jesus was the God of creation and covenant and promise, struck at the heart of the Christian message and had to be struck down in turn. That this dichotomy of the divine also lay at the heart of Irenaeus' objections to the Gnostic heretics is well known.[20]

Jesus Christ Has Come in the Flesh

It is commonplace to observe that one of the basic objections to Christian Gnosticism on the part of the ecclesiastical writers is that it is almost invariably docetic in its christology. Underlying the rejection of Gnostic docetism, however, is a good example of a broader issue, that of the influence of changing language on standards of orthodoxy. From first-century Christianity to second, there occurs a remarkable shift in the connotation and importance of the concept of *sarx*, "flesh," which culminates in the elaborate Pauline exegesis on the part of Irenaeus in *Adversus haereses*, Book V. Irenaeus is at pains to demonstrate, contrary to the evidence of the text before him, that the resurrection of the dead in Paul is in reality a resurrection of the flesh.[21] The shift in meaning of "flesh," by no means a univocal term in the New Testament in any case, is already visible in the Johannine literature, where its use may be related to the differing stances toward Gnosticism taken within Johannine Christianity.

Nowhere in the New Testament has the case for Gnostic influence on early Christianity been as strongly made as in the discussion of the Fourth Gospel.[22] This is not the place to review the history of the question, but it may be helpful to point out where the current debate lies. I do not believe that

[20]AH II.31.1 and frequently elsewhere.

[21]Ibid. V.7 and passim in Book V.

[22]In addition to the commentaries see James M. Robinson, "Gnosticism and the New Testament," *Gnosis. Festschrift für Hans Jonas.*

the fourth evangelist was a Gnostic, a former Gnostic, or even an opponent of Gnosticism. I regard it as very likely, however, that he was a somewhat sectarian Christian who was strongly influenced by Gnostic language and rhetoric and by the structures of Gnostic thought. A striking list of parallels to the Prologue of the Fourth Gospel has been observed in the Nag Hammadi work *Trimorphic Protennoia* and has led some interpreters to postulate a Gnostic origin for some of the key elements of the Prologue.[23] In addition, an analysis of the Gnostic revelation discourse form in *The Thunder* and a number of other Nag Hammadi tractates suggests that the fourth evangelist was influenced, not by a "revelation discourse source," as Bultmann and his pupil Heinz Becker postulated,[24] but by the style of such Gnostic discourses.[25]

Among the things that kept the evangelist from becoming a Gnostic in the full sense was his emphasis on the incarnation: "and the Word became flesh" (1:14). But as is well known, the word "flesh" is not consistent in the Fourth Gospel, and the use of it in 1:14, while not exceptional, does not convey the negative overtones of 3:15 or 6:63, where it contrasts with "spirit."[26] In the first epistle of John, however, the term is used in a credal formula in which the confession that Jesus came "in the flesh" (4:2) distinguishes believers from docetic heretics. I believe the author of the first epistle, who was distinct from the fourth evangelist, had recognized the danger inherent in the language and thought of the gospel and had experienced some fellow Johannine Christians who became out-and-out Gnostic docetists. He writes, therefore, in part in order to rescue the language of the

---

[23]The case is summarized by Robinson, ibid. For a criticism of it see R. McL. Wilson, "The Trimorphic Protennoia," *Gnosis and Gnosticism* (NHS 8; ed. M. Krause, Leiden, 1977) 50-54.

[24]Cf. Heinz Becker, *Die Reden des Johannesevangeliums und der Stil der gnostischen Offenbarungsreden* (Göttingen, 1956).

[25]The argument is briefly summarized in MacRae, "Nag Hammadi and the New Testament."

[26]Cf. Eduard Schweizer, "*Sarx, ktl.*," TDNT VII, pp. 138-41.

gospel for more orthodox purposes.[27] In so doing, he witnesses to the evolution in which "flesh" came to be used as virtually a shibboleth in the argument against Gnostic docetists, leaving far behind the original Johannine, and *a fortiori* Pauline, understandings of the word. Docetism is rejected, not simply as a denial of the humanity of Jesus, but as a denigration of the flesh, which in Christian thought in the second century is increasingly seen as the instrument of salvation itself. The Gnostics, because of their radical dualism of spirit versus matter, are the archenemies of the flesh.

A good example of the importance of the flesh in the argument against the Gnostics may be found in the apocryphal Corinthian correspondence which has survived embedded in the *Acts of Paul* and circulating separately in Papyrus Bodmer X.[28] Not only because it circulated separately in the third century, but because it does not fit the context of the *Acts of Paul* precisely, I believe the correspondence originated apart from the *Acts of Paul* as a piece of anti-Gnostic propaganda. The "pernicious words" of Simon and Cleobius, about whom the Corinthians complain, involve among other things a denial of the resurrection of the flesh and that the Lord has come in the flesh. The reply of "Paul" is almost a short treatise on the importance of the flesh, though, to be sure, it also answers the other allegations of the heretics. It emphasizes the incarnation of Jesus, "that he might come into this world and redeem all flesh through his own flesh, and that he might raise up from the dead us who are fleshly, even as he has shown himself as our example ... in order that the evil one might be conquered through the same flesh by which he held sway .... For by his own body Jesus Christ saved all flesh .... As for those who tell you there is no resurrection of the flesh, for them there is no resurrection ... you also

---

[27]See the similar argument in the commentary of J.L. Houlden, *The Johannine Epistles* (New York and London, 1973).

[28]See Wilhelm Schneemelcher in *New Testament Apocrypha* (ed. E. Hennecke, W. Schneemelcher, and R. McL. Wilson, Philadelphia, London 1965) vol. II, pp. 322-51, 374-77; M. Testuz, *Papyrus Bodmer X-XII* (Cologny-Genéve, 1959).

who have been cast upon the body and bones and Spirit of the Lord shall rise up on that day with your flesh whole."[29]

The question with which we began, namely, Why did the church reject Gnosticism?, has of course not been fully answered in these few pages. I have examined three reasons which I think pervaded the Christian opposition to Gnosticism from Paul, in the third case from the Fourth Gospel, to Irenaeus and have suggested that large issues are implied in the polemical use of these reasons. Whether or not these are the "real reasons" or the most important ones, the fact that they recur persistently in early Christian anti-Gnostic polemic warrants the attention paid them.

[29]Tr. Schneemelcher-Wilson, 376-77.

17

Prayer*

O God, who are the alpha and the omega,
    the first and the last, the beginning and the end,
    grace with thy presence all our endings and our
    beginnings.

Give us joy in the newness of life, humility in the
    moment of our accomplishment,
    gratitude for all that we have been given.

Thou who art, and who wert, and who art to come, be
    thou ever present in our transitions.

Lift our hearts beyond the satisfaction of the
    moment to the needs of the times,
    and sanctify our now with the memory of our then
    and the promise and hope of thy tomorrow.

*Composed for the Harvard College Commencement of 1982.

George W. MacRae: Bibliography

(Book reviews, abstracts, translations, forewords, short reports, etc., have not been included.)

"A New Date for the Last Supper," *American Ecclesiastical Review* 138 (1958) 294-302.

"Building the House of the Lord," *American Ecclesiastical Review* 140 (1959) 361-376.

"The Gospel of Thomas—*Logia Iēsou?*" *Catholic Biblical Quarterly* 22 (1960) 56-71.

"The Meaning and Evolution of the Feast of Tabernacles," *Catholic Biblical Quarterly* 22 (1960) 251-276.

"With Me in Paradise," *Worship* 35 (1961) 235-240.

"New Testament Theology—Some Problems and Principles," *Scripture* 16 (1964) 97-106.

"Prepare the way of the Lord," *The Way* 4 (1964) 247-257.

"The Coptic Gnostic Apocalypse of Adam," *Heythrop Journal* 6 (1965) 27-35.

"Miracle in *The Antiquities* of Josephus," *Miracles: Cambridge Studies in Their Philosophy and History*, ed. C.F.D. Moule (London: Mowbray, 1965) 127-147.

"Gnosis in Messina," *Catholic Biblical Quarterly* 28 (1966) 322-333.

Some Elements of Jewish Apocalyptic and Mystical Traditions and Their Relation to Gnostic Literature (unpublished doctoral dissertation; Cambridge University, 1966).

"Alexander of Abonoteichos," *New Catholic Encyclopedia* (New York: McGraw-Hill, 1967) 1:294-295.

"Atonement, Day of (Yom Kippur)," *ibid.*, 1:1026-1027.

"Bardesanes (Bar Daisān)," *ibid.*, 2:97.

"Basilides," *ibid.*, 2:160.

"Calendars of the Ancient Near East," *ibid.*, 2:1067-1069.

"Carpocrates," *ibid.*, 3:145.

"Chenoboskion, Gnostic Texts of," *ibid.*, 3:549-550.

"Dedication of the Temple, Feast of," *ibid.*, 4:714-715.

"Feasts, Religious," *ibid.*, 5:865-868.

"Gnosis, Christian," *ibid.*, 6:522-523.

"Gnosticism," *ibid.*, 6:523-528.

"Heracleon," *ibid.*, 6:1046.

"Hermetic Literature," *ibid.*, 6:1076-1077.

"Mandaean Religion," *ibid.*, 9:145.

"New-Moon Feast, Hebrew," *ibid.*, 10:382.

"Passover, Feast of," *ibid.*, 10:1068-1070.

"Purim, Feast of," *ibid.*, 11:1043-1044.

"Theodotus," *ibid.*, 14:27.

"Valentinus," *ibid.*, 14:518-519.

"Chenoboskion, Gnostic Texts of," *ibid.*, 1967 *Supplement* 16:83-84.

"Sleep and Awakening in Gnostic Texts," *The Origins of Gnosticism: Colloquium of Messina* 13-18 April 1966, ed. U. Bianchi, Supplements to *Numen* 12 (Leiden: Brill, 1967) 496-507.

"Anti-Dualist Polemic in 2 Cor. 4, 6?" *Studia Evangelica IV. Part I. The New Testament Scriptures*, ed. F.L. Cross, Texte und Untersuchungen 102 (Berlin: Akademie Verlag, 1968) 420-431.

"Coptic Versions," *The Jerome Biblical Commentary*, ed. R.E. Brown, J.A. Fitzmyer, and R.E. Murphy (Englewood Cliffs, NJ: Prentice—Hall, 1968) 2.579-580.

"Gnosticism and New Testament Studies," *Bible Today* 38 (1968) 2623-2630.

"The Fourth Gospel and *Religionsgeschichte*," *Catholic Biblical Quarterly* 32 (1970) 13-24.

"Shared Responsibility—Some New Testament Perspectives," *Chicago Studies* 9 (1970) 115-127.

"The Jewish Background of the Gnostic Sophia Myth," *Novum Testamentum* 12 (1970) 86-101.

"The Ego-Proclamation in Gnostic Sources," *The Trial of Jesus: Cambridge Studies in Honor of C.F.D. Moule*, ed. E. Bammel, Studies in Biblical Theology 2/13 (London: SCM Press, 1970) 122-134.

"A Nag Hammadi Tractate on the Soul," *Ex orbe religionum. Studia Geo Widengren XXIV mense Apr. MCMLXXII quo die lustra tredecim feliciter explevit oblata ab collegis, discipulis, amicis, collegae magistro amico congratulantibus. Pars prior*, Studies in the History of Religion (Supplements to *Numen*) 21 (Leiden: Brill, 1972) 471-479.

"The Apocalypse of Adam Reconsidered," *Society of Biblical Literature 1972 Proceedings* (Missoula: Scholars, 1972) 573-579.

(ed.) *Report of the Task Force on Scholarly Communication and Publication* (Waterloo, Ont.: Council on the Study of Religion, 1972).

(ed.) *Society of Biblical Literature. 1973 Seminar Papers* (2 vols.; Missoula, Mont.: Scholars, 1973).

Faith in the Word: The Fourth Gospel, Herald Biblical Booklets (Chicago: Franciscan Herald Press, 1973).

(ed.) with R.J. Clifford, *The Word in the World: Essays in Honor of Frederick L. Moriarty, S.J.* (Cambridge, MA: Weston College Press, 1973).

"Theology and Irony in the Fourth Gospel," *The Word in the World*, 83-96.

"'Whom Heaven Must Receive Until the Time.' Reflections on the Christology of Acts," *Interpretation* 27 (1973) 151-165; summary in *Theology Digest* 21 (1973) 216-221.

"New Testament Perspectives on Marriage and Divorce," in *Divorce and Remarriage in the Catholic Church*, ed. L.G. Wrenn (New York—Paramus—Toronto: Paulist, 1973) 1-15.

"Theological Diversity in the New Testament: Implications for Today," in *Perspectives for Campus Ministers*, ed. L.T. Murphy and J.W. Evans (Washington: US Catholic Conference, 1973) 103-127.

"The Thunder: Perfect Mind (Nag Hammadi Codex VI, Tractate 2)," *Center for Hermeneutical Studies Protocol 5* (Berkeley, CA: Center for Hermeneutical Studies, 1973) 1-8.

"Bible Books: Best on the Old and New," *America* 131 (1974) 324-333.

"Ministero cristiano e riconciliazione," in *Chiesa per il mundo* vol. 1, Saggi storico-biblici. Miscellanea teologico-pastorale nel LXX del card. M. Pellegrino,

G. Ghiberti, ed., Teologia Biblica 19 (Bologna: Edizioni Dehoniane Bologna, 1974) 177-191.

"Peter in the New Testament: Reflections of a Catholic Reviewer," *Worship* 48 (1974) 35-39.

(ed.) *Society of Biblical Literature 1974 Seminar Papers* (2 vols.; Missoula, Mont.: Scholars, 1974).

(ed.), H. Conzelmann, *1 Corinthians: A Commentary on the First Epistle to the Corinthians*, Hermeneia (Philadelphia: Fortress, 1975).

(ed.) *Society of Biblical Literature. 1975 Seminar Papers* (2 volumes; Missoula, Mont.: Scholars, 1975).

"Searching the Scriptures: New Books on the Bible," *America* 133 (1975) 358-367.

"The Gospel and the Church," *Theology Digest* 24 (1976) 338-348.

"The Judgment Scene in the Coptic Apocalypse of Paul," in *Studies on the Testament of Abraham*, ed. G.W.E. Nickelsburg, Jr., Septuagint and Cognate Studies 6 (Missoula: Scholars Press, 1976) 285-288.

"Adam, Apocalypse of," *The Interpreter's Dictionary of the Bible, Supplementary Volume*, ed. K. Crim (Nashville: Abingdon, 1976) 9-10.

"Nag Hammadi," *ibid.*, 613-619.

"Truth, Gospel of," *ibid.*, 923-926.

"'Unless Some Man Show Me': Books on the Bible, 1976," *America* 135 (1976) 375-385.

(ed.), *Society of Biblical Literature. 1976 Seminar Papers* (Missoula, Mont.: Scholars, 1976).

"Gospel of Truth," in *The Nag Hammadi Library in English*, ed. J.M. Robinson (New York—San Francisco: Harper & Row, 1977) 37-49.

"Apocalypse of Paul," *ibid.*, 239-241.

"Apocalypse of Adam," *ibid.*, 256-264.

"The Thunder, Perfect Mind," *ibid.*, 271-277.

"Authoritative Teaching," *ibid.*, 278-283.

"Gospel of Mary," *ibid.*, 471-474.

"Ministry and Ministries In the New Testament," *Living Light* 14 (1977) 167-179.

"Discourses of the Gnostic Revealer," in *Proceedings of the International Colloquium on Gnosticism. Stockholm August 20-25, 1973*, ed. G. Widengren, Filologisk-filosofiska serien 17 (Stockholm: Almqvist & Wiksell, 1977) 111-122.

"Books About the Book, Words About the Word," *America* 137 (1977) 380-388.

"Seth in Gnostic Texts and Traditions," *Society of Biblical Literature. 1977 Seminar Papers* (Missoula: Scholars, 1977) 17-24.

"The Development of Doctrine in St. Paul," *Lectureship: Mount Angel Seminary* (St. Benedict, OR: Mount Angel Abbey, 1978) 61-71.

"The School of St. Paul," *Lectureship: Mount Angel Seminary* (St. Benedict, OR: Mount Angel Abbey, 1978) 72-84.

"Eschatology," *Chicago Studies* 17/1 (1978) 59-73.

"Nag Hammadi and the New Testament," *Gnosis. Festschrift für Hans Jonas*, ed. B. Aland (Göttingen: Vandenhoeck & Ruprecht, 1978) 144-157.

"Prayer and Knowledge of Self in Gnosticism," *Tantur Yearbook* [Ecumenical Institute for Advanced Theological Studies Yearbook, Jerusalem] (1978-1979) 97-114.

"Heavenly Temple and Eschatology in the Letter to the Hebrews," *Semeia* 12 (1978) 179-199.

"The Annual Survey of Books on the Bible," *America* 139 (1978) 385-393.

Invitation to John: A Commentary on the Gospel of John with Complete Text from the Jerusalem Bible (Garden City, NY: Image Books/Doubleday, 1978).

"Apocalypse of Paul," in *Nag Hammadi Codices V, 2-5 and VI with Papyrus Berolinensis 8502, 1 and 4*, ed. D.M. Parrot, Nag Hammadi Studies 11, The Coptic Gnostic Library (Leiden: Brill, 1979) 47-63.

"Apocalypse of Adam," *ibid.*, 151-195.

"The Thunder: Perfect Mind," *ibid.*, 231-255.

"Authoritative Teaching," *ibid.*, 257-289.

"Gospel of Mary," *ibid.*, 453-471.

"Blessed Proliferation. Books on the Bible," *America* 143 (1980) 368-376.

"A Note on Romans 8:26-27," *Harvard Theological Review* 73 (1980) 227-230.

"Romans 8:26-27," *Interpretation* 34 (1980) 288-292.

"Reflections on Ecumenism," *Harvard Divinity Bulletin* 11 (Sept.—Oct. 1980) 11-13.

"Why the Church Rejected Gnosticism," in *Jewish and Christian Self-Definition. Volume One: The Shaping of Christianity in the Second and Third Centuries*, ed. E.P. Sanders (Philadelphia: Fortress, 1980) 126-133, 236-238.

(ed.), *Prayer in Late Antiquity and in Early Christianity*, Tantur Yearbook 1978-1979 (Tantur-Jerusalem: Ecumenical Institute for Advanced Theological Studies, 1981).

"A Kingdom That Cannot Be Shaken: The Heavenly Jerusalem in the Letter to the Hebrews," *Tantur Yearbook* [Ecumenical Institute for Advanced Theological Studies Yearbook, Jerusalem] (1979—1980) 27-40.

(ed.), *Spirituality and Ecumenism*, Tantur Yearbook 1979-1980 (Tantur-Jerusalem: Ecumenical Institute for Advanced Theological Studies, 1981).

"Limits of Formulations," *Commonweal* 108 (1981) 42-43.

(with C.P. Price), *Easter*, Proclamation Series 2 (Philadelphia: Fortress, 1982).

"A Note on 1 Corinthians 1:4-9," in *Harry M. Orlinsky Volume*, ed. J. Aviram et al., Eretz-Israel Archaeological, Historical and Geographical Studies 16 (Jerusalem: Israel Exploration Society—Hebrew Union College/Jewish Institute of Religion, 1982) 171*—175*.

"Apocalypse of Adam," in *The Old Testament Pseudepigrapha. Volume 1: Apocalyptic Literature and Testaments*, ed. J.H. Charlesworth (Garden City, NY: Doubleday, 1983) 707-719.

"Apocalyptic Eschatology in Gnosticism," in *Apocalypticism in the Mediterranean World and the Near East*, ed. D. Hellholm (Tübingen: Mohr-Siebeck, 1983) 317-325.

Hebrews, Collegeville Bible Commentary 10 (Collegeville, MN: Liturgical Press, 1983).

"The Temple as a House of Revelation in the Nag Hammadi Texts," in *The Temple in Antiquity: Ancient Records and Modern Perspectives*, ed. T.G. Madsen (Provo, UT: Brigham Young University, 1983) 175-190.

(ed.) H.D. Betz, *2 Corinthians 8 and 9. A Commentary on Two Administrative Letters of the Apostle Paul*, Hermeneia (Philadelphia: Fortress, 1985).

(ed.) with G.W.E. Nickelsburg, *Christians Among Jews and Gentiles. Essays in Honor of Krister Stendahl on His Sixty-Fifth Birthday* (Philadelphia: Fortress, 1986). Also published as *Harvard Theological Review* 79 (1986) nos. 1-3.

(ed.) with E.J. Epp, *The New Testament and Its Modern Interpreters* (Philadelphia: Fortress; Atlanta: Scholars, 1988).

"Messiah in the New Testament," in *Judaisms and Their Messiahs*, ed. J. Neusner (Cambridge, UK—London—New York: Cambridge University Press, 1988).

Index

Index